A DAUGHTER OF THE
"Enemy of the People"
VALÉRY DUNAEVSKY

ISBN-10: 1477586423
EAN-13: 9781477586426

"The long sobs of the violins of autumn
Wound my heart with a monotonous languor."

These first lines of Paul Verlaine's poem "Chanson d'Automne" were used as a BBC code to transmit information to the French resistance about the start of the operation Overlord, the Allied (British, American and Canadian) invasion of France in 1944.

These were also some of the most cherished lines of poetry for Alla Dunayevskaya. This was not only because of their poetical value but also for their association with one of the Allies' most longed-for events of WWII. She also romanticized all things French. Additionally, these lines were, I believe, a small window into Alla's spiritual world.

Contents

Preface vii

Chapter I Odessa (Ukraine): 1938
Arrest of Lev Shmulian, Alla's Father 1

Chapter II Fleeing to Taganrog and Move to Rostov-on-Don (Russia): 1938–1939 17

Chapter III Prewar Life in Rostov-on-Don and Evacuation to Semipalatinsk (Kazakhstan) During WWII: 1939–1941 39

Chapter IV Life in Semipalatinsk and WWII Episodes: 1941–1945 53

Chapter V Return to Rostov-on-Don After Evacuation: 1945 95

Chapter VI Move to Murmansk (Russia): 1947 105

Chapter VII My Return to Rostov-on-Don: 1957 157

Chapter VIII Alla and Victor Move to Riga (Latvia): 1960
I Join Them: 1961 169

Chapter IX Toward Emigration: 1974–1979
Emigration: 1979 177

Chapter X My Mother's Arrival to Pittsburgh, USA and Her Life There: 1982–2009 199

Appendix A Alla's brother, Witold Shmulian—a renowned mathematician and Soviet Army officer who was killed at the liberation of Warsaw 241

Appendix B On anti-Semitism 253

Appendix C R. Burns' Epigrams 263

Appendix D Documents 265

Alla's Family Tree 281

Additional Notes 283

Notes 285

Bibliography 287

Acknowledgments 291

Index 293

PREFACE

This book is dedicated to my mother, Alla Dunayevskaya*. Through kindness, cheerfulness, intelligence, dignity, and lack of cynicism (despite the severe blows her family suffered in the tumultuous events that shaped the former USSR in the 1930s–1950s), she became an inspiration to me and many who met her. Although she came to America at the mature age of sixty-two, she was able to adjust and be a valuable member of society to her last days. She was one of very few Soviet emigrants recognized in the Marquis' *Who's Who of American Women*, seventeenth edition.

Along with highlighting the image of my mother, I am trying to highlight the images of several other relatives, some of whom lived short albeit heroic and highly creative lives. These serve as examples of perseverance against all odds. Keeping memories about these people alive is a way of paying homage to them.

Among these relatives is my uncle, Alla's brother, Witold Shmulian. He was a renowned mathematician heroically killed at the liberation of Warsaw. From the trenches of WWII, he sent mathematic treatises into the USSR Academy of Sciences. There is also my maternal grandmother, Isabella Shmulian, who was a freelance playwright and poetess. She was remarkable in that she put various Russian fairy tales and pieces of literature into poetic form.

---

* The difference in the English spelling between my and my mother's names is because she transliterated her Russian name, and the name ending is gender-dependent

This book was written to provide my English-speaking daughter and her peers with a glimpse into the family history. This is naturally intertwined with the historical and spiritual fabric of the time. The goal of the book has been accomplished by:

- demonstrating the background and episodes from the life of my mother, other relatives, and myself and my reflection on them

- addressing the respective ideologies, policies, and events (especially of WWII and the Cold War) that directly or indirectly affected the life of my family and which, like the Holocaust that my parents narrowly escaped, continue long after to be a source of serious contemplation

- bringing up the pieces of poetry my mother and my maternal grandmother enjoyed or which are sound bites of the era. For some of these poems, it is the first time they are presented in English. The adaptations were done by myself. A few pieces of poetry from my maternal grandmother are also presented.

The book shows also how the extreme ideologies of Stalin's socialism and Hitler's Nazism resemble each other.

Valéry Dunaevsky.

NKVD[1] Order № 00447, July 30, 1937

"Register Families Of The Repressed, And Put Them On A Secret Watch..."

CHAPTER I

Odessa (Ukraine): 1938 Arrest of Lev Shmulian, Alla's Father

On January 17, 1938, in a sunny winter day, my mother, Alla Shmulian, was returning home after school. Approaching the third and top floor of the building at Novoselskaya Street (later Nezhinskaya) where her family had a flat, she was astounded to see a frightening picture. Her father, Lev Shmulian (1883–1945), was a well-known attorney and lecturer of law.[2] A witty and charming person who resembled Anton Chekhov, he was descending the stairs accompanied by a group of NKVD personnel. He was obviously under arrest.

On passing her, Lev said something like, "Do not worry. It is a mistake." Alla's mother, Isabella (Bella) Shmulian (1891–1975), was an elegant, slim lady with long hair. She was standing near the open door to the flat with her head and shoulders down and a grim expression on

[1] NKVD is the Russian acronym for the People Commissariat of Internal Affairs (regular and secret police).

[2] L. Shmulian graduated with a first degree diploma from the jurisprudence department of the emperor's Novorossiysk University in Odessa in 1912.

her face. Like her husband, Isabella had a law degree[3], but she never practiced. Instead she dedicated her time to bringing up three children and engaging in some literary activities.

As Alla entered the flat, she saw it had been ransacked. Everything was messed up. The drawers and doors of the furniture were swung open, chairs were thrown about, and books were strewn along the hallway and floor. Isabella later told me it was fortunate the NKVD could not open one bookcase and left it uninspected. If they would have opened it, they would easily have found additional incriminating evidence against Lev Shmulian. Namely there was a letter from Isabella's French cousin, Valentin Feldman.

At that time it was a liability to have correspondence with foreigners. Feldman, however, was not a complete foreigner. He and his parents immigrated to France after the Bolshevik Revolution. He graduated from the Sorbonne and at the time was starting his professorship there. It was reported later that, after the occupation of France by Germany in 1940, he was one of the university professors who formed an antifascist committee. Unfortunately his group was betrayed, and he and his colleagues were executed. Addressing his captors, he was attributed with the following words prior to his execution: "Imbeciles, it is for you I am dying."

Meanwhile, Lev Shmulian was accused of Trotskyism, which was a political ideology branded by Stalin and his sycophants as antisocialist and anti-Soviet. Anyone who happened to be accused of this fell automatically into the unenvied category of "enemy of the people." Shmulian was allegedly betrayed by some of his students or colleagues in the pervasive atmosphere of anonymous denouncements typical during the era of Stalin purges in the 1930s.

Shmulian was soon sentenced by the Troika[4] to seven years of hard labor for the aforementioned Trotskyism. He was shipped off to serve his term in one of the Gulag‡ concentration camps in the north European

---

[3] I. Shmulian received a second degree diploma from the jurisprudence department of the highest women courses at Novorossiysk University in Odessa in 1918.

[4] NKVD troikas or Troikas, in Soviet Union history, were commissions of three people employed as an additional instrument of extrajudicial punishment (*внесудебная расправа, внесудебное преследование*). They were introduced to circumvent the legal system and as a means for quick execution or imprisonment of anti-Soviet elements.

part of the USSR, which was in the Arkhangelsk Oblast. During the trials in Odessa, he was allowed family visitations. Grandma Isabella told me Lev described his prison environment as a fascist dungeon. He admitted, however, he was not personally beaten during interrogations. This was not the case for many other prisoners who refused to sign false incriminations for acts such as spying for other countries.

During one visitation, he told Isabella, pointing with grim sarcasm to one of the prisoners seating nearby, "This is a Japanese spy." Pointing to another prisoner passing by who was escorted by guards, he said, "That is a German spy." This was in reference to the absurd charges that were leveled against the innocent victims of Stalin terror. He attributed his relatively lenient treatment to his somewhat lesser charges than others, who were trampled by the juggernaut of political farce. Lev also believed his better treatment was because many interrogators and a whole investigative department were his former students at the university, where he enjoyed popularity for his intelligence, knowledge, humor, and good comradeship.

One example of the favorable attitude of Lev's students was the following. During the May 1 demonstrations, he was the object of a playful "swing" ceremony. This is when an admired person is literally thrown into the air and caught by a friendly crowd a few times. It is quite possible some of these cheerful folks took advantage of the essentially innocent jokes my grandpa liked to crack, and they turned him in to the NKVD. One had to be extremely careful with jokes at the time, as mutual denouncement flourished, and people often solved their personal problems by denouncing a boss, friend, or spouse.

The arrest of Lev Shmulian apparently untied the hands of those who had envied him, wished him ill for whatever reason, and conspired toward his downfall. After the arrest, the Shmulians' flat was requisitioned by the government. Almost all their belongings were confiscated, and my mother and grandmother were evicted. They found shelter in the tiny apartment of their former maid, Emilia. This apartment did not have modern conveniences and was located in a dilapidated building at the outskirts of Odessa in a poor neighborhood called Moldavanka.

---

‡ Gulag is an acronym for *G(lavnoye) U(pravleniye Ispravitelno-Trudovykh) Lag(erei)*, or Main Administration for Corrective Labor Camps.

Meanwhile, the main investigator of the Shmulian case moved his family into the Shmulians' flat.

During one of the family visitations, Lev advised Isabella that she and Alla must leave Odessa immediately to avoid arrest. It was common then for the families of persecuted people to follow in the footsteps of their arrested husbands, fathers, or brothers. Isabella and Alla heeded this warning and fled Odessa in June of 1938 after Alla graduated from school. They went to the small provincial city of Taganrog, Russia. Located on the north shore of the Azov Sea, one of Alla's brothers, Theodor Shmulian, had settled there since 1937.

Alla was born in 1920 and had two older brothers, Theodor (1912-1998) and Witold (1914-1944). Theodor (which is Edia for informal addressing) was working as an engineer at the *Krasny Kotelshchik* (Red Boilerman), a big pressure vessels plant in Taganrog. After an early childhood accident, he almost lost his hearing, but he eventually was able to communicate with others by lip reading, which he learned in special programs for deaf children. Isabella had dedicated a lot of time and effort to ensure Theodor would grow from a disabled child into a full-fledged human being. He responded well to her efforts, and while still in kindergarten, he learned to read, write, and count. He had an exceptional memory, often memorizing verses on the first reading. Isabella also taught him to play checkers.

In 1937 Theodor received his engineering diploma. He also became very proficient in checkers, which, along with chess, is very popular in Russia. It is considered a sport game, and Theodor quickly attained the official title of Master of Sport. In the 1950s, he wrote a fundamental book on the game of checkers and dedicated it to Isabella, writing "To my mother, who made me a person." He frequently won first place at the checkers tournaments.

Witold, which is also Anatolii, Anatoly, or Tolyia for a nonformal greeting, was a talented mathematician. At the time of the events described here, he was a mathematics PhD student at Odessa State University, and he lived with his wife, Vera Gantmacher, who was also a mathematician. From the memoirs of one of his professors (see Appendix A), it is known that when Witold applied for the postgraduate school, he presented a mathematical treatise. This proved an important mathematical theory that had been left without proof even by its original developer, the renowned mathematician Freshet. In 1940 Witold moved to Moscow for postdoctoral study at the prestigious Steklov's Institute of Mathematics. The name Witold Shmulian is well known in mathematical circles.

With the arrest of her father and her departure from Odessa, a chapter in Alla's life was closed. With the exception of the final page of the chapter—the downfall and unjust imprisonment of her father—Alla's childhood was quite upbeat. This was despite the political upheavals of the postrevolutionary period in the USSR, the constant shortages of common goods, and the starvation and famine in Ukraine during the early 1930s.

The Ukraine famine of 1932–1933 was one result of Joseph Stalin's brutal collectivization policy. During implementation, several million independent farmers and their families perished. People died as a result of hunger and famine and because millions of peasants were resettled in appalling conditions.

As a successful attorney, Lev Shmulian was able to provide a high standard of living for a family of five. The Shmulians lived in a spacious four-room apartment and had good furniture, delicate tableware, and a maid. The family was friendly and hospitable. Lev's colleagues and their wives often gathered at the Shmulians' flat. These were joyful parties with interesting conversations, witty toasts, and light flirting. Unusual for the times, Alla had a governess who taught her to speak French and play the piano. Mother recalled that, when she was still little, her father often took her into his home office, and she liked to sit on his lap while he wrote. The maid brought them tea in glasses on traditional Russian glass holders made of heavy silver.

Alla's mother fit into their upper-middle-class lifestyle with her love of poetry and all things beautiful and her sharp tongue. She was a feisty woman able to speak on equal footing with people of different backgrounds. She always retained her understanding and love for common people despite her privileged background. She was the daughter of a prosperous attorney, Solomon Nevelshtein. In his office in Kherson (a big port city in Ukraine just north of Odessa) she met her future husband. Nevelshtein, who somewhat resembled Omar Sharif in the role of

Dr. Zhivago, owned a law firm that was providing legal papers for large grain exports from southern Russia. He also was active in civic activities, serving as an elector to the Russian parliament (Duma) from a Kherson section of a party of cadets. Lev Shmulian was a junior partner in the Nevelshtein firm when Isabella met him.

Isabella's mother (Alla's grandmother), Tatiana Feldman, was also a professional. In the late 1880s, she finished midwife courses but, like her daughter, was a housewife. In addition to raising her daughter, she also raised her younger siblings. These included her sister Tamara (a future MD in neonatology) and her brother Grigori (a future professor of economic geography).

Alla was a doted-on daughter brought up in a well-to-do family of the Russian Jewish intelligentsia. They instilled in her the classical values of kindness and spirituality in terms of love for art, literature, poetry, philosophy, and tolerance. These values were cultivated by a big-city life in the flamboyant Odessa with its famous opera house and Potemkin Stairs.

After Moscow, St. Petersburg, and Warsaw, Odessa was the fourth largest city in the Russian Empire. It remained one of the largest cities in the Soviet Union, and it is currently one of the largest in Ukraine. Odessa was founded at the end of the eighteenth century on a site that was once occupied by an ancient Greek colony. The site of present-day Odessa was then a town known as Khadjibey. During the Russo-Turkish War of 1787–1792, it was captured by Russian forces for the Russian Empire.

From its birth, Odessa was a cosmopolitan city founded by several foreigners. Among them were Duc de Richelieu, who served as the city's governor between 1803 and 1814. Having fled the French Revolution, he served in Catherine's army against the Turks. Another Frenchman, Count Andrault de Langeron, succeeded him in office. Various city landmarks are named after these founding fathers. In addition, the main street, Derybasovskaja Street, was named after a Spaniard in Russian service. This was Major General José de Ribas who commanded a detachment of the Russian forces that took Khadjibey in the Russo-Turkish War.

Odessa became home to an extremely diverse population of Russians, Ukrainians, Jews, Poles, Romanians, Turks, Albanians, Armenians, Azeris, Bulgarians, Crimean Tatars, Frenchmen, Germans, Greeks, Italians, and peoples of other nationalities.

The cosmopolitan nature of Odessa was documented by the great Russian poet Alexander Pushkin, who lived in internal exile in Odessa between 1823 and 1824. In his letters, he wrote that Odessa was a city where "the air is filled with all Europe, French is spoken, and there are European papers and magazines to read."[25] In the Soviet era, a popular poet, Vladimir Vysotsky, echoed that feeling in a song he wrote for a movie set in the early twentieth century: "they say Odessa is closer to New York and Paris than to St. Petersburg..." Odessa has long, straight streets lined with chestnut trees and monumental buildings. In Alla's youth the city already had over twenty institutions of higher education and research, diversified industries, and two big ports. Odessa was the first city in Russia to introduce a horse-driven tram and later steam and electric streetcar service. Tram lines numbers fifteen and sixteen were near Alla's house.

Many renowned political and military leaders, poets, writers, musicians, and scientists were born or lived in Odessa. Among those were such internationally known figures as poet Anna Akhmatova, writer Isaac Babel, whose series of short stories *Odessa Tales* were set in the city, the duo of Ilf and Petrov (authors of the famous *Twelve Chairs* and *Golden Calf*), Ze'ev Jabotinsky (a founder of the Jewish emancipation movement Zionism), and Marshal of the Soviet Union Rodion Malinovsky (leader of the Red Army, which decimated the Japanese Army in Manchuria in August of 1945.) This was the critical event that led directly to the capitulation of Japan in WWII.

Odessa produced Pyotr Stolyarsky, who was one of the founders of the Soviet violin school. It also produced a famous composer, Oscar Feltsman, and a galaxy of stellar musicians. This included violinists Yuri Vodovoz, David and Igor Oistrakh, Boris Goldstein, and Zakhar Bron and pianists Sviatoslav Richter, Benno Moiseiwitsch, Vladimir de Pachmann, and Emil Gilels.

The most popular Russians in show business from Odessa are Yakov Smirnoff (comedian), Mikhail Zhvanetsky (legendary humorist writer who began his career as port engineer), and Roman Kartsev (comedian). This list would not be complete without mentioning Leonid Utyosov, 1895–1982, famous Soviet jazz singer and comic.

Many world-renowned scientists lived and worked in Odessa. Among them were Illya Mechnikov (Nobel Prize in Medicine, 1908), Igor Tamm

(Nobel Prize in Physics, 1958), Selman Waksman (Nobel Prize in Medicine, 1952), Dmitri Mendeleev, Nikolay Pirogov, Ivan Sechenov, Vladimir Filatov, George Gamow, Nikolay Umov, Leonid Mandelstam, Aleksandr Lyapunov, Mark Krein, Alexander Smakula, Waldemar Haffkine, and Valentin Glushko. Note that the aforementioned Mark Krein authored the paper about Witold Shmulian (See Appendix A).

Alla was good in school. When she was a little girl, she liked to cut out fashion models from the paper to resemble figurines and color them elaborately with colored pencils. The figurines could stand on their own by resting on both flaps of the folded sheet. Alla's delicate nature was shining already in childhood. Isabella told us how one time, when Alla was four, Alla categorically refused to go on a tram because she was barefoot. Her sandals were removed because of rain, and she was afraid to stain the floor of the tram's carriage.

Alla's spiritual values were formed during a time of enthusiasm for building a new society. The lyrics of patriotic songs of that era reinforced morale, and many people of different ranks in society believed the sacrifices the country endured were justifiable in the long run.

Fortunately Alla did not suffer the privation that touched the lives of so many in the USSR in the early to mid-1930s, which was a period of collectivization and industrialization. However, Lev's salary was not always sufficient to stave off hunger. To avoid starvation, Isabella traded the remains of her family heirlooms for meager food compensation in special stores set up by the government to encourage trade with foreign countries and relieve food shortages. The stores were called "TORGSIN," which is a Russian acronym that stands for "trade with foreigners."

Because of their good upbringing and supported by good nature, Alla and her immediate family did not develop the cynicism that prevailed among many in the Soviet culture, despite the blows life later dealt them. Alla grew up romantic, sensitive, and reserved in the expression of her feelings. She was delicate and correct in her relationships with people. While being a "hot number," she still had high moral and aesthetic standards. Some people considered her correctness to be somewhat excessive, but she was not a cold person, and the memories of her at various life events confirm it.

Odessa is famous for its jolly, humorous, and sharp-tongued people. Alla, her kin, and her friends definitely possessed these Odessa qualities and enjoyed them. I learned from her this quintessentially Odessa pun. When a young lady was asked, "Are you from Addis Abeba," she would answer, "No. I am Beba from Odessa." However, the family's humor and style of behavior were, in general, a notch above the folksy level now considered a trademark of Odessa and is still popular among Russians.

The family's humor, lexicon, and manners were those of the cultural elite. They did not like vulgar language and philistine conversations. In their verbal communications, they used images from literature and plays. (They often referenced Moliere, for example.) However, Isabella knew plenty of catchy Yiddish expressions and aptly applied them at suitable circumstances.

Placing stock in the honor of the status, occupation, or profession to which one belonged was a hallmark of the Shmulian/Nevelshtein family, as it was a norm in European and Russian imperial societies. These attributes were held in high esteem by this family and contributed to their sense of responsibility and moral duty to country, colleagues, friends, and family. It also contributed to their necessity to maintain composure in all circumstances. One of the oft-repeated sayings of Grandma Isabella was an expression meaning, "Even if you are bursting along the seams, you still have to try to retain your best image." Keeping a proper tone was everything. As Eleanor Roosevelt said, small people talk about people, average people talk about events, and high people talk about ideas. This was quite applicable to this family. Discussions of science, war, peace, and moral principles, as it was in Chekhov's dramas, were common among Alla and her family.

In the late 1940s, there was an anti-cosmopolite campaign in the USSR, but Grandma Isabella told me cosmopolitism was not always considered a negative thing. She recalled her father, Solomon, proudly declaring he was a cosmopolite. These family traditions and her classical upbringing helped make Alla an internationalist in her attitude toward people and events.

So, despite the tragedy that had befallen upon them, Isabella, Alla, and many other people of their ilk remained patriotic citizens. In Bella's case, she continued to believe in the virtues of a socialist system, associating it with cultural and social progress. Like her, Alla carried throughout her life a sense of attachment to the best attributes of Russian, Ukrainian, and Soviet culture.

Lev Shmulian also tried to appeal his conviction within the framework of the political doctrine. Grandma showed me letters written by Lev from the places of his confinement. In those letters, he tried to demonstrate his innocence by elaborating on his adherence to Stalinist rather than Trotskyite political doctrines. He tried to explain that the accusations against him were misinterpretations of his position. He asked Isabella to carry his letters to the appropriate judicial authorities. The letters were written on very thin paper, and the handwriting was very small in order to maximize the available space.

When Lev, aged sixty two, died in April of 1945 from a heart attack, he was still in a Gulag camp near small town Nyandoma in the Arkhangelsk Oblast. Although he already served his term (seven years), he was not allowed to leave the camp under the pretext that the war was not over. Already not feeling well, in his last letters he expressed his desire to live to the time when he could find out how the war ended and about the destiny of his son, Witold, whose death on the front in 1944 was concealed from Lev by the family.

Photographs and Documents

Alla's Early Years

Alla is seven years old.

Alla is fifteen years old.

Alla is seventeen years old.

Alla's Parents, Grandparents, and Brothers

Alla's father, Lev Yulyevich Shmulian, and mother, Isabella Solomonovna Shmulian (née Nevelshtein). 1911. Isabella was from Kherson, and Lev was from Golaya Pristan' (Naked Haven), Ukraine.

Alla's maternal grandmother, Tatiana Semenovna Nevelshtein.

Alla's maternal grandfather, Solomon Nevelshtein.

Isabella Shmulian, 1940. Her handwritten note at the lower right corner says (emphatically) that she is fifty years old at the photo.

Alla's older brother, Theodor Shmulian (1912–1998), at about thirty-five years of age (ca. mid-1940s).

Alla's younger brother, Witold Shmulian (1914–1944), at twenty-seven years of age after joining the army. November 1941.

"Rostov father, Odessa mother."

Russian folk saying

CHAPTER II

Fleeing to Taganrog and Move to Rostov-on-Don (Russia): 1938–1939

After moving to Taganrog, Isabella and Alla rented a room in a small apartment on Dobrolubovsky Street. Left without any financial means, they survived on small donations from Isabella's brother, Grigori, who was teaching at Leningrad's Pedagogical Institute. Possibly they also received assistance from Alla's brothers.

Taganrog was founded by Peter I (Peter the Great) as a fortress and naval base in 1698. It is located on the Azov sea in the place of one of the earliest Greek settlements around the Black Sea basin. In the nineteenth century, it developed into an important grain-exporting port. Although overshadowed by Rostov-on-Don, just forty miles southwest, Taganrog grew substantially to become a city with diversified industries funded by Belgian and German investors early in the twentieth century.

Taganrog retains a rich cultural and historic heritage. Alexander I of Russia built a palace there as his summer residence, and he died there in 1825. Alexander I was considered a highly traveled monarch. That fact and his death in Taganrog were captured by a rhyming Russian pun, *Vsiu zhizn' on byl v doroge , a umer v Taganroge*, which literally means that he spent all his life on the road but died in Taganrog.

Taganrog was the native city of Anton Chekhov, and the home where he spent his early life is preserved as a museum. The city has several institutions of higher education plus the A. P. Chekhov Theatre, which was founded in 1866. By 1911 the city already had eleven foreign consulates.

Soon after arriving in Taganrog, Alla applied to the Rostov-on-Don Medical Institute, which was the closest medical school in the area. Before she was allowed to take the entrance exams, she and other applicants had to be interviewed by a special commission made up of members of the administration and university faculty. In her interview, she had to mention the situation with her father. She was very worried that being a daughter of "the enemy of the people," as her father was branded, would automatically preclude her from entering school. She began crying.

After the interview, the chairman of the commission gently asked her to wait outside so her case could be deliberated. When Alla was invited back, she was told by the chairman that the commission had decided to allow her admission. They told her children do not bear responsibility for their parents. It was a big relief for Alla. In telling us later about this event, she mused that her nice looks and timid behavior played a role in the decision, as she knew a few individuals in similar circumstances that were not that lucky. The rule of children not being responsible for their parents was apparently seldom followed, and the reversal was generally the norm.

After passing the tests and being admitted to the school, Alla moved to Rostov where she rented a room with a roommate, Fanya Moroz. Moroz was a girl from Pyatigorsk, a city in the Northern Caucasus.

Sometime in the winter of 1938 or the spring of 1939, Alla met my father through his friends. At the time, Victor Dunaevsky (1918–1965) was a student at the Institute of Agricultural Machine Building, RISHM.

One of Victor's friends was Ted Zaltsman, a slender, attractive young man with a charming smile. I remember him from a photo taken on a winter evening when he was wearing a sport coat without a hat. When I reviewed these photos of Ted and Alla with Fanya Moroz and other friends decades after they were taken, they gave me a sense of well-being, calmness, and coziness. This instilled in me a sense of security and confidence, as if the photographs told me this benevolent atmosphere was extending to me as well. This was true in a way because I always felt love, support, and friendship from the friends of my parents, with whom I also became friends.

The photographic paper and the quality of the photographs probably played a role as well in creating a warm and fuzzy aura for these prewar years. The photos were taken by a Leica camera, which was a popular camera for the time. It had a large objective that ensured good resolution, and the photos were printed on Agfa photo paper, which brought some softness to the photo image. The name Ted, which was not a very typical Russian name, also created some magic. "Ted" was a Russian Americanism for Theodor.

I subconsciously received everything associated with America as positive. This was very deeply seated. From early childhood I heard the word "America" mainly with a favorable connotation. At least it was not unfavorable like the words "Germany" and "Germans." I remember those words in the following association. At about the age of two, I was asked who my enemies were. Born in the middle of WWII and at a critical time in the battle for Stalingrad, I was supposed to answer bedbugs and Germans. The bedbugs were definitely a scourge in many houses of the Soviet Union and not only in wartime. However, "The times they are a-changin'" as Bob Dylan said, and today I can list some Germans as my friends.

My father was an athletic fellow, and as I see it now, he somewhat resembled the actor Daniel Craig. He was an excellent swimmer and diver, and he played tennis well. He was also active in boxing. In one photograph, I saw him with his friends Tolya (Anatoly Tsipelzon) and Gleb Kurasov. They were brave-looking young men in sport shirts. When Grandma Isabella knew that Alla was dating Victor, she was pleased. She heard from someone that the Dunaévskys were a respectable family in Rostov.

Victor's father, Zélman Hilélevich (or Zinoviy Ilyich) Dunaevsky (1891–1968), was a quiet and intelligent person. He wore a pince-nez and was bald at an early age. Otherwise, he somewhat resembled Josef May, who was a handsome character from a portrait by the German artist, Otto Dix. Zelman graduated in 1921 from Don Institute of the People Economy with a degree in economics and was working in the system of people education in the departments of finance and planning. Prior to his stay with Don Institute, he studied medicine in London circa 1911–1912. For whatever reason, he did not finish school there. Instead he moved to the University of Toulouse in France where, in 1912–1914, he continued his studies. For reasons unknown to me, he did not take the final exams.

In prerevolutionary times, Zelman's family owned a business in Poltava (Ukraine) and apparently had the means to give an education to him and his two brothers, Jon and Abram (in 1940s-1950s they both occupied high level management/directorship positions in industry). Zelman (Zyama in a folksy tongue) was fluent in French and English and read the only available French and British newspapers in the Soviet Union, which were the Communist newspapers. In particular, the French *Humanité Dimánsh* was available after the war in street kiosks, and it provided political and general information not available from the Soviet press. Zélman was conservative in principles, reserved in manners, and inclined to follow a dress code. He was a bearer of classical culture with wide-ranging knowledge.

Zelman was also a kind and very decent person with a mild sense of humor. At the same time, he was strict in his demeanor and in confronting what he perceived as violations of the moral norms. I found this out firsthand because he was openly not fond of the escapades he learned about when I was a teenager and young adult. He also was often skeptical and sarcastic about various activities in the Soviet era, derisively calling them "*svistopliaska.*" This is a Russian word for bravura dances, which are often performed with saber rattling and accompanied by whistling in various operas or ballets. I remember another of his expressions directed at those who promised a lot but could not deliver. The expression translates to something like, "He has a dollar's worth of ambition and only a cent's worth of ammunition."

While on a winter vacation in Switzerland, Zelman met his future wife, Lyuba or Lyubov (love in Russian) Osherovskaya (1891–1966) from Rostov. She was one of the seven children of Abram Osherovsky, a merchant originally from a Novogrudok district in Belorussia. He settled with his wife, Leya, in Rostov in the 1880s. Of the seven children, five were sisters. Three, Lyuba, Ida, and Rose, received a medical education and worked as doctors in their respective fields. Lyuba was an ob-gyn, Ida was in ophthalmology, and Rose was in sanitary and hygiene. The oldest sister, Clara, the youngest, Vera, and Lyuba's brother, Iosif, got only some schooling, however. Another of Lyuba's brothers, Oscar, was an educated man and worked all his life as a math teacher in Rostov schools.

My paternal grandmother, Lyuba, started as a gynecologist and obstetrician and specialized later in radiology. She belonged to a cohort of physicians who, along with her brother-in law, Professor Alexander

Dombrovsky (the husband of her sister, Ida), were trailblazers in administering radiation therapy to oncology patients. She was a nice, petite, and serious woman with a pragmatic attitude and skills. One of her expressions that sticks with me is drawn from Greek mythology. "It is not the Gods who fire the pots," which means that one can achieve great success, even without exclusive abilities, by employing good old-fashioned hard work, diligence, and sufficient wisdom or common sense.

Toward midsummer of 1939, Alla and Victor were apparently friendly enough that Victor invited Alla to spend time with him at a Black Sea resort. In Soviet times, however, it was always a problem getting accommodation in resort areas, as there was an endemic shortage of available housing. In addition, the authority to provide accommodation was given to the trade unions and Communist party bureaucrats who made sure accommodation was distributed mainly to the employees of the factories and other organizations and party functionaries.

Party bosses, high-ranking employees (*nomenclaturnye rabotniki*), and the Soviet elite, which included famous writers, actors, teachers, scientists, promoted workers, military leaders, etc., were given priority. The government also provided summer houses (*dacha*) to a select group of individuals valuable to the Soviet state.

In order to get a room in any of the government-owned resort facilities, which were indeed free of charge in "the workers' paradise," an individual needed to present to the resort officials a special document. This was a sort of permit called a *putevka*, and it needed to be approved by a trade union leader from the organization to which the individual belonged. It was almost a game of chance for regular folks to get a *putevka* for a resort. Considering these complications and the desire to spend time at a resort, which often included medical facilities where workers could recuperate after illnesses and fatigue, people often went out on a limb and relied heavily on connections to get *putevka(s)*. This was the case even when the accommodation was merely a bed in a room of four to six people.

Victor asked his parents to help him get a *putevka* to one of the Black Sea resorts along the beaches at the foothills of the Caucasus Mountains. He asked for two *putevkas*. One was for him, and another was for his friend, Gleb. He felt it would be preposterous to ask for a *putevka* for his girlfriend,

Alla. His parents knew little about his dating, and they certainly would not have approved of him going with a girlfriend on a vacation. Using her connections in the medical world, Lyuba got two *putevkas* for Victor.

Victor and Alla enjoyed each other's company in a subtropical climate with balmy air and warm sea water. Subsequently, and most likely under Victor's insistence, they decided to get married. Without notifying their parents, they officially tied the knot in a municipality of the resort city, which was probably False Helendjik, on July 29, 1939. In describing the events surrounding their life in the resort, mother used to recollect a comical story.

It happened that in the same *Dom otdykha* (a resting house or hostel) where Alla and Victor were staying, Victor's uncle, Oscar Osherovsky, was also vacationing. Oscar was tall and blond with blue eyes, supporting the now-popular notion that Eastern European Jews had in their ancestry Slavic and Germanic DNA. With his straight bearing, muscular hands, blazing eyes, and expressions of wisdom, Oscar produced a prophetic image. This was reinforced by the appropriate mimics and gesticulations.

He was a bachelor and considered a bon vivant. He was apparently also a gourmand, and as a mathematician, he was a self-absorbed and absent-minded fellow. All of this probably led him to minor infractions. Mother related that Oscar was seen a few times coming down to breakfast before any of the vacationers had arrived at the dining room and, in apparent oblivion, skimming sour cream from a plate of his fellow resort-goer. The plates with sour cream were set at the tables before the resort-goers arrived to breakfast.

Oscar knew about Victor and Alla eloping but joined their conspiracy and did not inform Victor's parents when he returned to Rostov. This probably added some strain between Oscar and my grandfather.

So it was a complete surprise to Lyuba and Zyama when Victor returned home after his vacation with a young wife. This was a bigger shock to Zyama, who was an orderly and punctual person of old school manners and morals. Lyuba, however, had a softer heart. Fortunately Victor had a separate room in the flat where the Dunaevskys lived, which simplified the situation. Also Alla was an attractive and well-mannered young lady, which helped dissipate the tensions that could surface when a son brings a wife into the parents' house unannounced.

After Grandma Isabella visited the Dunaevskys, any ice that remained between Victor's parents and Alla thawed, even though she was somewhat detached from the mundane aspects of life and not very interested in the kitchen and household duties. A visit from Isabella, an elegant, intelligent, and witty person, did not leave any doubts that Alla, albeit the daughter of the "enemy of the people," was from a good family. The common ground between the Dunaevskys and Shmulians was love for and knowledge of modern and classical Russian and European literature, art, and music.

Alla's marriage was also a surprise for her former friend, Yuri Umilyanovsky. Alla met him in 1936 while on a summer vacation with Isabella to Kiev. Yuri was the son of a childhood girlfriend of Isabella. The friend was of Polish-Jewish descent. Yuri was a nice, serious, and matter-of-fact fellow a couple of years older than Alla. After their first meeting in Kiev, they kept writing each other and probably met a few times before the arrest of Lev Shmulian interrupted their communications.

Yuri and Alla retained a friendly relationship throughout their lives. The correspondence between them, mostly from Yuri's side, resumed after Victor's untimely death in 1965. Alla explained to me she decided to marry Victor instead of Yuri because she liked Victor's idealistic attitudes and his athletic and handsome appearance. Yuri became a military officer serving in counterintelligence spheres. He married a couple of times.

In the decade or so after we moved to America, with the appalling socioeconomic conditions after Gorbachev's *perestroika* in Russia, Yuri and his daughter, Natalia (Natasha) Kameneva, began asking Alla to help them settle Natalia and her daughter in America. In due course, Alla provided Natalia with connections to Yuri Mordwinkin. He was the president of a small American electrotechnical company, and Alla met and befriended him at a social outing. He was a second-generation Russian emigrant and son of a White Army officer.

Natalia, a computer science researcher, was able to secure a job with that firm in the early 1990s. Alla also helped Natalia with accommodation, allowing her and her daughter to stay with her for several months. Later she arranged for Natalia to stay with her Russian friends, the Shulikovs (recent émigrés from Russia), and later with their friends until Natalia could afford to rent an apartment.

Returning to the epoch of Alla's youth, in 1937 and 1938, Soviet dictator Josef Stalin unleashed mass terror on civilians, NKVD, and military personnel. Thousands of innocent people who, in one way or another, were associated with the main targets of Stalin's terror were also persecuted. The leading figures of political opposition (Kamenev, Zinoviev, Bukharin, Rykov, and Radek) and leading military commanders (Tukhachevsky, Yakir, Uborewitz, Blyukher, Rudzutak, and Gamarnik) were accused of Trotskyite, anti-Soviet activities, branded as the enemies of the people, tortured until they incriminated themselves[5], convicted, and executed. This was generally by a shot in the neck. Hundreds of thousands followed them.

Having eliminated the aforementioned individuals, who represented the Old Bolshevik Guard and were his former comrades, Stalin rid himself of potential or imaginary rivals.

Whole strata of the population were also targets for extermination. These consisted of *kulaks* (Russian for "fist," this definition applied to well-to-do peasants), who had been targeted since the early 1930s, and various national minorities, especially those living in the border areas. They were targeted for bourgeois nationalism and potential disloyalty. Stalin, ever the internationalist, harbored a bitter hatred for any perceived manifestation of national exclusivity, and he did not even spare his fellow Georgians, thousands of whom were accused of nationalistic activities and executed or exiled. Purges of individual ethnicities were known as NKVD national operations.

Former Russian citizens who returned to the USSR from America in the 1920s were also targeted. Those that returned were either lured by sumptuous offers from the Soviet government or they sympathized with Soviet socialist programs. Such was the story of the paternal grandfather of my second cousin, Natalia Kandror (a pediatrician in Boston). He returned to Russia with his family in 1927.

Being an established businessman in the electrotechnical industry, he was initially given the opportunity to lead important sectors of industrialization in the Soviet Republic of Georgia. Eventually he perished in the Great Purge. His son, the father of my cousin and an airplane mechanic during WWII, had been born in Russia before the family originally

---

[5] Stalin and his magnates often laughed about the NKVD's ability to get people to confess. Stalin told this joke to someone who had actually been tortured. "They arrested a boy and accused him of writing *Eugene Onegin*," Stalin joked. "The boy tried to deny it...A few days later, the NKVD interrogator bumped into the boy's parents. 'Congratulation!' he said. 'Your son wrote *Eugene Onegin*.'"

emigrated to America. He was executed by a firing squad at the end of the war for his attempt to defect to the Americans.

For this offense, his wife was imprisoned in Gulag camps for seven years and was finally released after Stalin's death. For a substantial portion of her life, my cousin lived with her family (mother, aunt, maternal grandmother and her husband, who was Natalia's grandfather and a journalist blinded by an accident in the 1920s) in a single room in a communal apartment in the center of Moscow. This apartment was shared by twelve other families.

In their room, they retained a humongous chest her grandfather brought from America in the 1920s. After almost fifty-five years on Soviet soil, this trunk returned to America with my cousin's luggage.

Meanwhile, minus the tens of thousands killed in the dungeons of Lubianka (NKVD headquarters), most convicts went into the system of labor camps and penal colonies of the Gulag. Many of these camps provided cheap labor for the great construction sites of communism. One of those was the White Sea-Baltic Canal. (The Russian abbreviation is "Belomor" from the two names.)

The Great Terror (the slaughter of Russians on an unimaginable scale[6]) was instigated by Stalin and promulgated by Nikolai Ezhov.[7] An ethnic Russian, he replaced Genrich Yagoda (a person of Jewish descent) in 1937 as chief of the NKVD. Yagoda supervised the arrest, show trial, and execution of the Old Bolsheviks Lev Kamenev and Grigory Zinoviev. These events, along with decimation of the ranks of Red Army high Command, marked the beginning of the Great Purge. Like many Soviet secret policemen of the 1930s, Yagoda was ultimately a victim of the Purge himself. He was demoted in 1936 from the directorship of

---

6 During the Great Terror (1937-1938), at least 1.5 million Soviet citizens were arrested for alleged crimes against the State. Some seven hundred thousand were shot. [32]

7 The name Ezhov has a connotation of hedgehog, which is "*ezh*" in Russian. The word "*Ezhovshchina*" is a euphemism meaning to take someone in hedgehog gloves, and it refers to the period of Ezhov's tenure, which was characterized by harsh repression. On a folksy level Ezhov came to be known as a "bloody dwarf."

the NKVD in favor of Nikolai Ezhov (also spelled Yezhov), and he was arrested in 1937. Charged with the standard crimes of wrecking, espionage, Trotskyism, and conspiracy, Yagoda, soon after his trial confession, was found guilty and shot.

Yagoda's fall from grace was associated predominantly with his failure to fabricate suitable for Stalin lies and distortions concerning the defendants during the first, 1936, and second, 1937, show trials of the leading Communists (The Trial of Sixteen and Seventeen, subsequently). He even provided Stalin with reports detailing the unfavorable public reaction to the show trials abroad and growing sympathy among the Soviet population for the executed defendants. Stalin interpreted these reports as Yagoda's advice to stop the show trials and purges. This enraged him. Yagoda also earned Stalin's enmity eight years earlier when he expressed sympathy for Nikolai Bukharin who Stalin had forced from power. (Bukharin was an economist who promoted a more moderate/less draconian process of industrialization than Stalin's.) Yagoda also failed to provide the forced labor he had promised for the Moscow-Volga Canal and the Moscow underground. These projects were completed with paid and voluntary labor. The economic uses of the Gulags were limited.

As one Soviet official put it, "The Boss forgets nothing." Solzhenitsyn describes Yagoda as trusting in deliverance from Stalin even during the show trial. With Stalin sitting in the hall, Yagoda confidently and insistently begged him for mercy. "I appeal to you! For you I built two great canals!" [26, 27, 28]

Ezhov was a very short (5'1") ethnic Russian who Stalin patronizingly called "shibzdick" (a Russian derogatory word for short people). Ezhov ordered the guards to strip Yagoda naked and beat him for added humiliation just before his execution. Ezhov would suffer exactly the same fate just two years later at the order of his successor and former deputy, Lavrenty Beria. Ezhov was even killed by the same executioner (NKVD chief executioner, Vasily Blokhin). His count of 7,000 shot in 28 days remains one of the most organized and protracted mass murders by a single individual on record, and earned him the Guinness World Record for 'Most Prolific Executioner' in 2010.[29]

Ezhov's reign of terror, which engulfed millions of people in 1937 and 1938, was somewhat eased during the "Beria thaw" of 1939–1940.

By the summer of 1938, Stalin and his circle realized the purges had gone too far, and Ezhov was relieved from his NKVD post and eventually purged. "Ezhov was taken in the dead of night to a slaughterhouse he himself had built near the Lubyanka. Dragged screaming to a special room with a sloping cement floor and a log-lined wall, he was shot there by Blokhin. Beria gave Stalin a list of 346 of Ezhov's associates to be shot. Sixty of them were NKVD officers, another fifty were relatives and sexual partners." [16]

Lavrenty Beria, Stalin's fellow Georgian (Mengrel) and confidante, succeeded Ezhov as head of the NKVD. On November 17, 1938, a joint decree of the Sovnarkom[8] USSR and Central Committee of VKP(b)[++] (Decree about Arrests, Prosecutor Supervision, and Course of Investigation) and subsequent orders of the NKVD were signed by Beria. This canceled most of the NKVD orders related to systematic repression, and it suspended the implementation of death sentences.

Despite some easing, the ideological and political terror still remained in force, although it became a bit more selective. It focused on cultural elites such as with the arrest of the renowned short story writer Isaac Babel, leading administrators, scientists, and upper- and middle-rank military commanders that had been spared during earlier purges. Stalin did not trust them. Decimation of the best military cadre cost the country dearly in the Finland campaign of 1940–1941 and the Great Patriotic War of 1941–1945.

This decimation continued even after the onset of WWII. Air force commander and twice Hero of the Soviet Union, Yakov Smushkevich (of Jewish descent), was arrested on June 8, 1941. This was just weeks before the German invasion of the Soviet Union. Smushkevich was arrested by Beria during a series of purges that centered on air force senior commanders. Particularly targeted were those who had participated in the Spanish Civil War. He was executed on October 28, 1941 while the Germans were still advancing toward Moscow.

---

[8] Sovnarkom—the *S(oviet) N(arodnykh) K(omissarov)* (Council of People's Commissars)
[++] VKP(b) is an acronym for All-Union Communist Party of Bolsheviks.

Twenty high-ranking Soviet officers of Jewish and non-Jewish descent were also executed along with Smushkevich. These included the commander of the 1939 battle with Japan, Grigori Shtern, ace fighter Lt. General Pavel Rychagov, Commanders Loktionov and Proskurov, and other. The arrests and executions of the scapegoated military and armaments production leaders continued well into 1942. All were posthumously rehabilitated after Stalin's death.

The motivation for these waves of terror was apparently the desire of Stalin and his cronies to eliminate potential rivals, real and imagined. (Stalin never forgot a person he couldn't dominate.) They also sought to consolidate power, completely subjugate the population to Stalin's vision of a socialist state, squelch even minor dissent, eliminate former comrades whose loyalty to current policies could be suspect, and express vengeance against former friends and even relatives for trivial offenses. Many innocent people were accused of destruction, sabotage, and being "servile fools." The vagaries of Stalin paranoia flourished.

The arbitrariness of the arrests is summarized in a joke of the time. Three arrested persons met in prison and began describing their offenses. One said, "I was late to work and accused of negligence." Another said, "I was early to work and accused of attempted sabotage." The third said, "I was on time to work and accused of being a spy since I had a foreign watch."

The madness of the situation was such that there were even theories that the waves of repression in 1937 and 1938 were needed to meet quotas for cheap, forced labor in the Gulags. This was due to the high rate of convicts' mortality from the waves of persecutions that took place during the civil war and collectivization. Interesting, however, that in Yagoda's last year of power the rate of mortality in Gulag dropped down to about 20,000. This would soar to over 90,000 in 1938.

Like many leaders of his ilk (e.g., Hitler or Mao Tse-Toung), Stalin considered himself one of the brightest luminaries in many fields, especially in art, literature, and poetry. The only form of art allowed at the time was socialist realism. Stalin and his government watched diligently to make sure no deviant material was published. Occasionally Stalin would call a writer to discuss his work, his thoughts about his colleagues, etc. Often these calls were an ominous sign of impending persecution against the author or a colleague. From the memoir of Boris Pasternak (the author of *Doctor Zhivago*) we know Stalin called him one time to inquire about the talented poet Osip Mandelstam, who was known for his unfavorable views of Stalin and Stalin's cruel policies.

Although Mandelstam had already been deprived of work and a means of existence, Stalin did not immediately decide on more severe punishment. In the conversation with Pasternak, Stalin asked his opinion of Mandelstam's talent. (An author who was talented in Stalin's eyes or who Stalin considered necessary at the moment might fare better than a more ordinary *comrade*.) Despite Pasternak's high appraisal of Mandelstam's poetical skills and talent, Stalin sealed his fate.

Mandelstam's nonconformist, antiestablishment tendencies were not heavily disguised. He opposed the increasingly totalitarian government under Joseph Stalin. In the autumn of 1933, he published the poem "Stalin Epigram." The poem, sharply criticizing the "Kremlin highlander," was described elsewhere as a "sixteen-line death sentence." It was likely inspired by having seen the effects of the Great Famine while on vacation in the Crimea. This was the result of Stalin's collectivization in the USSR and his drive to exterminate the *kulaks*.

Six months later, Mandelstam was arrested. After the customary pro forma inquest, he was sentenced not to death or to the Gulag but to exile in Cherdyn in the Northern Ural with his wife. Exile was considered nearly a miraculous event, and it is usually explained by historians as owing to Stalin's personal interest in the poet's fate. Mandelstam attempted suicide, after which the sentence was lessened to banishment from the largest cities. Otherwise allowed to choose his place of residence, Mandelstam and his wife chose Voronezh. In 1938 Mandelstam was rearrested and died in transit to the far east Gulag camps.

In 1956, during the Khrushchev thaw, Mandelstam was exonerated from the charges brought against him in 1938. On October 28, 1987, during the administration of Mikhail Gorbachev, Mandelstam was exonerated from the 1934 charges as well. Thus his reputation was fully rehabilitated. In 1977 a minor planet was discovered by Soviet astronomer Nikolai Stepanovich Chernykh and was named 3461 Mandelshtam after him.

Pasternak was not exiled or imprisoned. Despite this, a Bill Mauldin cartoon in the American press showed Pasternak and another prisoner in the Gulag splitting trees in the snow. In the caption, Pasternak says, "I won the Nobel Prize for literature. What was your crime?" The cartoon (Bill Mauldin Beyond Willie and Joe (Library of Congress)) won the Pulitzer Prize for editorial cartooning in 1959.

One of the Mandelstam poems, which reflects the poet's apprehension of the time, is presented below in Russian and my English adaptation:

Осип Мандельштам
Ленинград
Декабрь, 1930.

Я вернулся в мой город, знакомый до слез,
До прожилок, до детских припухлых желез.

Ты вернулся сюда, так глотай же скорей
Рыбий жир ленинградских речых фонарей.

Узнавай же скорее декабрьский денек,
Где к зловещему дегтю подмешан желток.

Петрбург! Я еще не хочу умирать!
У тебя телефонов моих номера.

Петербург! У меня еще есть аддреса,
По которым найду мертвецов голоса.

Я на лестнице черной живу
И в висок
ударяет мне вырванный с мясом
звонок.

Я всю ночь на пролет жду гостей дорогих,
Шевеля кандалами цепочек дверных.

Osip Mandelstam
Leningrad

I've come back to my city
With tears in eyes.
Everything from my childhood
In its silhouettes I recognize.

So you're back. Then swallow fast
The fish oil from the riverbank lamps
That you liked in the past.

Familiarize yourself quicker
And don't shy away
From the ominous tar
Mixed with egg yolk
Of the short winter day.

Petersburg! I don't want to die yet.
You still have my numbers
In your telephone net.

Petersburg! The addresses of my friends…
Plenty of them I still get.
So I can look up the voices of the dead.

I live in a room off a back door stairwell
Where torn from the wall
Jangles in my temples the bell.
And throughout the night,
Waiting my dear guests,
I am rattling the door chains-fetters
Without a rest.

December 1930

The metaphors of the last lines of the poem reflect the poet's apprehension of a possible visit of the NKVD in the night ("waiting my dear guests"). In his imagination, the door's chain transforms into heavy fetters.

Ironically, western liberals did not pay much attention to the stories about Stalinist abuses or even the semi-artificially created famine in the Ukraine in early 1930. People believed such stories were anti-Soviet or Nazi propaganda. Walter Duranty's reports in the *New York Times* contributed to this view. Many reporters of Duranty's time slanted their coverage in favor of the Soviet Union. This was either because the capitalist world was sinking under the weight of the Great Depression, or it was out of a true belief in communism. Perhaps it was a fear of expulsion, which would result in the loss of livelihood. Also many editors found it hard to believe a state would deliberately starve millions of its own people.

However, even considering this, Duranty's reports in 1932 were extreme. It is probably Durante who originated a saying exonerating the brutality of collectivization: "One needs to break a few eggs when making an omelet." Similarly Feuchtwanger, who is often praised for his efforts to expose Nazi brutality, praised life under Joseph Stalin in his notes about life in Moscow, *Moskau 1937*. He even approved of the Moscow trials. His book has been criticized as a work of naive apologism.[2]

Photographs and Documents

Alla, Victor, and His Family

Alla and my dad, Victor Dunaevsky, in summer of 1939 at the Azov Sea beach near Taganrog.

Alla (center) with girlfriends Sofa Mindlin (Teds's wife) (left) and Fanya Moroz from Piatigorsk (right) (1939).

Victor Dunaevsky (background) and his friend Gleb Kurasov at study (ca. 1938).

Alla (rightmost in front row) with friends at a sport outing (ca.1939).

Lyuba (Lyubov Abramovna) Osherovskaya, Victor's mother (ca. 1911).

Zelman Hilelevich Dunaevsky, Victor's father (ca. 1914).

Portrait of Josef May by a German artist, Otto Dix. There is a certain similarity between the portrait and Zelman Dunaevsky in his 60s and 70s.

CHAPTER III

Prewar Life in Rostov-on-Don and Evacuation to Semipalatinsk (Kazakhstan) During WWII: 1939–1941

On September 1, 1939, WWII started. This was a war that would profoundly change the geopolitical makeup of the world and the destinies of peoples and states. Following the Molotov-Ribbentrop Pact (a nonaggression treaty signed between Nazi Germany and the USSR on August 23, 1939) and almost immediately after the German invasion of Poland, Stalin expanded Russian territory westward to include almost all the countries, except Finland, that had belonged to Imperial Russia and were lost after the Russian Revolution of 1917. Instantaneously the populations of the newly formed soviet republics and "liberated" territories of Estonia, Latvia, Lithuania, Belorussia, Ukraine, and Moldavia began to experience Stalin's terror. This oppression was conducted under the slogan of struggle against the bourgeoisie and other antisocialist elements.

To prevent the rebirth of a non-Communist led Poland, which was currently occupied by German and Soviet troops, and possibly to avenge the beating the Red Army took at the walls of Warsaw in 1920, Stalin ordered the murder of thousands of Polish officers captured during his Polish campaign of 1939. The massacre took place in 1940 near the village of Katyn in the Smolensk Oblast. Ignored or whitewashed by Soviet propaganda, these criminal acts did not reach the general Soviet population, which was already cowed by the omnipotent NKVD secret police.

Fortunately, from the time of Victor and Alla's marriage in 1939 until Hitler's onslaught on the Soviet Union in 1941[9], the life of my parents was not appreciably affected by the turbulence. This was also a period of modest improvement in the living standards of the Soviet people.

Alla was studying medicine and Victor mechanics. He eagerly read the American magazines *Popular Science* and *Popular Mechanics* translated into Russian. The magazines were available in a local library that Alla and Victor frequented. Victor continued playing tennis and was trying to teach Alla. She was not necessarily athletic, but she liked to carry a tennis rocket, considering it stylish while strolling with Victor along the Rostov thoroughfares. With the massive industrialization of the 1930s, Rostov was becoming the capital of the agricultural machinery industry in the North Caucasus. It was also a big cultural center and a hustling and bustling city. Blocks of huge buildings, interconnected in the middle, were built downtown. They lined Marshal Budenny Prospect near its intersection with Engels (a main street) and toward the River Don. These buildings housed the enormous bureaucratic apparatus of the Soviet governmental structures responsible for commandeering southern Russian industry, agriculture, and many other walks of life.

The popular architectural styles of gigantism and constructivism found fertile ground in Rostov where avant-garde architects built a number of modernist structures. One of them was a theater in the form of a giant tractor overlooking the open steppe beyond the river Don at its lower left bank. The theater is still considered an international landmark.

---

9 The invasion was codified as plan "Barbarossa." This was Hitler's campaign with stated purpose to subdue the "inferior" Slavs and to win *Lebensraum* or "living space" in the east for racially "pure" German people. It started at 3:15 a.m. on June 22, 1941, and it was the largest campaign in military history.

A few blocks away from the three-story building on Gorky Street where the Dunaevskys lived, was a multistory, supermodern building. It housed some of the Rostov professional elites. This included government-supported scientists, specialists, and achievers in various fields. They lived there as long as they did not fall out of grace due to actual or perceived political incorrectness.

The building was constructed in a semicylindrical shape that ensured an unusual radial disposition of the bedrooms connected to a centrally located living room. I was always thrilled visiting this building where Ted Zaltsman lived with his family after the war. They lived in the flat which originally belonged to the endocrinologist Professor Mindlin, whose daughter, Sofa, became Ted's wife. Interestingly I recently found a similar building when I visited my friends in Houston who lived in that type of dwelling.

The prewar years in the USSR featured good, lyrical, patriotic songs and nice musicales, some of which were written by the famous mid-twentieth-century Russian composer, Isaak Dunaevsky. Although not a direct relation to me, he and my paternal grandfather were both born in the Poltava district of Ukraine. The American movies that reached the Soviet silver screen were also in great prominence, especially those of Charlie Chaplin. Alla and Victor liked the cultural side of life and attended movie theaters, musicales, and plays. There was one song that my mother sang even after the war, and she sometimes accompanied herself on the piano. It was the touching song of Suzette, a poor, blind flower seller from Chaplin's *City Lights*.

One of the popular and enthusiastic songs of the era glorified the budding Soviet air force. It had the following words. (In my adaptation below I tried to retain the rhythm and rhyme of the original.)

Higher and higher and higher
The flight of the steel birds we order.
And each propeller is breathing
The security of our border.

I recently found out that the melody of this song was borrowed from a similar song in Nazi Germany. Despite the differences in ideology and regime, both countries often extolled the same virtues. This included romanticizing technical progress and industrialization.

In the parallel universe of the Gulag prison system, life in the camps went on in its own way. Fortunately for Lev Shmulian the management of the camp to which he was assigned appreciated and utilized his legal skills. He was such a "dangerous enemy of the people" that he was allowed to travel unguarded to Arkhangelsk, the main city of the province where his camp was located, to justify a better food quota for the camp, which was meager at best, before some local authorities. In 1940 Alla, Witold, and Isabella were able to visit Lev in the camp. These were their last visits.

Witold, who was already teaching mathematics in Odessa University, became a post doctor of mathematics that year at the prestigious Steklov Mathematics Institute in Moscow. His mother, Isabella, and his brother, Theodor, continued to live in Taganrog, which still gleamed with the aura of Anton Chekhov. Isabella was a prolific freelance writer. One of the unique sides of her art was rendering various prose literature pieces into verse form. In particular, she transformed several famous European and Russian fairy tales, including "Red Riding Hood," and arranged them as verse plays for children.

She also made a verse adaptation of the comedy *Nedorosl* (*The Minor*) by renowned eighteenth-century Russian writer Denis Fonvizin. With a main hero, Mitrofan, and about the seamy side of Russian society, Isabella made it suitable for a children's play. Not having big support from the authorities in her undertakings, she still was able to produce these plays. They were performed with neighborhood children and with the assistance of the local school personalities. The plays were staged in backyards in the summer and in some cultural facilities in the winter.

There were only a few performances, and these took place in the late 1930s and early 1950s. It is very regrettable that not much remains from the scripts of these plays. One reason was the difficulty of typing her handwritten materials, which were often scribbled on small pieces of paper. This required special permission and clearance, considering the shortage of typewriters, the shortage of paper in certain times, limited access to either, and a general government clampdown on the free use of typewriting and copying facilities. This situation continued even through the 1990s.

Isabella was strict in her selection of actors for her plays. She was incorruptible and did not condone nepotism. Hence, as punishment for some of my mischief associated with a play rehearsal, I, who at the age of seven or eight coveted the role of the wolf in *Little Red Riding Hood*, was not given the role. Delving now into this subject and further introspection, I suspect that my latent resistance to assisting my grandmother type or preserve her writing developed as a reaction to not being given the role in her play. If so, this would be another example of how childhood memories can affect adult behavior.

Isabella also wrote lyrical verses and poems dedicated to her friends and relatives. In the Taganrog period, one such poem was for her first grandchild, Zhorzhick (a Russian diminutive for George), who was born to her son, Theodor, in 1940.

Many of Isabella's works reflect the politics and mood of the day. One play in verse was about a group of pioneers (a junior league of Communist membership that loosely resembled the Scouts) who, at their afterschool meeting, debated the possibility of the presence of an enemy of the people among them. The poem ends with the pioneers declaring there are no enemies among them. This positive ending probably did not dovetail well with the official doctrine requiring the population, including the pioneers, to be vigilant and hunt down "enemies" whoever they were.

A more palatable ending for the authorities would have been where the pioneers find the "enemy" and unmask him. That happened in a real-life story when pioneer Pavlik Morozov betrayed his father. A relatively well-to-do farmer (derogatorily called *kulak*), he allegedly concealed a portion of his crop from the government requisitionists. The ending of her play suggests that Bella, especially with the arrest of her husband, was disillusioned about certain aspects of Soviet reality, or at least she was not deeply indoctrinated by the Soviet "enemies among us" propaganda.

The opposite, however, was often the case. At least on the surface, many regular folks and even intellectuals were intimidated into accepting the notion that the ongoing purges and arrests were justified in the light of Stalin's theory that class struggle increases in reaction to the strengthening of a socialist state.

This theory, however, was a complete falsehood and farce. It was intended to cover up the nefarious deeds of the regime, particularly the murder of a Stalin rival, Sergey Kirov, in 1934. The murder was instigated by Stalin, who blamed an "attack" by anti-Soviet elements and orchestrated a witchhunt for the "enemies."

There were many personal tragedies, such as the arrest of my grandfather. Among family and friends, the victim was considered loyal to the regime, but the event had to be filtered through the prism of a popular rationalization of the period. Echoing the Duranty "broken eggs" analogy, it boiled down to the notion that the chips flew when the forest was cleared.

The Evacuation: From Rostov to Semipalatinsk, Summer of 1941.

After graduation in 1941, Victor began working as an engineer at the Red Aksay factory in Rostov, which produced certain types of agricultural machinery. When the war started on June 22 with the German invasion, his factory began transitioning to the production of military equipment. Victor got a deferment from military service perhaps because he now worked in a defense industry or because he had poor eyesight. Perhaps it was for other reasons altogether. In any case, he became involved in the development of manufacturing processes and designs for antiaircraft machine guns.

The factory, along with other big industrial enterprises and organizations, was located within territory that could potentially fall into enemy hands. As such it began preparing for evacuation to the eastern areas of the Soviet Union behind the Ural Mountains. Before the war, huge industrial complexes had already been built in this area.

The evacuation of the industry, organized by the government in the shortest time and not in the easiest of conditions, was overall an important achievement. (One needs to give credit where it is due.) It achieved two goals. It didn't leave industrial stock for the enemy, but it made it useful for the war effort. The central government was preparing to leave Moscow for the hinterland city of Kuibyshev on the Volga River in case the capital was captured.

Rapid advancement of the fascist hordes across the vast expanses of the European part of the USSR uprooted huge masses of ordinary citizens. People packed, if they had time, and fled eastward. More often, however, they left everything behind in panic and fled in whatever way they could.

This was mostly on foot and in horse-driven buggies because automobile transportation was very rudimentary. The railroads had ceased running in the occupied areas or had gone out of service due to bombing.

The extended columns of refugees were often harassed by low-flying Luftwaffe Messershmidts, Junkers, Fokke–Vulfs, and Stuka diving bombers. They strafed the human masses moving along the highways with cannon and machine gun fire to instill terror and sometimes for the pure amusement of the aircraft crews. Members of the Communist Party or Young Communist League (*Komsomol*), army officers, and Jews could expect the worst in case of capture. The *Officiren, commisaren, Juden* (German for officers, political commissars, and Jews) were the first targets of the advancing Nazis. Accordingly many of the people in territories expecting to be occupied destroyed or buried their membership cards. Many Jews also destroyed their passports[10] to hide their identities, fearing Nazi anti-Semitic attitudes.

In the frantic atmosphere of these territories, rumors become an important source of information. This was true even in areas still under Soviet control, because the regular sources of information, such as radio and newspapers, curtailed their operations, and individual radio receivers were often confiscated by the Soviet government under the pretext of minimizing exposure of the citizenry to enemy propaganda. Along with sources of information, many other elements of Soviet infrastructure were crumbling in advance of the enemy.

On one late September day, Zelman, my grandfather, returned from bazar, an open-air farmers' market close to the Don River, which was the major source of retail groceries. He was in a panic from the rumor that Germans were unexpectedly and quickly approaching Rostov. In the plans of Hitler's generals, Rostov was a city of special importance.

---

10 In the USSR everybody had an internal passport where a fifth point was reserved for the nationality of the passport bearer. Upon the introduction of Soviet passports in the early 1920s, people whose religious affiliation was Jewish or whose ancestors were Jewish received passports where they were identified as Hebrews. Subsequently children of Hebrew parents were automatically identified as Hebrews also. In the case of mixed marriages, children had the right to select the nationality of one parent when they received their passports at the age of sixteen.

It was a strategic railway junction, a river port, and a gateway to the Caucasus, which was rich in minerals, especially oil. The rumors about the German troops' proximity were taken seriously, and the family of Dunaevskys made the tough decision that their younger members, Alla and Victor, had to flee east. They had to get further away from the zones which would be potentially occupied by the fascists.

It was decided that the older Dunaevskys, Zyama and Lyuba, would stay behind. They would leave it up to destiny, which offered the following possible options.

- The Red Army would still be able to repel the advancing enemy troops.

- Means of transportation out of the city could be found later, if resistance to the enemy prevailed for some time, so they also could leave.

- They would meet their fate, whatever it would be.

Regardless of any rationalization, the hesitation of the older Dunaevskys to leave could be understood. There was limited information available about the extent of Hitler's anti-Semitic policies and about the horrendous crimes committed toward Jews by Nazis and their collaborators in the occupied territories. Even as Jewry was exterminated in the occupied territories, the Soviet government, except for on a few occasions, was reluctant to mention this peculiar situation.

The full extent of these crimes became known to the larger world only after the war. During the first year and a half after the start of WWII, the information for Soviet citizens about the mistreatment of Jews was concealed to some degrees by Soviet propaganda. After the Molotov-Ribbentrop Nonaggression Pact, the Soviets bent over backwards to placate Germany. They treated them as a friendly nation struggling with British and French imperialism. At the same time, the hostile attitude of Nazi Germany and its actions toward Jews were increasing slowly, but those actions were often presented to the world in a distorted form.

Zyama and Lyuba's decision to remain in Rostov also represented an attitude popular among many intellectuals and non-intellectuals alike.

This was the belief Germans were civilized and cultural people. In addition, many skeptical people, Zyama being one of the first among them, were inclined to dismiss certain leaked stories of Nazi abuses because they believed this was sheer propaganda from the Soviet government.

Lyuba's hesitation to move was probably also due to the fact she was working as a doctor in a Rostov hospital where her sister, Vera, was a long-term patient with some serious illness. Lyuba apparently believed that as long as she continued working in a hospital her sister would be protected.

Heeding a decision to flee, Alla, Victor, and Alla's mother left the Dunaevsky flat one day in early October, taking with them a minimum set of belongings and food supplies. A tram from a still-operating line took them to the outskirts of the city. From there they moved on foot toward Novocherkassk, which is situated about thirty miles east of Rostov. Novocherkassk was the former capital of Don Cossacks and a center for railroad connections. Rumor had it that trains were still leaving from there toward the eastern territories.

The Dunaevskys and Isabella were speeding toward Novocherkassk with crowds of other Rostovites. They spent a night in the fields near a haystack. In the morning they met people coming back from Novocherkassk who said the Germans had been driven back, and there was no imminent threat of a Rostov occupation. So they decided to return home. Upon their return to Rostov, Isabella probably went back to Taganrog on a train by a local, still-functioning railroad line.

Meanwhile the situation on the front remained critical, and many people and organizations continued evacuating from southern Russia, albeit in a haphazard fashion. Along with other big industrial facilities—and there were a number of those in Taganrog—the plant where Theodor was working began preparing to evacuate the equipment and workers with their families.

The strict evacuation rules stipulated that only the immediate family members could be taken on the evacuation train. Accordingly Theodor could take only his wife and son on the train, while he knew his mother and his sister's family would also like to be evacuated. (Victor's plant was apparently not ready yet for evacuation.) For Theodor it was an agonizing dilemma. He had to decide whether to evacuate with his wife and son and leave behind his mother and sister's family or not evacuate at all. The dilemma, however, was soon resolved.

Theodor's wife, Lyusia, decided she could not leave her parents behind. She also felt relatively safe since her passport showed her nationality as Russian. Her parents, though, were of mixed Russian/Jewish stock. So it was decided she, and Theodor's and her two-year-old son, George, would stay in Taganrog. This outcome allowed Theodor to obtain, with some effort, permission for Isabella to sign up for the evacuation train. Because Isabella did not want to be separated from Alla, Theodor eventually signed up Alla and Victor for the train too.

The train left Taganrog sometime between October 10 and 15. The Germans (the armored SS Divisions Wiking and Leibstandarte SS Adolf Hitler) arrived at the outskirts of Taganrog on October 17. After a heavy fight resulting in loss of thousands *Wehrmacht* soldiers and officers, the Red Army left Taganrog on October 22, 1941. From the first days of the German occupation, the new regime started mass deportation of the citizens to Nazi Germany for hard labor, and systematic genocidal action. By the end of October, 7000 Taganrogers (old men, women, communists, gypsies, Jews and anyone else suspected in aiding the resistance movement) were shot to death in a village near Taganrog. All Jewish population of Taganrog, 2,500 Jewish people, perished in that massacre.[36] The atrocities, fortunately, did not touch Theodor family.

The destination of the train carrying Alla and Victor was Makhachkala, a main city of the Dagestan Autonomous Republic within the Russian Federation. It is located on a Caspian Sea bank of the Northern Caucasus. The train, which consisted mostly of freight cars, some without a roof, had to pass through Rostov. This was where Alla and Victor were picked up. With its departure from Rostov, the evacuation train of Theodor's *Krasny Kotelshchik* plant began moving directly toward the North Caucasus.

Due to bombing raids by enemy aircraft and various irregularities in locomotive operation and railways maintenance, the train's movement across the Kuban steppes in the foothills of the Caucasian Mountains toward Makhachkala was slow and intermittent. In these conditions, it took several days to reach the west bank of the Caspian Sea. Typically it took one and a half days.

After arriving in Makhachkala, Theodor and a group of colleagues took a train to Derbent, a city about one hundred miles further south. Possibly they were in search of work. Meanwhile, Bella and the younger Dunaevskys continued to stay with other travelling families at the train. They were trying to decide what to do next. The timing and means for further transportation of the equipment and people were not clear. The next steps depended on the situation at the front, the opportunity to get booked on a ship across the Caspian Sea (with hopes of finding a job in the eastern part of the USSR), and the opportunity to stay at the Makhachkala station where the train had unloaded.

Ever since the civil war in the USSR, it was typical for travelers waiting for connections to spent days and nights under the roofs of railway stations. In the absence of available and affordable housing and hotels, people could find at the station temporarily shelter with toilets (albeit often very primitive and without plumbing), running water, boiled water, food, some medical facilities, and a special room for mothers with children. The railway stations in big cities boasted restaurants that were decent by the standards of the time. In wartime, these railway stations become magnets for desperate crowds who virtually lived there.

The overfilled hallways of railway stations always retained a bouquet of specific smells—food, human sweat, and unwashed clothes. Despite the unhygienic conditions of the evacuation, the country avoided any substantial outbreak of infectious diseases thanks to government-sanctioned anti-epidemic and sanitary services. At the most basic level, their presence was evident in the bitter smelling quicklime and chlorine powder, which was sprinkled on the toilets (*othozhie mesta*) for disinfection.

The pieces of equipment from the *Krasny Kotelshchik* plant that were transported via the freight train were unloaded and then loaded on a ship scheduled to go across the Caspian Sea. On the eastern shore of the sea, that equipment was reloaded on another freight train for delivery to the industrial city Zlatoust of Chelyabinsk Oblast, Southern Ural.

While the train was being unloaded, Theodor and his colleagues came back from Derbent and joined their families, who were still waiting at the train. One day, when Theodor and his family were at the Makhachkala bazar buying food, NKVD troops conducted a roundup. They tried to apprehend all those who had evaded military service or had questionable documents or no documents. They went after anyone else who had a hard time explaining why he/she happened to be there at that time.

At this unfortunate moment, Theodor was horrified to find he lost (or misplaced) his military card. This was where his exemption from service was certified. Because of his hearing problems, he had difficulties explaining why he had no military card on him. The explanations of the family members—that Theodor had traveled with them on the evacuation train and thus had a deferment from military service—were not taken into account. The NKVD apparently were not interested in letting him go once he was apprehended.

It was a severe blow to the family and particularly Isabella. She was apparently devastated by this new injustice done to her family after her husband's arrest—the removal of her son, who was essentially leading their dash to safety. It was almost three years later that the whereabouts of Theodor, who miraculously survived all the odd, bizarre, and dangerous situations in store for him, were clearly established.

Uncertainty about the future, hardships of the present, and anxiety about the relatives left behind raised the misery of the evacuees to the highest level. In a few days, however, the anxiety was somewhat relieved when my parents were pleasantly surprised by the appearance of the older Dunaevskys at the Makhachkala station. As it turned out, soon after the departure of Victor and Alla, Zyama and Lyuba also decided to flee, driven by the unfavorable news from the front.

The Dunaevskys were also encouraged to leave through their association with a doctor that joined them in Rostov. He was an energetic personality who had more or less a clear vision of where to go and how to get there. He was able to get tickets for one of the last trains to Makhachkala. His goal after that was a trans-Caspian trip and ultimately the establishment of himself and his fellow travelers as professionals in their fields in the towns of the republics of Soviet Central Asia. The doctor had a relative near Semipalatinsk, which is located on the right bank of the river Irtysh in eastern Kazakhstan. The doctor hoped his relative might provide some housing assistance if he and his group could reach him there.

Unfortunately, I don't have any knowledge about the efforts and time consumed in crossing the Caspian Sea from Makhachkala to

Krasnovodsk on the eastern shore of the sea. I also don't know what they went through on the railroad to reach Semipalatinsk and the small town of Zhana-Semey where the doctor's relative lived. Probably while still in Rostov, the doctor sent a cable to his relative telling him he and his friends might require housing assistance. Based on an agreement cabled back by this relative, the doctor and his party, which ultimately grew to six people, including Isabella and four members of the Dunaevsky family, arrived at the relative's house to his utter surprise. Everybody felt great awkwardness.

Although they must certainly have felt taken aback, the master of the house and his wife demonstrated hospitality and fed the guests. Each one received a piece of bread with fruit jam. This was apparently not a small deal at the time, as my mother remembered this event very vividly many years later. She explained they had run out of money and had not eaten for several days. There were only two small rooms in the house, so the lodging provided by the host for a few nights was very rudimentary. Fortunately the Dunaevskys did not stay long in this house. As was expected, Lyuba Dunaevsky quickly found a job as a doctor at a local military hospital treating wounded soldiers evacuated from the front. Lyuba's job simplified establishing permanent housing for the Dunaevskys. Their new home consisted of a single room in a two-story building with communal amenities.

In a few months Isabella was housed in another place where she rented just a corner of a room. Her living became dependent on the small subsidies her younger son, Witold, sent her. He was now serving as an artillery officer in the Red Army. At the beginning of the war, he and a group of coworkers at the Steklov Institute had joined a so-called people's army. This was reformed into a regular army, which fought long battles from the walls of Moscow to Warsaw. On August 27, 1944, a few days before his thirtieth birthday, he was heroically killed.

During his life on the front, Witold never stopped his scientific activity. He was always finding opportunities to continue working on the mathematical problems he was involved with at Steklov. Some of his completed works were (with assistance from friends) later published in the USSR's Academy of Sciences journals. Appendix A shows a tribute to W. Shmulian, which was prepared for his fiftieth birthday by his former professor. Witold's wife, Vera Gantmacher, was also a mathematician and the daughter of the renowned mathematician R. Gantmacher. She stayed in Odessa with her parents while Witold was in the army. She and her parents were murdered in February of 1942 by the Romanian fascists, who occupied the city on October 17, 1941. Roughly half of the 180,000-strong prewar Jewish population of Odessa perished in the Holocaust.

Following Lyuba, Alla also got a job in the hospital. From May 4, 1942 until September 13, 1945, when the hospital was liquidated following the end of war, she was listed there as a trained nurse. Victor found a job as a mechanic at the meat processing plant, and Zelman began working somewhere as an accountant. Nonmilitary service in the organizations helping the war effort was considered by the government as important and honorable as direct military activity at the front. The work was demanding. Not meeting the government quotas on the supply of goods, whether they were food, materials, armaments, etc., could be considered sabotage, and the party at fault could be prosecuted to the highest level—being shot by a firing squad.

"Rise up, huge country,
Rise up for a mortal fight
With the dark fascist force,
With the damn horde."
"Вставай страна огромная,
Вставай на смертнй бой
С фашистской силой темною,
С проклятою ордой."

Words from the Soviet patriotic song "The Sacred War," June 22/23, 1941. Music: A. Alexandrov. Lyrics: V. Lebedev-Kumach. [33]

CHAPTER IV

Life in Semipalatinsk and WWII Episodes: 1941–1945

Rostov was taken by the Germans on November 21, 1941. It was the gate to the Caucasus. The Axis armies thrust toward the Caucasus to seize the oil fields of Maikop and Grozny, the rich agricultural areas of the Northern Caucasus, and the refineries on the Caspian Sea near Baku, the capital of Azerbaijan. Hitler believed the threat to the Caucasus oil fields would force the Red Army to sacrifice its last reserves of manpower to protect them. If the Nazis conquered the oil fields, Germany's critical shortages would be filled. The Soviet Union could not survive long without the oil the Caucasus provided.

Rostov changed hands twice during the Second World War. The first occupation of Rostov was in November of 1941, and it lasted only a few days. It was, however, characterized by a brutal suppression of the city's armed resistance and bestial atrocities against Jews and others suspected of supporting partisans. The scale of the crimes committed was small, however, compared to the second occupation, which lasted longer.

Although the Soviet defensive line was overcome with relative ease and speed in early November, the torrential rain that followed the Germans' success forced another costly suspension of attack until the middle of the month. Rostov fell to Rundstedt's forces on November 20 in temperatures as low as -20 °C (-4 °F), but the Germans had no time to celebrate their victory. Just two day later, Marshal Semyon Timoshenko's southwestern front counterattacked strongly. With little hope of repelling the Soviets, Kleist, the commander of the 1st Panzer Group, sought permission to withdraw, lest his armor and men be annihilated. The desperate situation of the 1st Panzer Group was evident to Rundstedt as he looked at his map and listened to the latest news from the front. So he proposed a withdrawal of eighty miles to the relative safety of the River Mius.

Hitler, however, demanded the line be held around Rostov, and he sacked Rundstedt for failing to carry out his "no withdrawal" orders. Ironically Rundstedt's replacement, Field Marshal von Reichenau, saw the logic in the withdrawal proposals and asked the Führer to agree to them. Hitler gave his approval, and the withdrawal took place. [3] The advancing units of the German Panzer Army were driven out of Rostov. The Germans suffered their first significant defeat on the Eastern Front.

In some newsreels of that time, one can see the American tanks, distinguished by the big letters "USA" on the sides, situated in front of the German positions. This testifies to the speedy delivery of American help to the Soviet Army.

But on July 24, 1942, the German army managed to occupy the city for the second time after fierce battles and heavy bombardment. The second occupation lasted until February 14, 1943. When the city was recovered by Russia, it took ten years to raise it from the ruins and restore it. Rostov was among the fifteen Russian cities that suffered the most during the years of occupation. It was also the largest Russian city seized by the German army.

By various estimates, over 20,000 Jews lived in Rostov. Although many fled the city in the days prior to the first, short-lived occupation in November of 1941, a sizable portion of the Jewish population stayed behind. These were people who did not manage to evacuate with the factories and other enterprises, people who did not want to be evacuated because they did not believe in or know about the murderous Nazi intent toward the Jews, and people who had no means to flee because they were old, ill, handicapped, or refugees with no place to go. By the summer of 1942, the number of Jews remaining in Rostov had increased since many who left earlier had returned.

During the second occupation, starting in mid-August and lasting through the end of September, several genocidal actions against the Jewish population took place in different parts of Rostov. Along with Jews, a large number of Soviet prisoners of war, Communists, government functionaries and their families, handicapped and disabled people from local hospitals, and other undesirables were liquidated. Based on eyewitness accounts,[4] on August 11–12 nearly 11,000-13,000 Jewish people, including women, children, and the elderly, were marched through Rostov to a secluded ravine called Zmievskaya Balka, or Snake Gulch, where they were summarily executed and buried. Nearly five-thousand Jews were massacred at the Jewish cemetery. By some accounts, over 27,000 Jewish people perished in these genocidal events.*

* See also [19]

German authorities facilitated the assemblage of Jews for extermination. They even issued proclamations with false promises of protecting the Jews against the hostile actions of the local population (see Appendix B).

They also brought in gas vans to exterminate the remaining Jewish citizens, who were hunted down with the active assistance of the local collaborators who also formed the firing squads. Along with Jews, they also gassed several hundred captured Red Army soldiers. The bodies were disposed of in the same Snake Gulch and also in a shaft the prisoners of war and Jews who had arrived from Poland had been digging before being executed.

As Anton Laurer from the Police Reserve Battalion described,[5] "There were two gas-vans in use. I saw them myself. They were driven into the prison yard and the Jews—men, women and children—had to get into the van directly from their cells. I also saw inside the gas-vans.

They were lined with metal and there was a wooden grille on the floor. The exhaust gasses were fed into the inside of the van. I can still today hear the Jews knocking and shouting, 'Dear Germans, let us out.'" During one of these actions, Lyuba's sister, Vera, perished. She had been left in Rostov's general hospital after her siblings evacuated.

Zmievsakya Balka was the place of the largest-scale Holocaust massacres on Russian territory. A commemorating monument was erected there. Under the German occupation, atrocities against the Jewish population were committed in Taganrog as well. Fortunately these did not touch Theodor's family.

Back to the other members of the Dunaevskys and Shmulian families, the families of Isabella's sister and brother stayed in Leningrad during a substantial portion of the nine hundred days of blockade from 1941–1944. They barely survived in a city where six hundred thousand died from starvation. Their account of survivorship does not differ much from others who survived the blockade. They had a nominal daily ration, which consisted of 100 g of bread per adult. Factory workers received additional quotas of bread.

The bread benefits were not extended to Bella's brother, Grigori, who was teaching in the Pedagogical Institute, or her sister, Tamara, who was a doctor in a hospital. To supplement their rations, many people took chairs apart and boiled the glued connections to make soup. Anything with glue, including wallpaper and book bindings, was used for that purpose. The leftover bits of furniture and wooden planks from fences (usually found at the outskirts of the city) were also used to fire the stoves, as central heating and running water were mostly out of service during the three years of the blockade. Within a few months of the blockade, no wooden fences were left in the town. All cats and dogs were consumed. The cases of cannibalism were not infrequent. [40]

Fortunately Alla and her family members did not suffer from outright starvation during their life in Kazakhstan, but everything was scarce. Meanwhile the harsh Eastern Kazakhstan/Siberian winter of 1941 was coming. Food could only be bought at the farmers market, where Kazakhs from the surrounding rural areas brought the fruits of their pastoral life. This was mainly meat, butter, milk, and cheese. Since it was an outdoor market, the food sold in the winter was frozen because of the dangerously low temperatures. Milk was sold by pieces. For easy handling, the Kazakhs kept the pieces of milk, without any protective wrapping, in the folds of their traditional garb or in their pockets.

The radio brought news from the front in briefs from the *SovInform Bureau* (Soviet Information Agency). In a slow and metallic voice (to encourage confidence), the radio announcer Yuri Levitan (whom Hitler promised would be the first to hang upon the capture of Moscow) delivered the news, which was not good. With heavy fighting, the Soviet Army continued to retreat under the relentless German onslaught. Whole armies were encircled and decimated during the summer campaign. One and a half million Soviet military personnel were taken as prisoners of war and left to die from starvation and the elements. Huge swaths of the USSR European territory were occupied during the first weeks and months of the war.

Thousands of pieces of ammunition, tanks, artillery, and aircraft were destroyed. The relative ease with which all this took place is partially explained by the ineptness of the new military command, from which the most experienced cadre had been decimated by Stalin's purges and by the Germans having reliable information on the location of Soviet military equipment. They received this information through reconnaissance flights by the Luftwaffe over Soviet territory before the war and in the first days of war. These flights went unopposed by the Red Army either because Stalin wanted to avoid shooting at enemy aircrafts for fear of provoking a larger confrontation or because the orders weren't delivered in a timely fashion. Despite the appalling losses, dozens of senior officers were scapegoated on Stalin's orders. Subsequently they were imprisoned, tortured, and executed.

Meanwhile the Nazi invaders suffered their most serious defeat since the start of WWII in the battle for Moscow (code-named Typhoon by the German operation) at the end of 1941.

The transfer of four hundred thousand fresh Soviet troops and a mass of ammunition from Siberia and the Manchurian border to the Moscow front dealt a substantial blow to the *Wehrmacht* machine in this theater of war. As a result German troops, which were already within 30 km of the outskirts of Moscow, were thrown back by 100–250 km.

This turn of events was possible due to information primarily from Soviet secret agent Richard Sorge. In the mid 1930s Sorge was planted in Tokyo as a Nazi Germany journalist. He informed Moscow in September 1941 that Japan did not intend to attack the Russian Far East in the winter of 1941–1942.

However, on October 18, 1941 he was identified as a spy by the Japanese. He was arrested, tortured, indicted as a Soviet spy and hanged on November 7, 1944. Through his actions and handsome looks, Sorge (of German and Russian descent) became a hero. There have been books and movies about his life.

The Red Army troops went directly into battle after the traditional November 7 military parade in Red Square. Although many government institutions and plants were evacuated from Moscow, Stalin and some member of the Politburo decided to stay and watch the parade from the walls of Lenin's mausoleum. This measure was intended to boost the morale of the Soviet troops.

By the end of the battle in early January of 1942, there were over one million casualties from both sides. Along with fresh troops, other factors helped to defend Moscow. Particularly helpful was the appearance of the new T-34 tanks, which savaged the German panzers and were almost invincible. Due to an unusually cold winter, with temperatures often as low as -20-30°F, the fighting machines' engines on both sides faltered. However, the Red Army tanks fared better in these conditions thanks to the use of compressed air at the start-up.

While fierce battles were raging near Moscow, Imperial Japan attacked the United States naval base at Pearl Harbor, Hawaii, on December 7. This extended WWII to the Pacific as the United States declared war on Japan following the attack. Germany and Italy immediately declared war on the United States in accordance with the agreement between the Axis powers (Germany, Japan, and Italy). This turn of events finally allowed the United States government to break its pretence of neutrality toward the "European" war and declare all-out war on Germany and Italy on December 11.

However, hostilities toward Germany were already simmering with the United States helping to destroy German submarines menacing British shipping lanes. In May of 1941, the U-boats also attacked a United

States merchant ship. This was after the United States entered into the Lend-Lease Program with the UK Commonwealth, which allowed massive shipments of war material to the cash-strapped country. The Lend-Lease Agreement was extended to the USSR after it suffered tremendous losses in the wake of the Nazi invasion. These vital Lend-Lease shipments included war materials, armaments, land vehicles, and food. Lend-Lease was later extended to France and China who became allies with the USA, UK, and USSR in the war against the Axis powers.

Under the Lend-Lease Agreement, the Soviet Union received thousands of US-made trucks. By 1945 nearly two-thirds of the truck strength of the Red Army was US-built, and it consisted mostly of Dodge 3/4-ton and Studebaker 2½-ton trucks. Likewise the Soviet Air Force received 18,700 aircrafts, which was about 19 percent of Soviet aircraft production during the war.

The United States' supply of tanks, locomotives, railroad cars, telephone cables, aluminum, canned rations, and clothing were also critical. Delivery of these goods went through the Northern Atlantic and Vladivostok (a Pacific Ocean port at the easternmost part of the USSR), over the Trans-Siberian Railway, through Alaska and the Arctic, and through Iran, which was occupied by Soviet troops. Even Stalin admitted the victory in WWII wouldn't have been possible without the United States Lend-Lease Program. [6]

From the first month of Russia's entry into the war, Stalin demanded that Great Britain and later the United States open a second front in France. At that time military wisdom held that the Russians would collapse in defeat within three months or less. It was only because of the Russian army's heroic resistance, the vast landmass the Germans had to cover, and the onset of winter that the Nazi offensive came to a halt outside Moscow in December. A second front, mounted by England alone (America had yet to join the war), was impractical. However, Churchill and Roosevelt could not tell Stalin they had no intention of invading France until some distant date, which turned out to be 1944.

As time passed Stalin became convinced his allies were prepared to let the *Wehrmacht* break itself upon the crucible of the Russian people. He gave little thought to the difficulties involved in mounting an amphibious assault on a heavily defended coastline, and at one point he offered four divisions of Russian troops for the purpose. (Churchill was sorely tempted to take Stalin at his word and would have done so if he could have spared the shipping.) At the same time, Stalin showed little gratitude for the assistance he was receiving from his allies, although assistance had a high cost in both shipping and men lost. Indeed, as Stalin's letters demonstrate, he took pains to conceal this foreign aid from the Russian people, insisting planes be delivered outside the Russian territory and without the pilots the Allies had offered to help train the Russians. [6]

Hopes for the opening of a second front were constantly on the minds of the Soviet people, including Alla and her family. The topic of a second front continues even today among Russian people whenever they get together and start their famous soul-searching conversations. Often these conversations surface around Memorial Day and D-day. This is when the American media glorifies the Normandy landing and attributes the defeat of Nazi Germany exclusively to that event, thus shoving aside, in the eyes of Russian émigrés, the tremendous sacrifices of the Soviet people. After all the Eastern Front accounted for nearly 90 percent of German military losses in World War II. Moreover, in the months following the Normandy landings, the war in western Europe was fought between only fifteen Allied and fifteen German divisions, whereas on the Eastern Front more than four hundred Soviet and German divisions battered each other for three years.

Witnessing the current might of the United States, and not being savvy about the difficulties of a channel-crossing invasion of the Nazi-fortified European coastline, many Russian emigrants still question why a Normandy invasion did not happen earlier than the summer of 1944. Many forget America was fighting on several fronts during WWII. First there was the Pacific front, then the African front in 1942, then the North Atlantic, and finally Europe after the capture of Sicily in July of 1943. Some historians believe, however, the western Allies, particularly Churchill, intentionally delayed opening the front in France. They speculate Churchill's secret hope was that Germany and the Soviet Union would exhaust each other on the Eastern Front, leaving the western powers free to deal with them easily when the time came. According to these historians, the invasion of northern France in 1944, when it was apparent the war was no longer going smoothly for Germany, was needed to prevent communism from gaining more of a foothold in Europe.

In the USSR we read books about life in Nazi-occupied Europe, and one of those was Hans Fallada's *Every Man Dies Alone*. This left a big impression on my mother and other members of the family, and often it was a topic for family conversations. After emigrating to America, we learned more details about the preparation and execution of Operation Overlord (the Allies' invasion of Normandy on D-day). Alla's sensitive nature romanticized the French resistance, and she was touched by the poetical nature of the code the BBC issued to resistance fighters to inform them about the invasion. It was described in *The Longest Day* by Cornelius Ryan [7], which I presented to my mother on her sixty-fourth birthday.

The code was based on a phrase from French poet Paul Verlaine's poem "Chanson d'Automne." The first translated line, "The long sobs of the violins of autumn," signified a British and US invasion was imminent. The second line, which signaled an attack within forty-eight hours, was, "Wound my heart with a monotonous languor." Alla loved and knew poetry and often recited memorable pieces at various occasions. She retained that habit to the end of her days. When she became elderly, Mother staved off mental decline by reciting from memory various verses and checking their correctness with me. That phrase from the code was one of Alla's favorite lines to recollect.

The Allies went to great lengths to keep the actual incursion date a secret, hoping to fool the Germans into believing the air and seaborne assault would take place across the Strait of Dover in the Pas-de-Calais area rather than right across the Channel. Even down to the last day, when Eisenhower ordered the invasion fleet to return to port rather than face a raging storm, the worst to hit the Channel in some twenty years, there was fear the Germans had spotted the ships and were prepared for the landings. They hadn't. Adolf Hitler, even after the Allies had landed, still believed the Normandy beach fighting was only a cover for the "real thing" to come. Even more astonishingly, the German *Wehrmacht* high command had plenty of warning. A German spy at the British Embassy in Turkey told his superiors in Berlin that the BBC in London would alert the French Resistance to the invasion by broadcasting a two-part coded message. The message would be taken from the aforementioned poem by Paul Verlaine, "Song of Autumn."

When the second part of the quoted message aired on June 5, 1944, it set off a wide range of railroad demolition and other destructive activities by the French Underground. German intelligence intercepted those messages and even notified Berlin, but the high command didn't put the troops on alert. At least they didn't put the German Seventh Army Corps, which had been stationed along the Normandy coast. The Germans had called war games for June 6 in Rennes, France, some eighty miles southwest of Omaha Beach, and many top-ranking officers were absent from their north coast redoubts. Most importantly, Rommel, in charge of all the German defenses, was far from his headquarters at La Roche-Sur-Yon (seventy-five miles south of Rennes on the Atlantic Coast).

Rommel had gone home to Germany to visit his wife and see Hitler. To make things even worse, the German high command shifted its last remaining fighter wing from Normandy back to Germany, leaving just two planes capable of taking to the air. They promptly attacked the British invasion force and then hightailed to the interior.

The Germans weren't alone in their mistakes. On the Allied side, there were errors galore. The most glaring involved a press message on June 3. Originating from Eisenhower's headquarters, it stated, "General Eisenhower today announced Allied landings in France." It turned out to be a mistake, of course. It was a careless machine "test" by a Teletype operator in the pressroom, yet the Germans received it. Seeing no maritime activity on the Channel, they actually ignored it.[7]

Russian expectations for the opening of a second front by the Allies in Europe were not just an abstract thought. The expectation of its early occurrence were propped up by the Soviet government and actually used to reinforce a fighting spirit in Red Army soldiers. Expressing any doubts about the reality of this event occurring in the early war years was prosecuted. A doubter could be court-martialed. Mother told me a related story.

In 1943 my father signed a letter in support of the innocence of his friend, Yuri Menikov. He was an army officer accused of some infringement of the aforementioned political doctrine and was thus under threat of a court-martial. This would automatically banish him to a penal battalion or concentration camp. My father's petition on behalf of his friend was a very courageous action for the time.

The "infringement" was a letter Yuri wrote to his parents, expressing doubts that the Allies (America and Britain) would open a second front during 1943. As we know now, he was right in his assessment. The second front was opened only in 1944. Deviation from the rules of political correctness is always, even nowadays, potentially troublesome, but in those days in Russia, it was a matter of life and death. Fortunately my father's friend was spared the worst (imprisonment or execution).

As 1942 rolled on, the advances made by the Soviet Army in the battles for Moscow were stalling and bitten back in some cases. Military historians explain this as overextension of the Russian supply lines and poor military judgment of army commanders, who underestimated the enemy. An example of the latter is the doom on the Volkhov Front. To relieve Leningrad, whose 2.5 million civilian inhabitants were entering the depth of mass starvation, Stalin overruled his generals and insisted on a counteroffensive along the entire front. This spanned from the Baltic in the north to the Black Sea in the south.

"Launched at first sight on January 6, 1942, Stalin's Leningrad offensive began with a bloodbath. Attacking on foot over the frozen Volkhov without artillery preparation, air cover, or winter camouflage, Russian infantry were cut down by the thousands by German gunners shelter ring in well-built firing points on the Volkhov's River higher west bank. Thrown into battle the following morning, the 2nd Shock Army…in the first half hour of its assault…lost more than 3,000 men." [23] As one of the survivors of the battle recalled: "Uniquely for January, the river ice started to break up and drift. The grey Volkhov boiled with shellfire, and turned red with human blood. We were getting used to war by then, but seeing human arms and heads sticking up out of the river and human bodies under the transparent ice, we recklessly cursed those who, through stupidity and irresponsible thoughtlessness, plunged infantrymen alive into the frozen river…Later I was in the battles for Kishinev and Budapest, but the sight of the bloody mortal Volkhov stays with me to this day."[23]

"Red Army tactics also remained rudimentary. German soldiers were amazed to see Russian infantry advancing across open ground in line abreast, shouting loud 'hurrahs,' which, one German veteran observed, 'told us where to shoot.'"[23] It was also at the Volkhov Front that General Andrey Vlasov (who earlier played a key role in the defense of Moscow) was captured. After his capture, Vlasov began to cooperate with the Germans. He was made the commander of the anti-Soviet Russian Liberation Army (ROA) that, by 1944, was a division-sized unit made up of other turncoat POWs. He was captured by the Russians in 1945 and executed for treason in 1946. [24]

Still the Germans were not able to fully recuperate after the debacle at Moscow in the winter of 1941, and having not captured Leningrad, the German command was looking for opportunity targets. In the spring and summer of 1942, one of these targets was the Caucasus. The Red Army continued their stiff resistance but the relentless German onslaught gradually rolled them back. The Red Army surrendered important population centers and military targets such as Sevastopol, a navy base in the Crimean Peninsula.

The surrender of Sevastopol was largely attributed to the inept and reckless leadership of Lev Mekhlis, Stalin's preeminent commissar. The Soviet military actually had a double command. One was strictly military and another was the Communist commissars. The military coordinated their plans with the commissars or subjugated the commissars to their vision. Oftentimes, and particularly with Mekhlis, the situation was reversed. The commissars imposed their nonprofessional views on the military commanders.

Along with their direct push toward the Caucasus, the Nazi troops also advanced toward Stalingrad, a large industrial center on the Volga River situated only forty miles east of another arterial waterway of European Russia. This was the Don River, at the mouth of which the Rostov-on-Don was located.

The capture of Stalingrad was important to the Axis leaders for two primary reasons. First the city was an important transport route on the Volga River between the Caspian Sea and northern Russia. As a result, the German capture of the city would effectively sever the transportation of resources and goods to the north. Second its capture would secure the western flank of the German armies as they advanced into the oil-rich Caucasus region. They had the strategic goal of cutting off fuel to Stalin's war machine. The fact the city bore the name of the leader of the Soviet Union, Joseph Stalin, would also make its capture an ideological coup.

Soviet leadership realized they were under tremendous constraints of time and resources, and the Soviet command began exerting extraordinary efforts to defend Stalingrad and annihilate the advancing Axis armies. At this stage of the war, the Red Army was less capable of highly mobile operations than the German army. However, combat inside a large urban area, which would be dominated by handheld small arms rather than armored and mechanized groups, minimized the Red Army's tactical and supply disadvantages.

The Stalingrad Battle (SB)[8,9] took place between July 17, 1942 and February 2, 1943. The battle's outcome was disastrous for the Axis war machine and marked the turning of the tide in favor of the Allies. The battle involved more participants than any other on the Eastern Front and was marked by its brutality and disregard for military and civilian casualties. It was amongst the bloodiest in the history of warfare. The upper estimates of combined casualties came to nearly two million. The Soviet side seized a strategic initiative and did not relinquish it until the full defeat of the enemy. The SB established favorable conditions for the advancement of Soviet troops in the southwest.

Defeat of the Romanian and Italian armies in the course of the SB initiated a political crisis in these countries. Victory in the SB improved the image and authority of the Soviet Union in the international arena and created respect for the Soviet people.

Despite the stiff resistance offered by Soviet troops, assisted by the mobilized workers of the Stalingrad factories, the German offensive to capture Stalingrad proceeded rapidly in the late summer of 1942. It was supported by Luftwaffe bombing, which reduced much of the city to rubble. This would later help defenders hide themselves in the resulting war of attrition. Though vigorously started, the German offensive got bogged down in house-to-house fighting. Despite controlling over 90 percent of the city at times, the *Wehrmacht* was unable to dislodge the last Soviet defenders, who clung tenaciously to the west bank of the Volga River as the weather turned rainy and cold.

The Battle of Stalingrad, although localized predominantly in Stalingrad, was often concentrated in specific areas such as the Mamaev Kurgan and Railroad Station. It was also influenced by military actions in the larger area northwest and southwest of Stalingrad, an area about 150 miles northeast of Rostov. The Soviet Don Front and the 64th Army in the south of that large area were still functioning, and they harassed the Germans to provide relief for Stalingrad defenders.

On November 19, 1942, Soviet Army forces under the command of Gen. Leit. K. K. Rokossovsky (who was earlier accused of being a Polish spy and spent time in Lubyanka dungions where he was tortured) and under the general command of Marshal G. Zhukov (a brutal but often brilliant commander), a deputy of Supreme Commander-in-Chief Josef Stalin, launched Operation Uranus. This was a two-pronged attack on the exposed flanks of the German forces in Stalingrad. General Friedrich von Paulus, commanding the German Sixth Army in Stalingrad, asked permission to abandon Stalingrad and retreat before the pincers closed, but Hitler refused. He created Army Group Don under von Manstein and charged him with the relief of the Sixth Army in the SB. Manstein advanced to within thirty-five miles of Stalingrad, but Hitler would not allow the weakened Sixth Army to break free of Stalingrad and link up.

Following this the Soviet Army smashed the German flanks (weakly held by Romanians, Hungarians, and Italians), and the German forces engaged in the Stalingrad Battle were cut off and encircled between the Don and Volga Rivers. About 330,000 German troops fell into this encirclement, which was enforced by an external ring created from the forces of the Soviet Southwest and Stalingrad Fronts. It extended from the internal front by 40–100 km.

In fierce battles between November 24 and 30, Soviet forces squeezed the German fascist troops into a territory half the size they had occupied. The area was only 70–80 km west to east and 30–40 km north to south. With the Russian winter setting in, German troops were also weakening rapidly from cold, starvation, and the ongoing Soviet attacks.

In December a German attempt to break the encirclement failed and subsequently all attempts at German resupply collapsed.

One of the factors contributing to the German demise was their inadequate lubricants. In Stalingrad's subfreezing winter temperatures, the motors of their vehicles and fighting machines often stalled and jammed. The Soviet Army by and large did not experience these problems thanks to oil additives developed by Lubrizol, a petrochemical company based in Cleveland, Ohio. These additives were supplied via Lend-Lease to the USSR and the Allies.

On January 30 Hitler promoted Paulus to *Feldmarschall*. No German marshal had ever been made prisoner, and Hitler expected Paulus to commit suicide rather than surrender. Nevertheless Paulus surrendered on January 31, turning his pistol over to an officer of the Soviet Army who happened to be Jewish.

Paulus's promotion and surrender took place in the basement of a bombed-out Stalingrad supermarket, which had been Paulus's headquarters. By early February 1943, German resistance in Stalingrad had ceased. Six hundred thousand men had invaded Stalingrad, and only ninety thousand were left when Paulus surrendered.

Reflecting on the decimation of the foreign invaders who found their infamous end on Russian soil, many of whom were young soldiers, Soviet poet Mikhail Svetlov wrote the poetic monologue "Italian Cross" (1943). It was full of dreams of peace and the fraternity of nations. In this poem about a fallen Italian soldier, Svetlov denounces the nefarious interests of those who sent that young soldier from Naples (a city Russians idealized as beautiful and romantic) to occupy foreign lands and kill people who had not even the slightest inkling of invading the soldier's wonderful country. In the poem a cross the Italian was wearing grew allegorically to the size of a grave marker. Alla liked this poem, remembering and reciting it often. Its English adaptation, produced by me with the help of a friend, is given below with the Russian text.

Mikhail Svetlov, 1942
The Italian Cross
V. Dunaevsky/E. Aivazian adaptation of M. Svetlov;

A plain black cross
on the Italian soldier's chest…
His family for the only dear son
Had it blessed.

Me who shot you not far from the town,
I could hardly remember the noun,
Me who dreamed of the volcano exotic
And with me dreaming gondola floating.

Was it me who arrived with rifles
To destroy and ruin your Naples?
Were my bullets ringing like a cello
On the land of your Saint Rafaello?
Here I shot you. Your body lies on the ground
Where voices of my friends forever will sound.
We both have plenty of legends and stories.
Why did you come here to darken the glories?

Young Italian soldier from Nápoli,
What did you forget in the Russian field (*na pole*)*?
Why couldn't you have been happy, content
In your fairy-tale, beautiful land?

But you were brought here by a military train
to oppress my people and seize the terrain
Where your small holy cross
Will grow to a grave mark size, a symbol of your family loss!

……………………………………………

**Na pole*: Russian transliteration for "in the field"

The original text in Russian

Черный крест на груди итальянца.
Ни резьбы, ни узора, ни глянца.
Не богатым семейством хранимый
И единственным сыном носимый.

Я убивший тебя под Моздоком
Так мечтал о вулкане далеком!
Как я грезил на Волжском приволье
Хоть разок прокатиться в гондоле!

Но ведь я не пришел с пистолетом
Убивать итальянское лето,
Но ведь пули мои не свистели
Над священой землей Рафаэля.

Здесь я выстрелил. Здесь, где родился

Где собой и друзьями гордился,
Где легенды о наших народах
Никогда не звучат в переводах.

Молодой уроженец Неаполя,
Что оставил в России ты на поле?

Почему ты не мог быть счастливым

Над своим знаменитым заливом?

Но тебя привезли в эшелоне
Для захвата далеких колоний.

Чтобы крест из ларца из фамильного
Вырастал до размеров могильного.

Another of Svetlov's most significant works was the "Song of Kakhovka" (1935, composer Isaak Dunaevsky), which became extremely popular among Soviet soldiers during the Second World War.

The battle for Stalingrad turned the tide in Germany's expansion and put constraints on their ability to supply the resources needed to capture the Caucasus. However, Germans did take the Maikop oil fields in the foothills of the Caucasian Mountains, and the German Alpine Army, Edelweiss, took the highest Caucasian peak after fierce battles. They erected German flags on that peak (Elbrus) and on Kazbek.

In the mid 1960s, during an alpine excursion across the main Caucasian ridge, I met a one-handed tourist from the German Democratic Republic near Elbrus. When I asked why he decided to come here, he responded that in the summer of 1942, he was one of those who erected a German flag on Elbrus, and he lost his hand in the firefight with Russian troops. He added jokingly he hoped to find his hand somewhere frozen in the ice that covered the mountains.

By mid-September 1942, the Germans had to withdraw without reaching their main objective of the Caspian oil fields near Makhachkala and Baku. Another of Hitler's objectives, the liquidation of the Jewish population, however, continued unabated. In the occupied resort cities of Minneral'nye Vody (Mineral Waters), Kislowodsk, and Esentuki, several thousand Jews were murdered.[19]

It is believed there were other factors than the shortage of manpower that led to the German retreat. Military historians indicate that by the middle of 1942, Soviet military industry had recuperated from the shattering blows of 1941 and was alive and kicking in the Urals. This industry was the product of a modern state and was able to sustain mass production of armaments, which were often superior to those of the Germans. The Soviet Army benefited also from quick resupply of lost or destroyed weaponry. It was critically important the rate of resupply was faster than that of the German Army, despite all of Europe being at the service of the *Wehrmacht*. The Red Army had also learned to fight fluid, mobile battles, which was especially important in the mountains. The resolve of the Soviet Army was also ensured by Stalin's order number 227, which came to be known as Not a Step Backward. It placed the NKVD

SMERSH[11] detachments (*zagraditel'nye otriady*—the blocking squads) behind the frontline troops to prevent desertion, panic, and sabotage. They were also there to shoot anyone who broke ranks.

Fierce battles on the front brought a steady stream of wounded and maimed troops to the hospitals in the rear of the country. Lyuba, Alla, and others on the medical staff of the hospital worked around the clock treating wounded warriors. Alla worked as a general nurse cleaning and dressing wounds, administering injections, providing medications, and later (after taking special courses) assisting in taking X-rays. At the time of the war, X-ray procedures were not very safe due to limited protection. After the war, Alla developed an illness she associated with the extra exposure to X-rays from the lack of safeguards for the auxiliary personal to which she belonged.

Living with exposure to war's mayhem, cramped living conditions, constant fears for her imprisoned father, Witold at the front, and Theodor detained in Dagestan, Alla had to decide in the spring of 1942 what to do about her pregnancy. Should she bring a new life into this inhospitable, insecure world in a time full of the uncertainties and tribulations of a bitter war?

She could find no unambiguous answer among her family members and friends. One of them was openly trying to discourage her, derisively saying that only *kazashki* (Kazakh women), the majority of whom were then simple uneducated nomads, would go through childbirth in wartime. As I understand it now, another serious concern was of an existential nature, especially toward a new life.

The family knew they had escaped the clutches of a murderous enemy (the word "holocaust" was not coined yet), but for how long? Many were afraid that if the war was lost (and it was far from clear during 1941–1942 which side would win), Stalin might sue for peace and deliver the remaining Jews to Hitler. There were already signs of anti-Semitism rearing its ugly head.

---

[11] SMERSH (*СМЕРШ*: acronym of *СМЕРть Шпионам, SMERt' Shpionam,* "Death to spies") was the counterintelligence agency of the Red Army. It was formed in July of 1942.

Since the establishment of the Soviet government, the well-entrenched anti-Semitism in Russian society had been generally in check. However, German propaganda, the prewar friendship with Hitler, and the attempt to invigorate Russian nationalism in the service of war needs had loosened the grip restraining anti-Semitism. It is documented that various Jewish military and civilian leaders were dismissed from their posts starting in 1942–1943. This was done under the pretext of introducing an employment quota that would reflect national origin and avoid the overrepresentation of Jews in various walks of life.

So no quick decision was taken about whether Alla's pregnancy would go to childbirth or be stopped by abortion. While time passed, my life hung on a balance that began tipping toward abortion. Alla's mother-in-law, Lyuba, was an experienced gynecologist and obstetric doctor and could perform the operation herself. As a doctor in the hospital, she could get the needed facilities, assistance, and perhaps understanding from colleagues who, along with some immediate family members, might have considered the delivery of a child an unnecessary burden in wartime. Having entertained these thoughts, Lyuba and Alla prepared to go to the hospital for the procedure. Knowing my mother, I see her calm at the anticipation of either outcome, abortion or birth.

I wonder, however, what thoughts about her pregnancy Alla would have had if all the aggravating circumstances of war were not there. I guess the attitude of her and her twenty something peers, having grown up in the constantly changing, boisterous atmosphere of industrialization and enrolled in schools of higher education, could have been formulated by the words (suitable perhaps for our time) sung by Alexander Vertinsky. He was a famous Russian cabaret singer, a darling of the Russian people, and a white émigré who lived in Paris after the Revolution. In one of his songs, the hero, contemplating whether or not to have children after marriage, says with abandon:

"I was against it…
The wet cloths will begin…
And why burden your own life?"

A similar note sounds in the words of Bernard Shaw: "Youth is a wonderful thing, and it is unforgivable to spend it for children."

At the very moment Alla and Lyuba left the apartment to perform the abortion, my life was spared. My dad, Victor, finally made a decision. He waved his hand in a conciliatory gesture and said something like, "Let Alla give birth. Whatever will be with us will be as well with a child."

As told to me by my mother, this situation brings to mind a passage from the Bible where the hand of God stops Abraham from slaughtering Isaac.

However, it might not necessarily have been a hospital where the intended abortion or, later, my actual birth took place.

Until the age of four or five, I believed in a cabbage patch story told by my grandmothers about my mom and pop walking in the garden and finding a cute child under the cabbage. By the age of ten or eleven, I was given a more prosaic account of my birth, namely that I was born on bags of potatoes.

This suggests that instead of a hospital, Alla and Lyuba would have gone to a secluded place. This could have been somebody's apartment or even a basement with conditions barely sufficient for obstetric procedures (whether abortion or birth). On the other hand, the bags of potatoes could be seen as a metaphor for the overall cramped and simplistic conditions of my family life in the evacuation (and for many families well after the war). During these times bags of potatoes were commonly stored within living quarters.

I don't know how much time elapsed between the aborted abortion and my birth on December 25, 1942. It could have been months, days, or even hours. My birth certificate says nothing about it (as one would naturally expect) or about whether the birth took place in a hospital, home, or other place. It does show the name of the town, which was Zhana-Semey of the Kalinin District of Semipalatinsk Oblast. The town is located in or close to the area that, starting in 1949 with the first Soviet atomic bomb, became a nuclear test site. In wartime, life in that city was tough. After 1949 it became not only tough but unsafe due to radiation pollution. Fortunately our family left the town at the end of 1945 and returned to Rostov-on-Don.

Despite all the preceding worries, everyone in the family received my birth as a joyful event. It was even taken as a positive sign. I see confirmation of this in verses written by my Grandma Bella circa 1960, which I found only recently. In them she sentimentally compared my birth to a spark of light in the life of a family suffering the throes of war.

My emergence in the world certainly coincided with other signs of hope in the course of the war. This included the aforementioned defeat of the Germans at the Caucasus and the tightening of the noose around the German 6th Army at Stalingrad. For the Allies, however, 1942 was in many ways reminiscent of the series of debacles the Soviets experienced in 1941. These included the Japanese rout of thousands of US troops in the Philippines, the surrender of Singapore with its 80,000 British, Australian, and Indian troops joined by 50,000 more taken by the Japanese in their Malayan campaign, and the exhausting battles with German troops in North Africa.

Early in 1942 American troops invaded French North Africa and, with little opposition, defeated German forces stationed there. This enabled the French forces in North Africa to break with the Vichy regime and defect to the American side. The American romantic drama film *Casablanca* captured the spirit of the era.

At the same time British General Montgomery was able to defeat the German Marshal Rommel, the "desert fox," at Al Alamein, Libya, thus eliminating the threat to the Suez Canal and the Middle East. Decisive naval battles took place in the Pacific, helping to stem the Japanese advance.

....

With the decimation of the Nazis at Stalingrad, trainloads of captured fascist troops, including Germans, Romanians, Slovaks, and others, began rolling to the hinterlands of the USSR. From those only a few thousand of the more than one hundred thousand taken prisoners ever returned alive to their home countries. Some of the prisoner trains passed through Semipalatinsk to the concentration camps further east. This flow of POWs unexpectedly affected Zelman, who was sucked in by his curiosity. Probably while buying newspapers, Zelman was at the train station when a train of POWs stopped there. While strolling along the platform, he heard a conversation in French coming from a sealed railcar.

Being fluent in French and carried away by a desire to practice his foreign language skills (and to satisfy his interest about news from the front delivered uncensored by Soviet editors), Zelman approached an open but barred window from which he'd heard the French. He greeted the soldiers in French. Peering through the window, they struck up a small conversation. He asked them where they came from and where they were captured. As I heard the story, a real conversation did not ensue because Zelman was interrupted by two NKVD troops. Appearing suddenly they swiftly carried him away to their local headquarters, the *comendature*, where he was interrogated for a few hours and released with his promise not to get involved in unauthorized conversations with POWs in the future.

The Kursk Salient and German Operation Citadel

As a result of their Stalingrad victory, the Soviets extended their front lines several hundred miles eastward and liberated Rostov, Kharkov, and Kursk. Various tactical blunders of the Soviet advance were exploited by Manstein (considered one the ablest German generals and tacticians) and gave the Germans the opportunity to retake Kharkov.

However, they failed to retake Kursk, which left an immense bulge, or salient, in the Soviet lines surrounding the city. The bulge had a frontage of 250 miles, requiring the Red Army to commit nine valuable armies to its defense.

Although Germans stretched their resources to the breaking point, Berlin was determined to regain the initiative on the Eastern Front. The Führer was immediately tempted to take Kursk, which would require the *Wehrmacht* to go on the offensive and nip out the bulge.

In light of intelligence reports that the Germans were preparing an attack into the salient, the Soviets (under the command of Georgy Zhukov) decided to beef up the defenses and wear down the enemy. They would defend the Kursk salient, destroying German tanks and throwing in fresh reserves at the end for a general offensive. Against his instincts but revealing a growing military maturity within the Soviet high command, Stalin acceded to arguments that the Red Army should focus on defending Kursk rather than immediately launching an offensive in the area.

The attacking German force consisted of almost 800,000 men, 2500 tanks and assault guns (70 percent of the German armor on the Eastern Front), and 7400 guns and mortars. This was opposed by Soviet forces amounting to almost 2,000,000 men, over 5000 tanks and self-propelled guns, 31,500 guns and mortars, and over 3500 aircrafts. [10] The Red Army's meticulous defenses were 70 miles deep with fallback positions up to 175 miles behind the salient.

On July 5 Germany initiated Operation Citadel to annihilate the Kursk salient. This was a tank battle on an unprecedented scale. The battle lasted until July 23. Despite the Germans' tactical success (they were able to destroy more enemy armor than they lost), it was clear the Soviets' tenacious defense and superior resources had run Operation Citadel into the ground. Manstein lamented that the last German offensive in the east ended in fiasco, even though the Russians suffered four times the German losses in prisoners, dead, and wounded. Rokossovsky and Vatutin lost almost 180,000 men, 1600 armored vehicles, and 460 aircrafts. Model and Manstein suffered nearly 57,000 casualties and lost 252 tanks and 159 aircrafts. [12] [10]

The losses on the Kursk battlefield were not as strategically critical to Moscow as they were to Berlin. "As a result of the Kursk battle, the Soviet Armed Forces had dealt the enemy a buffeting from which Nazi Germany was never to recover," the Soviet chief of the general staff, Alexander Vasilevsky, later wrote. As a consequence of the failure of Operation Citadel, the Kursk battle was not only a pivotal moment in the campaign in the east but in the entire Second World War.

A paper in a military history magazine suggests, based on analysis of the writings of several German generals about the battle at Kursk, that a) the Germans could not have won even if they started the battle earlier, and b) even if the German won the battle, it would not have greatly changed their overall personnel losses, since the losses during this battle constituted only 3 percent of their total losses on the Eastern Front in 1943. That was approximately 1,700,000 people.

Italy in the War

Considering the prominence of post-WWII Italian art (movies and plays) in the cultural life of the USSR, the following are some of the Italian experiences in WWII.

---

[12] The exact number of the fighting armored vehicles, aircrafts, and men participating in and lost during the Kursk battle varies in different sources.

Under Benito Mussolini Italy was one of the Axis powers in Hitler's coalition. Italy declared war on the United States on December 11, 1941. The Italian forces under Rommel in the African campaigns were defeated by combined American, British, and French forces. After being badly beaten by the Soviets in Stalingrad, by the summer of 1943, Rome withdrew the remaining Italian troops from the Soviet Union. Many of the over-65,000 Italian POWs captured in the Soviet Union died in captivity due to the harsh conditions in the Soviet prison camps.

In November of 1942, the Italian Royal Army participated in the invasion of southeastern Vichy France and Corsica. In December 1942 the Italian military government of French territories east of the Rhône River was established, and it continued until September 1943 when Italy quit the war. This provided a de facto temporary haven for French Jews fleeing the Holocaust. In January 1943 the Italians refused to cooperate with the Nazis in rounding up Jews who lived in the occupied zone of France under Italian control. In March the Italians prevented the Nazis from deporting Jews in their zone. German Foreign Minister Joachim von Ribbentrop complained to Mussolini that, "Italian military circles…lack a proper understanding of the Jewish question."

On July 10, 1943, a combined force of American and British Commonwealth troops invaded Sicily. German generals again took the lead in the defense, and although they lost the island after weeks of bitter fighting, they succeeded in ferrying large numbers of German and Italian forces safely off Sicily to the Italian mainland. On July 19 an Allied air raid on Rome destroyed both military and collateral civil installations. With these two events, popular support for the war diminished in Italy.

On July 25, 1943, the Grand Council of Fascism ousted Italian dictator Benito Mussolini, and a new Italian government, led by General Pietro Badoglio and King Victor Emmanuel III, took over Italy. The new Italian government immediately began secret negotiations with the Allies to end the fighting and come over to the Allied side. On September 3 a secret armistice was signed with the Allies at Fairfield Camp in Sicily. The armistice was announced on September 8. By then the Allies were on the Italian mainland.

On September 3, 1943, British troops crossed the short distance from Sicily to the "toe" of Italy in Operation Baytown. Two more Allied landings took place on September 9 at Salerno and Taranto. The Italian surrender meant the Allied landings at Taranto took place unopposed. The troops simply disembarked from warships at the docks rather than assaulting the coastline.

German troops, once they discovered the Italians signed an armistice, moved quickly to disarm the Italian forces and take over critical defensive positions. These included Italian-occupied southeastern France and the Italian-controlled areas in the Balkans. Only in Sardinia, Corse, and in parts of Apuli and Calabria were Italian troops able to hold their positions until the arrival of Allied forces. In Rome one lone infantry division, Granatieri di Sardegna, and some small armored units fought the Germans with commitment, but by September 11 they were overwhelmed.

On September 9 a German "Fritz X" guided bomb sank the Italian battleship *Roma* off the coast of Sardinia.

On the Greek island of Cephallonia, General Antonio Gandin, commander of the 12,000-strong Italian division, resisted the German attempt to forcibly disarm his force. The battle raged from September 13 to 22, when the Italians were forced to surrender after suffering some 1300 casualties. The ensuing massacre of several thousand Italian POWs by the Germans stands as one of the worst war crimes committed by the *Wehrmacht.*

After the German invasion, the deportations of Italian Jews to Nazi death camps began. However, by the time the Germans got to the Campagna concentration camp, all the inmates had already fled to the mountains with the help of local inhabitants. Rev. Aldo Brunacci of Assisi, under the direction of his bishop, Giuseppe Nicolini, saved all the Jews who sought refuge in Assisi. In October 1943 Nazis raided the Jewish ghetto in Rome. In November 1943 Jews of Genoa and Florence were deported to Auschwitz. It is estimated that 7500 Italian Jews became victims of the Holocaust.

About two months after he was stripped of power, Benito Mussolini was rescued by the Germans in Operation Oak. This was a spectacular raid planned by German General Kurt Student and carried out by Senior Storm Unit Leader (*Obersturmbannführer*) Otto Skorzeny. The Germans relocated Mussolini to northern Italy where he set up a new Fascist state, the Italian Social Republic (*Republica Sociale Italiana* or RSI).

The Allied armies continued to advance through Italy despite increasing opposition from the Germans. The Allies soon controlled most of southern Italy, and Naples rose against and ejected the occupying German forces. The Allies organized some Italian troops in the south into "cobelligerent" or "royalist" forces. These Italian forces fought alongside the Allies for the rest of the war. Other Italian troops, loyal to Mussolini and his RSI, continued to fight alongside the Germans. From this point on, a large Italian resistance movement, which was located in northern Italy, fought a guerrilla war against the German and RSI forces. [11]

....

Unaware of the terrible events shaking the big world thousands of miles away, I was growing in Semipalatinsk until autumn of 1945 in a semi-pastoral atmosphere surrounded by people who loved me. Because my parents and the older Dunaevskys were preoccupied by their work during the long business days (which included Saturdays), I was watched, tended, and brought up mainly by my maternal grandma, Isabella.

She taught me manners, among which basic table manners were considered critical from the age of one and a half, when I could sit with grown-ups at the common table in my high chair. One of the most critical table manners was using a fork during a meal and especially when consuming watermelon. If I was impatient and grabbed a piece of melon before the edible portion was separated from its thick skin, I got gentle reprimands, mostly from my mother and Grandmother Isabella.

Another important rule was that a bowl with soup should be tilted away from you, not toward you, when scooping out the last spoonfuls. Tilting the wrong way might have entailed a reprimand that I was behaving like a *kolkhoznik* (a worker of the collective farm). This implied someone poorly educated and boorish.

The reprimands were often in the form of grown-ups making surprised faces and exclamations as if something really bad had happened. I sensed these strict rules were bothersome even for my father. He skipped them sometimes, and that prompted me to do the same. However, the result was that both of us were reprimanded. Despite these reprimands, I cherished Mother, and when I was asked to show how much I loved her, I demonstrated my affection by squeezing my small fists and straining myself.

This pantomime can possibly be deciphered as a child's expression of the desire to prevent his mother from being taken away from him. At gatherings of guests and friends, I was often asked to perform that antic, which they considered entertaining. When we later discussed my behavior with Mother, she told me she could hardly go anywhere without me crying. But life is life, and within a year after I was born, Mother had to leave me for several months to go to Tomsk (a Siberian city northeast of Semipalatinsk) to continue her medical studies. She stayed there with the family of Ida Osherovskaya (the aunt of my dad, Victor). During her life in Tomsk, Alla forged a friendship with Lyalya (diminutive for Helen), who was the daughter of Ida and her husband, Alexander Dombrovsky. The Rostov Medical Institute, where Dombrovsky was a radiology professor, evacuated to Tomsk.

Mother brought to the family an air of elegance radiating with calmness and confidence, which balanced Isabella's wariness and sadness. Along with instructions on manners, I imbibed from Isabella those humanistic attitudes she gave to Alla and her brothers during their childhoods. At the age of two, I was taught to appreciate the domesticated animals for sustaining our life. In that vein and as a form of good humor, I was even encouraged to express gratitude to one particular cow on a nearby farm. I said, "Thank you cow, Gasha, for giving us milk." As a child I carried this gratitude to the extreme by trying to thank each cow we met when we walked at the outskirts of the town.

Despite the stresses of the war, anxiety, and privation, Isabella continued her artwork. This was expressed in the verses she dedicated to me. She spiced them with humor while addressing some of my attitudes. Here is one of these verses in Russian along with a free verse English translation.

Isabella Shmulian, 1943.
To Valerick* on his first birthday.

Original Russian text
Я проснулся на рассвете
И давай кричать:
Целый год живу на свете
Можно ли молчать?

Я хочу всем однолеткам
Черным, рыжим, белым деткам
Рассказать о том, о сем
Поделеиться опытом.

Я узнал что есть коровки,
Свинки и лошадки
И что очень, очень вкусно
Кушать шоколадки.

Пусть теперь узнает всяк:
Делают часы тик-так.
Взрослых детки вы не бойтесь,
По утрам водой не мойтесь.
Можно ль взрослых уважать-
Заставляют ночью спать.

V. Dunaevsky, a free verse translation of the above text
I woke up at dawn and began screaming.
I already lived a whole year in this world
And can't stand to be silent.
I would like to tell all my peers,
Black and white kids and red-haired kids,
About many things,
And share with them my experience.

Let everybody knows
That the clocks do tick-tock.
I have learned also that there are cows, piglets, and horses and
That chocolate is very, very tasty.

As far as the adults,
You, children, should not be afraid of them,
And thus don't wash yourselves in the morning.
And how can one respect them
If they demand you sleep in the night?

*Valerik is a diminutive for Valery.

Death of Witold

The family was eagerly attuned to all the information from the front, especially letters from Witold. One day in September of 1944, a notice came from a local post office that a military mail package for Alla had been sent to the attention of Isabella. They went to receive the package, worried it was possibly bad news about Witold. While Alla joined the line leading to the post office service desk, Isabella left to wait for her near a container with drinking water. Her hand was lying on the faucet. Alla finally received the package, opened it, and began reading the document it contained.

By the expression on Alla's face, Isabella understood that her worst worries were justified, and in a spasm of anxiety, she squeezed that faucet and broke it off. In recollecting this event many years later, Isabella said anxiety pushed her strength over the limit. The package contained the death certificate of Witold, which informed them he was heroically killed on August 27 while fulfilling his military duties (see Appendix A). The certificate was the basis for application to a meager pension for Isabella. Because of disruption in the military mail service, several letters from Witold arrived after his death. In one of them, he wondered how long destiny would allow him to stay alive. In another he expressed expectations for a speedy victory in the war before the end of 1944 and his confidence of meeting his loved ones again. These types of expectations were cultivated in the army.

The death of Witold was a traumatic experience for the family and especially for Isabella. The event was concealed from Lev Shmulian, considering his heart problems. Witold's death added to Isabella's sadness. Even long after the war, she used to sing some sad songs when I was alone with her. She put these songs together herself. In them she expressed her inconsolable sorrow that she would never see her son again. Meanwhile, against all reason, she still had a slight hope Witold might not have perished but, because of his mathematical significance, had been assigned some super secret work for the military. In this scenario his whereabouts were made unavailable for the outside world. At every opportunity to strike up a conversation with military people (during the war and for a long time afterward, there were plenty of such opportunities), Isabella always asked the soldiers or officers whether they had seen or knew Witold.

She always proudly described Witold's mathematical aptitude and his good nature, and she showed reprints of Witold's papers in academy magazines. The reprints were on crummy, brownish paper and displayed myriads of mathematical symbols that were strange for me. Watching Isabella's demonstration of this mysterious material, seeing her exaltation, and hearing her explanation that it was all created under enemy fire subconsciously filled me with a sense of being exposed to something of the highest significance. The memories of these war papers and the intuitive appreciation of the difficulty that surrounded creating them had a deep impact on me, and it helped me many years later to cope with various engineering and life challenges.

Along with pride for her son, Isabella jealously guarded his image. As such, to those people she considered inferior to Witold, Isabella avoided giving any encouragement to reach Witold's level in anything, especially science. Isabella, unfortunately, assigned me to this category of people, even though she loved me. Surprisingly she was not very secretive with that attitude and openly told me I was not Uncle Witold, and I shouldn't strive to reach or exceed his level. I shouldn't go beyond what I was, which was a regular person. She retained this attitude from my childhood through when I decided to go to postgraduate school. She advised me, however, to strive to be a good engineer instead of a scientist. In that she expressed an extreme attitude. She thought a scientist could only be someone on par with Uncle Witold or the academician Kolmogorov.

Even though I understood Uncle Witold had superb intellectual and mathematical abilities, I did not lose hope in myself, despite Grandma Isabella's prophecies. I relied instead on Grandma Lyuba's philosophy that not only the Olympian gods know how to kiln the pots. A quotation from Einstein, which my father often invoked, was that the "The most practical solution is a good theory." This also helped me justify studying theory in order to be a good engineer. Thus, one way or another, I went in the direction pointed by Isabella, or at least I did not go in the direction of abstract science.

The significance of the above attitudes, specifically Isabella's and the more accommodating views of my father and Lyuba, can be understood in the context of a family tradition that children were not forced into early specialization in any discipline. For example, nobody pushed Witold to study math; his interest in it was natural. Grandma Isabella told various stories about his early childhood mathematical proclivities. Alla, although she did not demonstrate special mathematical interest, had a steely logic in her expressions, conversations, and behaviors. As I mentioned earlier, she was also very correct. She intuitively knew how to verbally disarm her opponent without going into a rage, as sometimes happened with me.

For me, the Witold saga yielded a lesson in perseverance. His ability to produce the highest feats of intellectual activity in conditions least suitable to this activity (literally under the enemy fire) was emblazoned in my memory.

The stresses my family members experienced through the war years in Semipalatinsk were periodically relieved by trips to the movie theater. Trailers with war chronicles usually preceded the movies. All military events were obviously presented from a politically favorable angle, whether the Soviet army was actually advancing or retreating.

After the Stalingrad victory, trophy movies began to penetrate the Soviet silver screen. One of them was about Tarzan. Several American and British pre and wartime movies, which were also shown, left a lasting impression on my parents. One of them was a musical with J. Strauss melodies entitled *Tales from the Vienna Woods.*

Another one was a wartime detective movie containing a clever British plot wherein the musicians in a restaurant located near the seaport of a Scandinavian country were actually British military intelligence agents. According to my rendition of the plot, told to me by my father, the band was able to observe the German military vessels passing through the port. The observed information was then coded into music the band played, corresponding to the type and number of ships that passed. The local radio broadcast the music. Further on, this musical code was intercepted by British headquarters and used by the British navy to destroy the German vessels. The name of the movie, in a Russian translation, was something like *John from Dinky Jazz.*

My parents also enjoyed the sharp and witty verses of Soviet poets satirizing invaders and their inevitable demise. They often recited these verses (like humming a favorite tune), and thus they stuck in my memory. Many of them were written by Samuil Marshak who was mostly known in the USSR for his children's poems. However, as we recognized, he was also a very prolific poetry translator from different languages. The epigrams and epitaphs of Robert Burns and several other British poets remained most memorable in their sardonic humor and unexpected endings and as treasure troves of keen observations of life's follies. To her last days, Mother and I treated some of these epigrams in our conversations as cherished intellectual possessions.

During the war, a number of memorable Russian songs were produced. One of those was "In a Forest Near the Front" (В Лесу Прифронтовом/V Lesu Prifrontovom) with Michail Isakovsky lyrics. Another one was "Dark Night" (Темная Ночь/Tyomnaja Notch) with lyrics of V. Agatov on musics of Nikita Bogoslovsky. [34] The song was from a 1943 movie "Two Soldires" (Два Бойца/Dva Boitsa) performed by Mark Bernes.

My father was a good mechanic. He could use parts from rejected mechanisms and apparatuses to make various mechanical toys for me. Toys were completely unavailable for purchase during wartime, but rejected parts were easy to find for someone working in industry. One of the toys mimicked a butterfly flapping its wings. A butterfly portion was attached to wheels adjacent to a stick. In order for the butterfly's wings to flaps, I had to pull or push the stick while walking with the device. The motion of the wheels forced the flapping.

Dad also helped me debunk the mystery of time, which in our Semipalatinsk apartment was controlled by a large, round timepiece with one arrow moving around a white circle, which had a scale of twelve uniformly placed divisions. It was glued to the round of a yellow-colored device arrogantly looking down from a high place on the wall. Somehow I think it was the metal housing of an antitank mine with a clock mechanism.

These types of things were probably available from Dad's work where the internals of the mine were used for some automation. Because of the expected disrepair of the prewar watches the family had and the difficulty of repairing them or purchasing new ones (all industries were only producing goods for military needs), the one-arm clock was perhaps a thing to rely upon while checking the time.

In the late forties, when we were living in Murmansk, Victor made running lights for my New Year's fir. (This was our substitute for the Christmas tree.) The achievement of such a feat, which brought immeasurable excitement for me, was possible because Dad found some rejected relays from an aircraft. There were many military dumps around Murmansk with all kinds of technical pieces, and he reworked the components for controlling the running lights. Although religious holidays were not condoned, the attributes of a Christmas celebration were borrowed and attached to the New Year's festivities. All groups of the population, regardless of national or religious origin, joyfully celebrated New Year's without paying too much attention to the original pagan or Christian origins of the customs.

The mechanical toys made by my father were perhaps a step toward fostering my interest in mechanical engineering. This was also supported by a story he told me about his resolution of a technical problem at the food processing plant during the war. A problem threatened to put some food processing machinery out of service, and he could expect harsh penalties for any delay in fixing the problem. In explaining this and similar stories to me, he was trying to convey the necessity of looking for nontrivial or revolutionary directions when resolving demanding or complex problems.

Later on, when I became an engineering student and asked Dad for advice, I was amazed how well he remembered various principles of mechanical design and machining processes. He even remembered those which require keen understanding of the underlying complexities. It was even more remarkable considering he graduated from a relatively new and provincial engineering school (the Rostov Institute of Agricultural Machine Building) and not from the prestigious Bauman Engineering School in Moscow, which he attended for the first two years. He is a good example of the excellent technical education the Russian and Soviet higher education system provided and which enabled rapid and advanced military developments in the most critical time. One such example of this was the special metallurgy of the armor and the design of the T-34 tank, which made it nearly invincible under enemy fire.

Images of Alla during her life in Semipalatinsk (Kazakhstan) and Tomsk (Siberia) (1942–1945)

Alla in Semipalatinsk (1942).

Копия

Архив
Министерства Обороны
Союза ССР

Отдел "4"
"26" ноября 1960 г.
№ 70931
г.Подольск Московск.обл.

гор.Мурманск, пр.Ленина дом 23,
кв 89 Дунаевской А.Л.

Сообщаю, что в приказе №126 Эвакогоспиталя 3592 от 4 мая 1942 года значится:

"Зачислить на должность медсестры
ШМУЛЬЯН А.Л.

Основание: оп 603130 д 16

В приказе №218 Эвакогоспиталя 3592
от 13 сентября 1945 года значится:

"Уволить в связи с расформированием госпиталя
мед.сестру ШМУЛЬЯН А.Л.

Основание : оп 603130 д.26

печать

Зам.начальника 4 отдела
подполковник /подпись/

(Печать)

Пом.начальника архивохранилища /подпись/

A copy of the record from the Archive of Ministry of Defense of the USSR informs:

- **Order #126 of the Evacuation Hospital 3592 on May 4, 1942 reads: "Hire Shmulian, A. L. as a medical nurse."**
- **Order #218 of the Evacuation Hospital 3592 on September 13, 1945 reads: "Lay off medical nurse Shmulian, A. L. in connection with a dismissal of the hospital."**

Seals, signatures, and notarization of the copy.

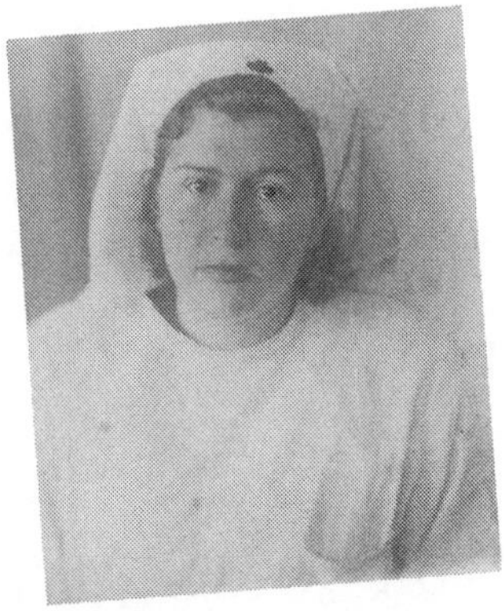

Alla in the medical nurse uniform at a Semipalatinsk military hospital (ca. 1942).

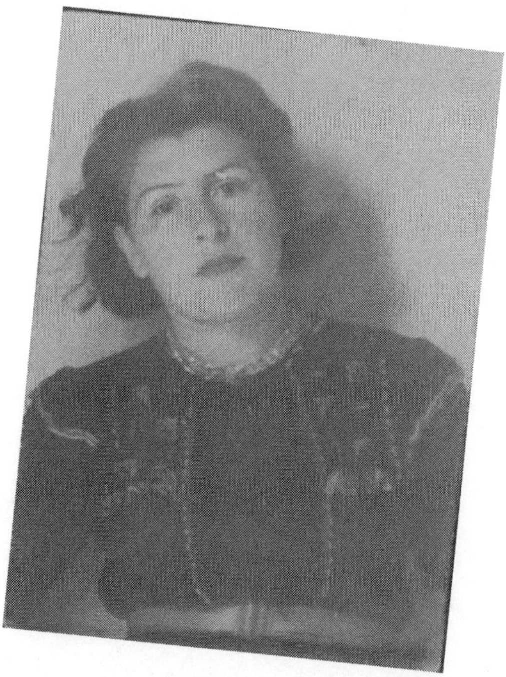

Alla in Tomsk, when she attended the Medical Institute there (1944).

Alla in Tomsk. On the right is Alla's note from the back side of the picture. It says, "To dear Victor from Alla. 3/25/1944."

Alla, and Victor's cousin Lyalya in Tomsk (ca. 1944).

Alla in kitchen, Tomsk (ca. 1944).

Below are images of the struggle and victory of the USSR during WWII, as shown in the Soviet post stamps.

A common theme and logo is "Death to German occupiers."

The theme is "Heroes of the USSR." ***(Above right)***
The stamp is dedicated to a Soviet female officer
who was captured in the fight, tortured, and executed by Germans.

Theme and logo: Stalingrad is a hero city (1945).

Theme and logo: Hail to our victory (1945).

Theme and logo: Everything to the front (1944).

Above is an American postal envelope with an image of J. Stalin. The wording celebrates Russia's declaration of war on Japan and states that, "On August 8th Japan's worst fears became a reality." (1945).*

---

* A message of this unique artifact implies an apparent prevailing opinion of the time, (which is now often forgotten) that it was the military invasion of the Soviet Union in Manchuria and not the American atomic bombing of Hiroshima and Nagasaki, that was the major blow to Japan. (The invasion took place three days after Hiroshima and on the day of Nagasaki bombing.) One week after the invasion and following a speedy defeat of the Kwantung Army, Japan surrendered.

The Russian military campaign against Japan started exactly three months after the surrender of Germany, just as Stalin had promised to Roosevelt at the Yalta conference in February of 1945. It was a short but fierce war. Moreover, despite a strategic and tactical advantage over the Japanese forces, the war resulted in large casualties on both sides. The Japanese's losses were, however, ten times those of Russians.

A family friend and medical doctor Captain Gershkovich, who participated in the campaign, told about the difficulties of defeating the well-entrenched enemy. Some of the most difficult to destroy fortifications included concrete pillboxes attached to the top of thin vertical steel poles. Such a location made these bunkers almost invisible through the canopy of the forest, the steel poles almost indistinguishable among the trees. All of which made it that much more difficult for the Russian artillery to stop the fire that rained from the elevated machine gun nests.

Suppressing these fortifications, (where it was later learned, Japanese gunners were chained to their weapons) finally proceeded due to the direct action of the infantry. However, it resulted in large losses among the Russian fighting men.

After the surrender of Japan, the Soviet Army discovered secret installations for experimenting with, and producing chemical weapons and biological weapons of mass destruction. At these locations, the Kwantung Army was also responsible for some of the most infamous Japanese war crimes, including the operation of several human experimentation programs using live Chinese, American and Russian civilians and POWs.

CHAPTER V

Return to Rostov-on-Don After Evacuation: 1945

In September of 1945, several months after the war with Germany was over, the hospital where Alla and Lyuba worked closed. The family went back to Rostov via almost the same route they used four years earlier. Upon returning to Rostov, they reoccupied their old flat. It had been left under the supervision of a neighbor (Elena Vasilyevna) who lived in one of the rooms. The war years added one more neighbor to the flat. This neighbor was a single woman of low rank who was allowed to stay in a small, windowless room. It was a sort of walk-in closet located at the intersection of the hallway and Elena's room that faced the street. When in my adolescent years I lived in Rostov again, I empathized with that poor woman, called Tanyka, with her round, pockmarked, peasant face. Although this sentiment was somewhat shared by my grandparents, the original owners of the flat, they considered the women a simpleton and intruder.

Alla continued her medical education and graduated from the Rostov Medical Institute in 1947. Victor began working as a machine design engineer in the petrochemical industry. Specializing in gynecology, Lyuba went back to work in a general hospital. Zelman returned to the educational system and taught math part-time in a railroad college during the night shift. The students there were already serious, grown-up people. Many had active military service behind them. They respected Zelman, remembered him many years after they left school, and cheerfully greeted him when they occasionally met him on the streets. "How are you, Zelman Ilyich?"

From 1945–1946 in Rostov, I was still a bereaved kid following Alla, who left me with my grandparents whenever she had to go somewhere. Isabella, who lived for some time with the Dunaevskys, probably taught me to tell my mother, "You are only a coquette and a tomboy." I told her this when she and Victor went out for some entertainment or for the evening, strolling along Engels Street. This was the main street of Rostov, and it was always crowded with people in their best attire.

As I mentioned, Rostov was heavily damaged by bombing. The house where we lived, however, was spared from the damage. The house was built before the revolution by Lyuba's father, Abram Osherovsky, for his many children. It was (and still is) a big three-story building with nine individual multiroom flats. Height-wise, the building was similar to a modern four-story dwelling. All rooms had high ceilings, perhaps exceeding modern standards by one or two feet. The windows had internal, vertically hinged, wooden blinds which were shut tight at night. Considering the poor street lighting, this created complete darkness in the rooms. I was sometimes scared to death waking up in these dark rooms in the night. Not seeing anything I thought I had gone blind and began crying. My sobs, which awakened the adults, resulted in a light being turned on, and only then was I convinced everything was all right.

The building was nationalized after the revolution. However, several of Abram's children and their immediate and extended families managed to live there. These included Lyuba's family (on the first floor), Lyuba's sister, Ida, her husband, MD Prof. Alexander Iosifovich Dombrovsky, and their family (on the second floor), and Clara and her family (on the third floor). On the first floor, across the stairwell from the Dunaevsky's flat, lived Lyuba's brother, Iosif, and his wife, Polina Borisovna. Before the war Iosif's son (Victor's cousin), Yuri, also lived there. He later became a military doctor with the rank of army colonel. In the 1960s and 70s, he was director of the military hospital in the Western District of the

Soviet Army. This was in Riga, Latvia. Polina was a petite and not very remarkable woman. We thought she did not speak well in Russian. Some of her expressions became a source of family jokes about her.

On the second floor lived also the family of a large-animal veterinarian, A. Subbotnik, and an army colonel who was the husband of one of Lyuba's cousins. As a cavalry officer, he wore on certain celebratory occasions a full uniform that even included a saber. He was a tall and handsome man, and seeing him in all his regalia incited some instinctive pride and awe in belonging to his clan. Wearing a saber was outmoded by the late 1940s or early 50s.

On the first floor lived a couple more Jewish families. One was the family of Raphail Tymyansky, a navy doctor, who shared a flat with Polina Borisovna (her husband Iosif died earlier) and someone else. Another family was that of an engineer named Fridman. They lived in the flat adjacent to Polina's but used the entrance from the side of the building.

Tymyansky attracted my attention with the dashing appearance of his navy uniform and his very hairy chest and athletic build, which I could see in the summertime when he appeared shirtless on the backyard deck. His wife was also attractive. They both balanced the overall gloomy atmosphere of the communal flat in which they lived. A poorly lit hallway sustained the gloom. That hallway was connected by a narrow and completely unlit corridor to the section of the flat with utilities (kitchen, bathroom, and toilet). It was also packed with some old chests. All the flats in the house shared a similar arrangement.

Despite the fact many Jewish siblings lived in the same house, a rare and curious demographic anomaly for post-WWII Russia, there was not much cohesion between the families. Each lived its own life with minimum mingling, even in cases of joy or grief. I realized when my father lived in the house before the war, his main friends were not the siblings living in the house. This may have been because of the age difference between him and his cousins.

Victor's friends were from the cohort of Russian and Jewish young men and included Tolya Tsipelzon, Gleb Kurasov, Yuri Menikov, and the aforementioned Ted Zaltsman, with whom he was involved in sports, comradeship, and engineering studies.

In postwar Rostov German prisoners of war were extensively used for reconstruction projects. One of these projects was the restoration of a building that was part of the Mechanics-Mathematics Department of Rostov University. It was located along Gorky Street and shared a wall with our house. The L-shaped university building surrounded a very large backyard that was separated from our backyard by a brick wall. The wall was not very high, reaching only to the windowsills of the first floor on the back side of our house. These were about eight to ten feet above the ground. Each story of our house had a deck on the back side, which extended along the whole length of the building. And everyone could easily observe, even from the first floor deck, which almost butted into the brick wall separating the two yards, what was going on behind this wall at the construction site.

There was a high watchtower with a sentry who carried his submachine gun with its round magazine always at the ready. The large quantity of German prisoners scurried at the bottom of the tower, around the backyard, and inside the building doing various kinds of construction work. At the far corner of the large university backyard was an open latrine where the Germans relieved themselves. The latrine consisted of a wooden deck with several holes in a row, and it was level with the second floor. A narrow staircase led to it. The waste accumulated through the months and years of their work on the site. Nobody removed it, and it kept piling up, finally almost reaching the level of the latrine itself.

Watching the Germans working across the wall was a favorite game for me, four and a half, and the neighborhood boys, who were older than me. According to my family's judgment, they were street boys or hooligans (children without obvious supervision). Sometimes we threw pieces of bread I was able to snatch from home across the wall, which was topped by barbed wire. The Germans rushed to get these small pieces of bread, sometimes fighting over them. One day I brought a toy rifle and began aiming at the prisoners.

A tall German approached the wall and, with a smile on his face, asked me something and pointed to the rifle. Through his gesticulation I understood he was asking me to give him a rifle. He then stretched his hand over the barbed wire and was able to grab my toy rifle. I was not sure what to do but did not leave the rifle. A sentry, realizing the situation, began yelling something at the German and training his submachine gun on him. The German released his grip on my toy rifle and ran away. With that my "Stalingrad Battle" with real Germans was over. My family heard the screams and popped out from our flat to the deck. After my explanations, the bread in the house was watched more closely, and my parents demanded I not play near that wall.

There is a sublime message in the above paragraphs detailing the dismal life of captive German soldiers and children's altercations with them. It was a rare and almost symbolic event in which a little Jewish boy fed his now-broken, formerly murderous enemy.

Myself (center) with two friends (street boys) on a backyard deck of our house in Rostov, behind which was a construction site with German prisoners of war (1946).

Alla and Victor (c. 1946).

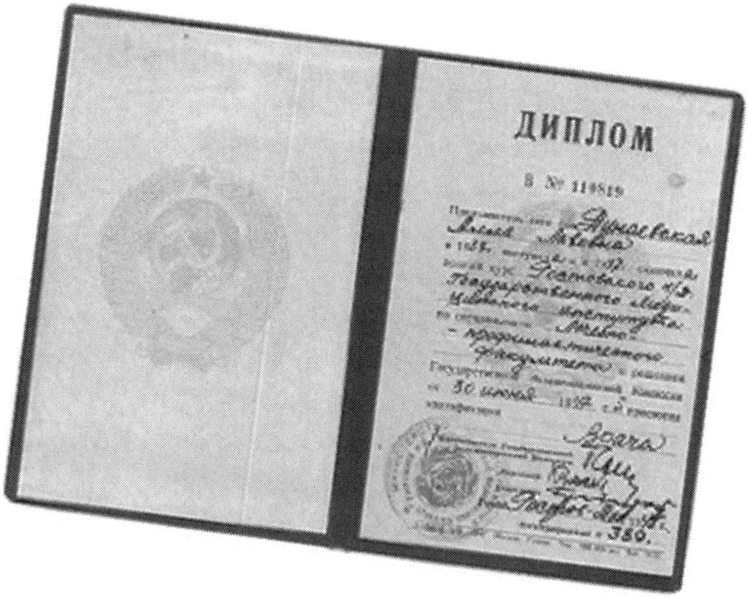

Alla's MD diploma, conferred on her by
the Rostov-on-Don Medical Institute (1947).

Me and my parents (Victor Dunaevsky and Alla Dunayevskaya) in Rostov. My left hand with a damaged finger is on a slinger and covered by the coat (1950).

The wages my parents and grandparents received were on par with their colleagues, who were white-collar workers. That is to say, the wages were relatively low and hardly sufficient to support an affluent lifestyle and separate living accommodations. The destroyed economy and continuous food shortages exacerbated the situation. The salaries of engineers and doctors were often not sufficient to put food on the table. Oftentimes I went to bed hungry and complained, "I am little. I did not eat anything." I probably exaggerated this problem and was simply repeating what someone suggested in my presence. To allay these financial needs, and on the recommendation of one of Victor's cousins, Boris Osherovsky, my family decided to relocate to Murmansk. This was a growing city inside the polar circle, located on the banks of Kola Bay and open to the unfrozen Barents Sea.

CHAPTER VI

Move to Murmansk (Russia): 1947

Warmed by the Gulf Stream, the Barents Sea was free of ice year-round. This was a crucial factor that made the Murmansk Port a destination in the supply route for the Allied convoys during the war. The Murmansk convoys were instrumental in keeping Russia in the war, carrying a substantial portion of the Lend-Lease supplies. The convoy route went around occupied Norway to the Soviet ports of Murmansk and Arkhangelsk (on the White Sea). This was particularly dangerous due to the proximity to German air, submarine, and surface forces. There was also the likelihood of severe weather, frequency of fog, strong currents, drift ice, and icebergs. This is not to mention the difficulties of navigating and maintaining convoy cohesion in the constant winter darkness and around-the-clock attacks in constant summer daylight.

Preyed upon by U-boats and Luftwaffe bombers, of nearly eight hundred convoy transports, ninety-seven ships and countless men were lost in the inhospitable waters of the North Atlantic. Scholars and historians still differ vehemently over the contribution of Lend-Lease deliveries to the outcome of the Great Patriotic War of the Soviet Union. One thing is certain, though. Arctic combat forged a partnership that no ideological differences could destroy. It was there, and in the USSR's hour of need, that the United States and Great Britain offered a hand, helping stop the *Wehrmacht*'s onslaught on the bloody battlefields of 1941–1942 and achieving a turning point in the war that brought closer the victorious May of 1945.

Victor's cousin, Boris, was already living in Murmansk with his family and was the chairman of a big construction organization. One of the advantages of life in Murmansk was attractive employment compensation. It typically included double salary and special, "polar," bonuses. They were often equal to the salary. These benefits were justified by the relative remoteness of Murmansk, its harsh climate, and the long polar night. The sun essentially disappeared from the sky for months in the winter and then seemed to overcompensate for its "bad behavior" by staying day and night over the summer months. High pay was also justified by the strategic significance of the city, which was near the Soviet Union North Sea navy and the base of a large fishing fleet. There were also other economic reasons for the government's support of city progress and attraction for the workforce. The magnificent northern lights (aurora borealis) somewhat compensated for the gloom of polar night.

During WWII the city was bombed by the Luftwaffe, and most of it was destroyed. After WWII, Murmansk was built up again, and it played an important role in the connection between the Soviet Union and the West. After all it had the only ice-free harbor on the Atlantic coast of the USSR. Murmansk became a modern and very active city with more contact with the Western world than most other parts of the country because many sailors worked on ships that went abroad. In addition to the merchant marine and fishing fleet, ship building, fish processing, and import and export activities made Murmansk a prosperous city with a higher income than most other places in the USSR. Murmansk also became a center for education, research, and culture. In the best years, the city had almost 500,000 inhabitants and was as big as Oslo or Helsinki. After the collapse of the USSR, Murmansk lost a lot of its former importance and a fourth of its inhabitants. Now it has 370,000 inhabitants but is still the biggest city north of the Arctic Circle in the world.

My father relocated to Murmansk late in 1947 after securing an engineering position. He worked in a department that was supporting R & D in the fish-catching and processing industry. In early 1948 the rest of the family (Mother, Grandma Isabella, and I) joined him. When we arrived in Murmansk, there was almost complete darkness outside the train except the area near the middle of the train, which was dimly lit by a couple of lights attached to the tops of tall electric poles. There was no visible station house. The luggage was unloaded into that area, and Victor met us. After our papers were checked by police with barking dogs, we were allowed to leave the station. Even many decades later, I still remember my uneasy feeling upon arrival in Murmansk. A solid station building was erected in the early 1950s, replacing the small, wooden shack that served as the station before.

We lived in a single room of a communal flat on the fifth floor of a seven-story building. We faced the main street, which was named after Stalin. The house had elevators, but they never worked. A government-subsidized apartment was provided to my father through his work. This was perhaps with the help of Boris Osherovsky, who had good connections. The flat had another room where a single mother, Mrs. Belovalova, lived with her daughter, Zhanna, who was my age, and her mother. Belovalova also worked for the fish-processing industry in a plant producing fish oil from the cod caught in the North Atlantic.

Except for Zhanna's cat, who menaced my father's galoshes (god knows why he disliked them), there were normal relationships within that family. At least the relationships were as normal as possible in a communal flat with a common kitchen and a single bathroom. Because of the cat's misbehavior and because I did not like the cod oil I had to take regularly to avoid scurvy from the lack of vitamins, fresh vegetables, and sun in winter, I developed some animosity to Mrs. Belovalova who I associated with the hated cod oil. Similarly I disliked her mother (Zhanna's Grandma), who I thought looked like an old witch. One time when I was home alone, I was able to express that animosity in an act of vengeance against the older Belovalova, who was not aesthetically appealing to me. I tried to destroy some of their food from the communal kitchen by throwing it out the kitchen window. Fortunately my rampage was resolutely cut short by Isabella when she returned home.

At the time of our arrival, the main housing in Murmansk consisted of two- and three-story log houses. Stalin Street, approximately a mile long and running parallel to Cola Bay, and several other downtown streets, which extended from Stalin Street to the fishing and commercial ports of the bay, sported big brick buildings. There was no pavement. Sidewalks were made of wooden planks.

The word "downtown" had a literal meaning in Murmansk. A few blocks behind the main street, the city's hilly area, with predominantly wooden housing, commenced. The more affluent members of the Murmansk population lived downtown. That included the families of the army brass, the Communist Party, and government officials. It also included better-off white-collar workers such as engineers, doctors, officers of fishing and commercial shipping, and higher-up workers in industrial and cultural organizations. The rest of the Murmansk citizenry, numbering at the time to approximately 50,000, lived in housing sprawled along the hills. Most of the fishing and commercial fleet sailors and their families lived there.

The main access to the fishing port facilities, where my father and Zhanna's mother worked, led through a long walkway with high fences on both sides. Behind the fences were fields containing huge salt piles. The air in the vicinity was salty. The walls of the fences were scrawled with bad words, as is typical for Russia. Somewhat off the port area, even many years after the war, one could see rusting oceangoing vessels with huge torpedo or bomb holes lying on the banks of Kola Bay. The unloading of convoy ships often continued during the bombing. These abandoned ships stirred the imagination of me and other ten- to twelve-year-old boys, and we satisfied our curiosity by crawling inside these dead behemoths during low tide.

After arrival in Murmansk, Alla began working as a doctor at the emergency ambulance station. In March of 1948, she took a four-month long course in radiology at the State Institute for Qualification of Physicians in Leningrad, and she passed the tests with the highest grades. On returning to Murmansk, she assumed the position of head of the radiology department at the district polyclinic, which served the general population. The clinic was located in one of the wings of an imposing building. Overlooking the port in the Kola Bay, it was utilized predominantly as a long-stay hotel or rest house for sailors recuperating between shifts at sea, which sometimes lasted up to six months.

Alla continued working as the head of radiology in the clinic for the next eleven years until the family moved to Riga, Latvia. I often visited Mother at her office when I needed to see other physicians for various childhood ailments. The somber atmosphere of her office, her image in the white coat tightly tied at the waist, and seeing her working with mysterious equipment all instilled in me a sense of awe.

At the same time she was very much into joyous and laughing moments. To my pleasant surprise, she and her assistant could laugh infectiously and for quite a long time over issue known only to them. Despite their amicable relationship and young age (not even thirty in the late 1940s), they addressed each other in the customary formal way. The assistant's name was Olga Grigor'evna, and she addressed my mother as Alla Llovna (not L'vovna or Lvovna, which would be the formal parlance). In that way, Anna Pavlovna would be called Anna Pallna and Anna Ivanovna as Anna Wanna. A patronymic name, modified in that manner, speeds up pronunciation of rather long Russian salutations, and it confers an added respect for the person addressed.

The last name of Olga Grigor'evna was Tasso. That was not a typical Russian name, and combined with the regular name Olga, it kept me amused until I learned her husband was of a Greek descend. This knowledge added an aura of mystery to Mother's work and her surroundings, as I had already heard from Grandma Isabella about the ancient Greeks and their fantastic myths.

At home Alla often liked to sing the popular songs of the1930s and 1940s. These included a Latin American song about Chilita (a beautiful but poor girl who, despite many rich suitors, loved a simple baker). Another was a Russian love song that started with the words, "How many attractive girls there are, how many tender names, but only one of these names brings a sweet longing and takes away peace of mind and a night's sleep." Another song was about the beautiful Odessa fisherman Konstantin and a fisherwoman, Sonya, who manned her own fishing sailboat. In the song Sonya attempts to strike up a conversation with handsome Konstantin, who she's heard a lot about but is only seeing for the first time. This song, the "Odessa Song," was also from the aforementioned 1943 movie "Two Soldiers." The alternative name of the song is "Scowls

Full of Mallet" (Шаланды Полные Кефали/Shalandy Polnye Kefali) which is based on the first line of the song. [35]

Still another song was about Odessa street toughs, which were called *úrkas* or *urkagáns*. Odessa was notorious for its criminal underworld, which was glamorized in songs. The vocabulary of these songs (*blatnýe*, which in loose translation is a colloquialism for things that are not fully legal in the straight world) consisted of slang. This could be used as the main parlance in common conversation on any subject. Using this slang was considered cool. The song explained that from an Odessa *kichmán* (prison) several *úrkas* (gangsters) ran away. Because of a skirmish with police, some *úrkas* got wounded and for recuperation hid in a safe place called *malína* (strawberry bushes).

Alla also liked the American song of 1943 "Comin' in on a Wing and a Prayer." (It was by composer Jimmy McHugh with words by Harold Adamson.) It was a joyful song about bomber pilots who returned safely to the base even though their aircraft was seriously damaged after successfully carrying out the required bombing raids. The Russian translation become very popular in the USSR and was performed by the famous Soviet jazz singer Leonid Utyosov. Alla also liked the early 1930s song with a fox-trot melody and funny repetitive line: "How do you do, do, Mr. Brown?" Alla sang the song, and my dad used to whistle it. And sometime they sort of danced to the tune.

They also liked "Tango Magnolia" ("V bananovo-limonnom Singapure," "In the Banana-Lemon Singapore"). In the words of the British researcher Richard Stites, "Vertinsky bathed his verses in images of palm trees, tropical birds, foreign ports, plush lobbies, ceiling fans, and 'daybreak on the pink-tinted sea'"[30] These were precisely the things wartime and postwar audiences craved. They also liked and sang a lyrical song of Sormovo about the love of two factory workers. The words of the song were by E. Dolmatovsky, and music was by B. Mokrousov.[31]

I was under Isabella's supervision when my parents were at work until I went to school in 1950. Isabella continued to teach me manners and was trying to teach me French. She was also trying to teach me Latin using the words from the old-school song "Gaudeamus Igitur" ("So Let Us Rejoice"). This was traditionally performed at university graduation ceremonies in many European countries. Despite its use as a formal graduation hymn, it is a jocular, lighthearted composition that pokes fun at university life while reminding about brevity of human life. Here are the first lines of this ancient song.

Gaudeamus igitur, juvenes dum sumus
Post jucundam juventutem,
Post molestam senectutem,
Nos habebit humus, nos habebit humus.

Vita nostra brevis est, brevi finietur
Vita nostra brevis est, brevi finietur

The translation goes something like this:

Let us rejoice, therefore, while we are young;
After the joys of youth,
After the troubles of old age,
The Earth will have us.

Our life is short, it will shortly be finished,
Our life is short, it will shortly be finished.

Isabella certainly opened a window to the world for me, giving me history and literature lessons. These were wholesome lessons where I learned not only the names of prominent leaders and literary heroes such as Alexander Makedonsky and Don Quixote but the names of their passions (Dulcenea in the case of Don Quixote). I even learned the names of their horses, which were Bucephalus and Rossinante respectively. These lessons, Greek fables, and fairy tales, which Isabella read to me, formed in my head a mosaic picture of the world. I imagined past and present, real and unreal all bound together. It was a child's world. Some of the Russian fairy tales about people transforming into animals and the Brothers Grimm fairy tales about wicked gnomes and dwarfs tinged this world with suspense and anxiety.

The strange reflection of low polar sunlight from the windows of houses on the hills (in polar latitudes the summer sun is very low over the horizon) dovetailed with this anxiety and created an impression in me that something was lurking behind these windows. A story Grandma told me added to my surreal perception of the outside world. Claiming to have had an extrasensory experience, she told me one day in 1905 she woke up early in the morning from a loud voice repeating the words "Tsusima, Tsusima, Tsusima." She did not know the meaning of this word. Upon complete awakening, she realized she'd heard it in her dream, and there was no one around to say these words.

Later in the day, her brother came into town with a newspaper that brought fresh news about a historically and politically overreaching marine battle in the Tsushima Strait (Tsusima in Russian). It was between the Russian and Japanese navies, and the Russian fleet was defeated. The outcome forced Russia to sign a peace treaty with Japan, which ended the bloody and unpopular Russo-Japanese war of 1904–1905. She could never find a good explanation for that experience. She was convinced she had never heard the name before and could not have known about the battle over there.

Some tales and stories Isabella invented for me. My favorite was a sequel that lasted many years. This was about the life and adventures of an imaginary folksy character called Phon'ka (from the Russian name Aphonasy). I guess it was her rendition of the popular stories about Ivan the Fool. I realized later the main character loosely resembled the good soldier Šveik—a personage from the famous novel of the same name by the Czech writer J. Gašek—in his often hilariously absurd behavior. She would tell me these stories sitting near my bed until I fell asleep.

In 1950 we began receiving by subscription a new edition of the *Big Soviet Encyclopedia*. Isabella voraciously read it and discussed various topics with me. She also taught me to play checkers and chess, and she played these games with me. She also introduced me to the world of postage stamp collecting. I found it fascinating and was enchanted with stamp collecting for many years.

I learned from her that our family was of Hebrew descent. In the past, before the revolution, there were pogroms against Hebrews who were accused of anything, including being wickedly smart. She recalled one time when she was a schoolgirl in the women's gymnasium in Kherson. The Russian girls in the classroom were frantically talking about the rumors that the Jews poisoned the well. Upon hearing it she approached that group of girls, and she told them she was a Jewess. She said she felt really smart because she understood that Jews could not have poisoned the well from which they themselves fetched water.

Isabella was proud of her Jewish heritage. She associated it with such towering figures as microbiologist Waldemar Haffkine from Odessa (1860–1930). He did pioneering work in the development of the anticholera and antiplague vaccines, which he tested on himself. He stayed in India a long time inoculating tens of thousands.

She associated her Jewish heritage also with great thinkers of the past such as Baruch Spinoza of the seventeenth century. He was actually excommunicated from his synagogue by the Amsterdam Jewish Religious Hierarchy. (Interestingly the ban is still in force.) There was also Uriel Acosta who also was excommunicated for attacking rabbinic Judaism as nonbiblical. She told me that while writing his treatises, Spinoza had to support himself by polishing optical lenses. Even when he became famous, he refused to abandon his trade when offered a lucrative position by an enlightened nobleman. That notion of self-reliance and supporting oneself financially by an activity other than the favored intellectual occupation set deeply in me from an early age. It helped me in the future to realize my academic aspirations while working in modest engineering positions.

I learned also from Isabella about the Italian philosopher Giordano Bruno, who was convicted as a heretic by the Inquisition and burned at the stake in Rome. Learning of the unenviable fates of these men apparently established in me from an early age a resistance to clericalism of any persuasion.

The moral lessons I learned from Isabella, which were later reinforced by Alla's mentoring, were often aimed at boosting an attitude of responsibility. The lessons were administered as recommendations to behave myself with equal decency in public and private. I was told to behave even when nobody could see me.

Decency of behavior (in Russian *poryadochnost'* or "*intelligentness*" was considered one of the most important traits a person could possess. Explaining it to me, Isabella often told the story of Diogenes, a Greek philosopher, who carried a lamp around in daylight as part of his search for an honest man in a society of scoundrels.

A human being, Isabella told me, is essentially a tabula rasa (Latin for a clean sheet of paper). Upbringing and life experiences are paramount in forming a person. I recently learned this expression is attributed to John Lock.

I also picked up pieces of wisdom from Isabella's conversations with Alla and other people of relevant intelligence. They talked about the works of philosophers such as Schopenhauer, Nietzsche, and Kant and of writers and playwrights such as Ibsen, Oscar Wilde, Chekhov, Ostrovsky, and others. Isabella and Alla liked that famous expression of Descartes, "I think therefore I am." Among the modern Russian poets, Isabella and Alla liked Esenin and the prerevolutionary Igor Severianin. Upon growing up I memorized several of Severyanin's poems. In later years Alla and I used to recall the lines of his famous "Pineapples in Champagne."

The lines of several R. Burns' poems, filled with ethical and social pathos, became a sort of credo for Grandma Isabella. Ideologically she was rather left wing, and she upheld the principles of honest poverty over ill-gotten riches. Considering that official religion was not very popular in the Soviet Union, and considering that even my great-grandparents had already left orthodox religious dogma along with much of the Russian/Jewish intelligentsia in the last quarter of the nineteenth century, through its sheer brilliance and underlying social commentary, Burns' poetry became a part of the written moral code for members of our family. (His work was skillfully adapted to Russian by Samuil Marshak.) Isabella's reading and reciting of Burns' verses became a conduit to the relevant ethical and moral norms.

For better or worse, I felt an attachment to some of these norms throughout my life. At least I used to find solace in them when my ambitions fell through. On the other hand, I used them as justification to not exert ambitions when they were possibly justified. Several memorable Burns' epitaphs along with Marshak's adaptation and my adaptation to modern English are shown in Appendix C.

When we were alone, Isabella often sang some touching and melodic songs. Some were based on lyrics of Sergey Esenin, a famous Russian poet of the first quarter of the twentieth century. The government ostracized him for not promoting the party line in his creativity.

Other songs, which are probably not traceable now, she apparently heard in the days of her youth.

One song was about the cruel end of a young and tender lady at the hands of mobsters who threw her out of the window of a high-rise building. Another song expressed sympathy to a poor Chinese man who was deprived of visiting the Forbidden City in Peking where life was plentiful for foreigners. Isabella sung also in French. One French song was about a French legionnaire falling in love with a beautiful Indochinese girl (*annamitte* in French). A few words of these songs ring in my memory. "Annamitte, le petite…l'amour…l'amour…toujours." The song was from the period when Indochina was part of the French colonial empire. French Indochina comprised the territories of the modern Vietnam, Cambodia, and Laos. And Annam was a French protectorate in the central region of Vietnam. Shown below are also a few lines from Ukrainian and Russian songs (with my English adaptation) Isabella used to sing.

Excerpts from several Russian and Ukrainian melancholic or sentimental songs Isabella used to hum.

A Ukrainian song.
Ukrainian transliteration/English translation.

Reve ta stogne Dnipr shirokyy,
Serdity viter zavyve…

Roars and moans
The wide River Dnieper
When a fierce wind howls…

A song of the Ukrainian patriots.
Ukrainian transliteration/English translation.

Ne nado nam tsaria Mykoly,
Ego z prestola my zspihnem.

Napishem novue zakony,
Gramatsku radu soberem

We don't need Tsar Nicolas,
We push him from his throne.
We will write new laws
And will create our own government.

A Russian lyrical song.
Russian text/English translation.

Река извиваясь, волнуясь бежит
И с каждым ее поворотом
Является новый чарующий вид-
Нет счета природным красотам.

Here runs the river twisting and wavy.
And with each of its turns
A new and beautiful view appears—
There is no count to nature's beauties.

A Russian sentimental song about the
charming hussars leaving provincial girls with broken hearts.
Russian text/English translation.

На солнце оружием сверкая,
Под звуки лихих трубачей,
По улицам пыль подымая
Проходил полк гусар усачей.

With their weapons shining under the sun,
Following the sounds of the dashed horn players,
And raising the dust clouds,
A regiment of the mustachioed hussars
Marched along the streets of a small town.

She also used to sing, as I mentioned earlier, her own sad songs, in which she expressed her unabated grief over the loss of Witold. The repertoire of Grandma's songs included one popular prewar patriotic song known as "March of the Soviet Tankmen." The melody was catchy, and the lyrics, which was filled with fighting spirit, was captivating. She usually sang only one quatrain of the song, which ended with these words, "when Comrade Stalin will send us to the fight, and the First Marshal (i.e., Comrade Voroshilov) will lead us." Isabella's performance carried overtones of light sadness, and her blue eyes filled with tears.

Isabella's other son, Theodor, was arrested in a police roundup in 1941 for not having a proper identity card. His whereabouts were unknown for three years, but he survived the upheaval of the war including service in the army, wounds, hospitals, and a series of bizarre experiences. He was now working and living in Taganrog. After his arrest in 1941, he was employed digging trenches near Makhachkala. Eventually he was released and shipped with other evacuees to work in the Asian republics of the USSR.

In his diary, Theodor vaguely recorded his travels, identifying the main cities he passed along the way. These included Krasnovodsk, Ashgabat, and Chardzhou. Then he went down the Amu-Daria River to a small town where he got a job as a school teacher in a nearby Turkmen village (*aul*). His diary depicts the life and customs of the Turkmens. It also depicts humiliation, which he sustained from the schoolchildren who taunted him for his hearing handicap.

The records in his diary of 1942 list the following titles: Departure from the aul, illness on the road, Hiva, Work at the state park, Work in the orphanage, Who educates whom?, Drafted in the army, Mosquitoes, Aralsk, Murom, Work at the defense construction, and Saratov.

Despite his almost complete lack of hearing, Theodor was mobilized for duties at the army front in 1943. After a short training period, he was sent to the sapper detachments. His lack of hearing multiplied his chances of being killed. There were situations he described where his comrades would hear the whistle of flying artillery ordnance and fall to the ground for cover, but he continued to run. The 1943 records of his diary also describe the liberation of Kiev, roundup by the enemy near Vinnitsa, life in the conditions of a roundup, escape from the roundup, and New Year's night. Their listed titles were "Katiushi," biography in verses, and poems of the war years. The titles of the 1944 list were work of supper in winter, wounding on February 12, hospitals, two months wandering across the Ukraine, demobilization, work in civil construction, and return to Taganrog with the soles of my boots tied on by wires.

Theodor's hearing handicap and intellectual upbringing made him somewhat reclusive. He did not always fit well into the mold of a typical combat soldier where a comradely familiarity and absence of a good code of conduct prevail. This was not always appreciated by his superiors. He described one time when his regiment liberated a town in the Ukraine, and his commander invited the soldiers to drink vodka for the success of the operation. Theodor, however, did not join the company as he never drank. The commander was furious for his refusal to drink and shouted at him, "Why don't you drink with us? Are you a Jew-face? Aren't you glad for our victory?" (See Appendix B, p. 260.)

Theodor did not hide from this abuse and answered the commander he was glad for the victory, but "for your bad-mouthing you'll now get it." He hit him in the face. The commander pulled out his revolver and was going to shoot Theodor on the spot. However, other comrades stopped the commander and dissuaded him from shooting Theodor immediately. He was jailed with the intention of being shot in the morning before the regiment. However, as happens in war, the situation can be very fluid. In the morning, the enemy attacked. Theodor was released from his confinement, and the incident was put to rest.

Isabella did not always hum sentimental or sad songs. She knew quite a lot of humorous songs, satirical rhyming poems, and jokes that she apparently picked up attending artistic performances in the pre and early postrevolutionary years in the famous Odessa café "Fancony." Some of them were quite frivolous. Others were definitely politically incorrect, satirizing Lenin himself.

I was only eight to ten at the time, but this did not stop Isabella from sharing with me anecdotes and satirical poems (about Lenin). There was the provision that in no way should I tell this stuff to anyone else, since, "You don't want to bring trouble to us, do you?" She would ask this before divulging to me these apocryphal (for the Soviet regime) stories. I hope divulging some of the most benign of these stories now is less preposterous and serves the purpose of showing the early sources of the Soviet dissident culture.

In one of the jokes, a boy asks his father, "Who was Nicolas the Second?" The father answers with an Odessa accent, "Oy wey! He was a tyrant. He put us in chains." The boy then asks who Lenin was. The father answers, "Oh! Lenin was a great liberator. He liberated us from the chains. Don't you remember my little golden chain from my watch?" For the clarity of the joke, remember that in the first years of the revolution, jewelry was expropriated by the Soviet government.

Another joke takes advantage of the fact that Lenin's portrait (with a caption that read, "You died, but your business lives") was exhibited ubiquitously, even in small businesses. As the joke goes, a father is answering a boy's question about who Lenin was by saying he was a businessman and a store owner. As proof of it, he points toward the Lenin portrait hanging with the aforementioned caption in the store. The pun here is built on the double meaning of the Russian word for "business," which is *delo*. In Russian, *delo* was used to signify both a commercial enterprise and any kind of activities in general. So in the joke, Lenin's *delo* (i.e., his major undertaking of building communism) is compromised by placing attention on the commercial meaning of the word. Currently the word "business" is used widely in Russia in its proper meaning.

No doubt had these jokes about Lenin gotten into the wrong hands, our whole family would have followed the footsteps of Grandpa Shmulian. In telling me these stories, Isabella probably had some sense of satisfaction that, in a small way, she could express her revulsion to the injustice that had befallen her husband. It is equally possible that for Isabella the jokes were nothing more than an abrasive political satire whose sound bite she enjoyed. Regardless I was a good boy and did not tell anyone these jokes, including my parents.

They probably wouldn't have condoned this type of indoctrination from Isabella, but I don't think they would have objected to it either. I already sensed their ambivalence and ironic attitude about many things that could be considered political. Politics began with taking out a bucket of trash. I was reminded to be careful I did not throw out newspapers with images of Stalin inadvertently soiled or defaced into the garbage bin in the backyard.

Isabella and the rest of the family were pro-Soviet in a good sense. wGrandma often described how pitiful life was for many poor people and especially poor Jews in Tsarist Russia, and she appreciated the positive changes the Soviet government gave them. My parents fit well in their respective positions, improving the postwar life of the country and enjoying the spirit of booming construction and development. The repressions of the 30s seemed a matter of the past, and knowledge of a new wave of repression had not yet reached the wider population.

Despite periodic shortages of bread and the subsequent long bread lines where Grandma spent many early mornings in 1947 and 1948, the food supply of Murmansk was quite decent on the scale of the Soviet distribution system. A huge supermarket on a corner of the central street always boasted frozen fish and delicacies such as red and black caviar, smoked fish, smoked bacon, etc. The frescos on the walls depicted in a lackluster manner the joyful life of the people in various Soviet republics engaged in their traditional occupations. The busty Caucasian women harvested grapes, in their colorful robes, the peasants of the middle Asian republics collected huge watermelons, and so on. Still there were always shortages of meat, poultry, potatoes, and fruit. Yet, the attributes of the Stalin cult were ubiquitous and fashioned to create a joyful atmosphere. At the corner of the building where we lived, there was a clothing store. Since everything was politicized, even that store sported a sculpture of Stalin holding his daughter Svetlana in his hands. This was an image famous in the era.

Murmansk was growing rapidly. Construction site cranes filled the horizon. On the ground, the most hard, dirty, and odious jobs were performed by teams of women led by a male supervisor. Considering permafrost, it took special efforts to build roads and foundations for buildings. Using huge mallets, the women hammered iron spikes into the ground to ensure its construction worthiness. The prevalence of women in these operations was due to a general shortage of men (from losses in the war and imprisonment in the Gulag) and because of the very low wages for these jobs.

In the early 1950s, the main streets of Murmansk were asphalted, and many new buildings were erected. One of these was the House of Culture, which had a stage for performances and also served as a movie theater. There were numerous rooms for activities. These were targeted to engage the population, and especially the youth, in professional studies such as radio technique. It also encouraged cultural undertakings such as choir or attending lectures on various topics. A few times, Isabella managed to stage some of her plays there.

The aura of Murmansk was like the northern lights. Life was not stagnant. Many Murmansk residents were recent transplants from Moscow or Leningrad, and this added to the cultural level of the city. On good summer days or nights (usually the summer nights had more sunlight than the days), big crowds of people swarmed along the two main Murmansk thoroughfares, Stalin Prospect and the road running perpendicular to this street and starting near the railroad station. Somewhere along this street was a city park with a structure commemorating fallen defenders of the city during the civil war and Second World War. Across the street from the park was a big restaurant with a live band. A huge stuffed polar bear, standing on his hind legs, nearly filled the restaurant lobby.

My parents celebrated New Year's there a few times. More regular celebrations such as family birthdays were conducted in our apartment. Dad's kin, Boris Osherovsky, was often present with his family at these festivities. He knew a lot of funny stories and anecdotes, and he delivered them effectively. As I recollect now, he somewhat resembled the French comic actor Louis DeFunet, who had a characteristically sardonic face. Having that type of face or making it while cracking jokes made Boris more humorous.

Despite the jovial atmosphere of these parties, I found more thrill in the birthday parties given by the neighboring family for Zhanna. They had lived in Murmansk longer than we had, and apparently they had more acquaintances with children. Many kids attended these parties, which were festooned with Bengal lights and other extravaganzas. I also enjoyed the larger variety of snacks at the Zhanna parties. This was probably attributable to the more focused culinary interests of Zhanna's grandma compared to mine, who was more involved with my cultural upbringing and her own literature exercises. Both grandmothers prepared the food for their families.

In the flat above us lived the captain of a long-haul trawler and his wife. The captain spent almost all his time with his ship and crew catching fish in the far-flung reaches of the Northern Atlantic. They often reached Georges Bank near Newfoundland. The walls of the rooms in their flat were covered with exquisite wallpapers, and the rooms were filled with various eye-catching products of the land and sea. From the sea, there were shells of humongous starfishes and crabs, seashells of any kind, and stuffed, exotic deepwater fishes. The land products of notice were fine china, vases, and decorative plates that were apparently received through the reparation process from the Soviet Occupation Zone in Germany. Other exciting items displayed in the rooms were souvenirs bought in the foreign ports where his ship stopped for resupply.

I viewed all of this with admiration when Grandma and I visited that flat by invitation from the captain's wife, Varvara Varfolomeevna, who became friends with our family. On the rare occasions the captain and his wife attended our parties, the captain, to my surprise, was extremely shy and silent and could not master even a simple toast. I could not comprehend this. I expected from a captain a torrent of exciting sea stories.

Good friends of my parents were also my dad's boss and his wife. In the late 1940s, the boss was a chief engineer with the last name of Khronovsky. He was a nice, tall fellow of Russian/Polish descent who often wore a leather coat. Something in his face was very appealing and suggested a decent and resolute nature. His wife was a slim, petite, attractive, and mercurial lady. Although she did not occupy any prominent position in the city's social life, she was self-assured, well-spoken, and most important in the judgment of my mother, who liked to be with her, in possession of good taste in women's attire.

Being well-dressed in a practical and fashionable way was not easy. The garment industry in Soviet times was far inferior to European standards, and there were financial hurdles to take into account. In that regard, the ability to sew a dress or mend it (or to know a good seamstress) was important. One such seamstress happened to be the wife of one of my father's acquaintances, engineer Goldshtein. We often visited them, and I very much enjoyed the borscht his wife used to feed us during dinnertime.

This was after the issues of making or mending a particular dress were discussed. To my grandmother's dismay, I openly said at one of these dinners that I liked the Goldshtein's borscht more than Grandma's.

Despite the good dinners, the acquaintance with Goldshtein brought certain troubles for my father. He was called into the *Ministerstvo Gosudarstvennoj Bezopasnosti* (MGB) headquarters. The Ministry of State Security, it was the successor to the NKVD and the predecessor to the Ministry of Internal Affairs (MVD). In Murmansk the MGB occupied a large, street-block-sized building. It was here my father was asked to be an informant and keep tabs on Goldshtein's family, reporting on all their guests, correspondence, etc.

This invitation coincided with the anti-cosmopolite and anti-American campaign instigated by Stalin. It predominantly targeted the Jewish cultural and professional elite. Goldshtein was targeted because he had some interaction with Americans. It is also possible he either stayed in America during WWII for some time due to his line of duty, or he had a relative who did so.

The American contact was sufficient to blackball Goldshtein and make him a suspect in anti-Soviet activity. The wartime Soviet-American alliance gave way to the Cold War, with mutual accusations of spying and warmongering. According to my mother's accounts, my dad refused to cooperate. The security apparatus did not easily forgive this disobedience, and as I understand, he was periodically blackmailed and threatened into cooperating.

One of my father's major responsibilities at work was the mechanization and automation of fish processing. This was a field in which he made several inventions that were implemented in the industry. This job also made it necessary to go to sea on trawlers to test his new equipment for freezing and processing freshly caught fish. For these expeditions, he used to wear a crimson American waterproof Windbreaker with a hood and lining of extremely light and warm alpaca fur. He possibly got it from the port authorities, who apparently retained a limited quantity of this stuff from wartime.

This elegant Windbreaker (*alpahovka* in Russian parlance) became, for me and my friends, a symbol of my father's status and a source of dreams about America, which made such practical and attractive things. Not very many people in our surroundings had *alpahovkas*.

Meanwhile, an even more serious challenge than seagoing arose. It was very trivial in form but potentially incapacitating. That was the traditional Russian heavy drinking. It usually accompanies parties celebrating the successful conclusion of business activities or simply a business meeting. It was apparently after one of these meetings that my father came home dead drunk.

Fortunately he was able to come home safely. He was, however, in a condition that he had to be put to sleep on the floor right in the middle of the communal kitchen in his high winter boots (*sapogi*) and that *alpahovka*. This was to the chagrin of my mother and Isabella and to the displeasure of Zhanna's grandma and her cat, who apparently did not like the smell of alcohol.

Dad was an avid sportsman, and the Murmansk weather presented more than ample opportunities for winter sports. On Sundays, three of us (Mother, Father, and I) used to go skiing in the hills behind the city. The proper adjustment of our outfits was essential in enduring the brutal Arctic cold and enjoying the skiing without frostbite. Dad was a good engineer and understood well the principles of thermal insulation.

Accordingly an important part of ski trip preparation was wrapping our feet in several layers of paper before fitting them into the ski boots. Our faces and ears (if they were not protected by a fur hat) had to be smeared with goose grease, and mittens were used instead of gloves. By ten to eleven years of age, I already well understood the basic elements of skiing, ski/boot fastening, and selection of the proper ski size, poles, and ski grease. From that age, I often used to go skiing in the hills by myself. Interestingly my parents and grandma were not very worried about me skiing alone.

I was even encouraged to go skiing and not sit at home. The types of crime rampant today such as kidnapping, sexual molestation, etc., were not heard of then. In walking toward the skiing areas, I usually took shortcuts and crossed the poor sections of the city. I saw the appalling conditions (without plumbing and running water) in which people in the outskirts of the city lived. Organized snow removal in that portion of the city was irregular at best, and by the end of winter, the snow piles often reached the roofs of the one- and two-story dwellings.

The children living in these districts were not very friendly to downtown kids such as me, and they could gang up on somebody to expropriate anything they considered of value. Typically it would be gloves, hat, pen knife, or pocket change. To avoid this harassment, I usually followed a route where the presence of these young rascals would be minimal.

This skiing frenzy was part of a general awareness and respect for physical fitness that was supported by both sexes and all age groups. "*Brust hieraus, bauch hinunter*," which in German means "pull in your stomach and push out your breast," was one of Alla's favored expressions when conversations touched a subject related to physical culture. The expression, which she learned in school, was apparently borrowed from German military lingo. Similar expressions exist in the armed forces of various nations, and this is certainly true of the Russian army. These expressions are used by commanders calling upon subordinates to stay at attention and demonstrate readiness. Taking physical culture (*phyzcoolture*) classes and passing the tests were a must in the regular schools and higher education establishments. Along with promoting various kinds of sports, the government established a two-tier system of tests for an individual's level of physical readiness.

The lower level was called BGTO (Be Ready for Labor and Defense), and the higher level was GTO (Ready for Labor and Defense). Each of these test programs included nongame types of sports such as running, jumping, pull-ups on a horizontal bar, rope scaling, rowing, and others. The performance requirements of the GTO approached Olympic levels. The water exercises, cold showers, and rubbing oneself with wet towels in the morning were considered important additions in the total system for beefing up body defenses. This was called quenching of the organism (borrowing the lingo of the heat treatment of steel to improve its strength).

There were always debates between Mom and Dad about what degree I should be subjected to these Spartan therapies. Dad was eager to put me through all nine yards of the strenuous physical exercises. Alla argued I was a sickly child (I often suffered from sore throats and other child maladies) and needed a nuanced approach. As a result, and to my satisfaction, I was sometimes able to skip the intense cold-water treatments prescribed by my father.

In 1950 I went to school. It was a junior four-year school and a field base for the local Pedagogical Institute, whose students were often present in our classrooms. The school was across the street from our house. Boys and girls studied together, and wearing a uniform was obligatory. The boys wore navy blue cadet suits that were relatively expensive. Although the salaries of my parents were relatively high, they still barely covered all the needed expenses, so all possible thrifty measures were put in use. This particularly applied to clothing, where remodeling and alterations were very popular.

In one of the provided photographs, I am with my parents in the summer of 1950, and I'm wearing a coat obtained by altering my grandfather's jacket. My left arm is under the coat, and it's in a sling because of an injury I sustained a few months before school started. I accidentally chopped off the tip of the little finger on my left hand by trying to investigate the principles of operation of some sort of water pump rusting in a backyard of our building. The pump had heavy levers. After I managed to swing a lever upward, I did not have enough strength to hold it. It came down swiftly, crushing my little finger before I completely withdrew my hand from under the falling lever with the sharp edges.

I did not feel pain in the first moments, and with the tip of my finger hanging on a thread of skin, I ran home. Mostly I worried I would be punished by my parents for such a gruesome prank. Several times my father had already strictly reprimanded me for my mischief. After coming home, I began crying and asking my parents not to punish me because it was just an accident. Of course, I was not punished but immediately taken by Mother to her clinic. Despite being a Sunday, some services and the emergency room functioned. It was decided not to attach the loosely held portion of the finger but to separate it completely and continue treatment of the remaining portion. In the absence of penicillin, the antibiotic was streptoceid powder, which was placed on the wound after it was cleansed. The treatment continued through the whole summer, and fortunately I was able to start the school year on time and attend a ceremony on the first day where pupils present flowers to the teachers.

The girls' uniform consisted of a dress with an apron over it like a waitress. The majority of students were children of professionals, high-ranking government employees, Communist Party functionaries, and military officers. The classes were crowded. Sometimes thirty to forty children were in the room. My neighbor, Zhanna, was a year older than me and went into another class. The classmates whose names I remember include Vladimir Portniagin, the son of the editor of the ma jor regional newspaper, *Polar Truth* (*Poliarnaja Pravda*), with whom I engaged in postage stamp collecting, Vsevolod Rudin, the son of a colonel, the son of the high-ranking General Sukhomlinov (who, with his family, lived in a building with a sentry sitting at the entrance of the building), the daughter of another high-ranking general, Zaremba (he was possibly the commander of the whole northwest military district), and Irina Kalinina, the daughter of one of the bigwigs in military or government service.

In the fourth grade, when we were already eleven to twelve years old, some boys from my class began openly demonstrating their budding sexual interests. These interests were prompted by pictures and toys with explicit sexual content, which the fathers of these children, sailors that visited the foreign ports, brought home with them. The boys sometimes brought this stuff into the school. During recess or after hours, it was observed with interest by the larger crowds of boys. The material prompted wrestling matches between the groups of boys for possession of the aforementioned Ira Kalinina, who was an attractive girl. These matches were accompanied by raucous noise. Although I did not object to peeking at the prohibited material, I was disgusted by the rampages. Kalinina did not suspect what role she played in the minds of some of her classmates.

In 1951 my father got a government-subsidized, one-bedroom flat in a new five-story building on Stalin Prospect. It was several blocks down the road from where we lived. It was a large L–shaped building the size of a football field. The longer leg ended in a five-cornered square, behind which was a railroad station. The flat had a kitchen where my dad set up a small lab in which he conducted various sophisticated experiments. These demonstrated to me numerous principles of physical laws and phenomena. These augmented and expanded my classroom curricula. I remember I was especially amazed seeing moving or rotating objects "frozen" when viewed with a strobe light.

Unfortunately there was no telephone service in the building, as there was none in the overwhelming majority of the city's housing. This was typical for all cities except possibly the biggest, Moscow, Leningrad, Kiev, Rostov… To place a telephone call to a relative living in another place or to receive a call, one had to go to the telephone station, from which a telegram could also be sent. Shortages of landline telephone service remained, in general, well into our time there. Telephone communication was substantially improved with the advent of cellular phone service.

As the following example shows, there were definite downsides associated with life without telephones, even in the Soviet Union.

One time we woke up to a woman's screams coming from the apartment across the hallway from ours. Because we couldn't call the police without a phone, we couldn't do much to help. My dad, Victor, pulled on some clothes to be ready for assistance if needed. He went to the door and swung it open to the limit permitted by the chain lock. At the same time, the door from the apartment from which the screams came burst open, and a seminude lady ran out. She was followed by a man (her sailor husband) with a knife. The couple ran up and down the stairs a few times with the woman continuing to scream. Victor intended to restrain her husband. I provided Dad with a hammer for defense. Alla and Isabella were persuading him not to venture out the door and pulled him back. They considered it an unwinnable situation, and they told him his interference would only aggravate it. Perhaps they were right. Eventually the woman ran back to the apartment and slammed the door. She probably barricaded herself in one of the rooms, as we did not hear much noise after her husband ran back to the apartment. It was also possible his drunken rampage fizzled out.

…………………………………………………………………………

The episode with Goldshtein was a relatively mild example of the anti-Semitism that flourished in the USSR from 1948 to the death of Stalin on March 5, 1953. There were several intertwined motives for this postwar atmosphere. The Cold War, which started in 1946 between the United States and the USSR, and the Israel orientation on America were a feeding ground on which Stalin continued his chess play of permanent witch hunts and periodic mass purges of the population. The "enemy" within was needed for the system that Lenin and Stalin envisaged to function. Essentially it was the old adage, "Beat up your own so the enemy will fear you." The anti-cosmopolitan campaign also started with a chauvinistic platform of overrating everything Russian and Soviet and underrating everything foreign and "bourgeois."

The following joke satirizes the mentality of the time. "In France a monograph was published called *Introduction to the Study of Elephants.* So the USSR published a book called *The USSR Is the Motherland of the Elephants.* In turn, Bulgaria, a satellite of the USSR, issued a book with the name *A Bulgarian Elephant Is a Younger Brother of the Russian Elephant.*"

Under the political and ideological terror of the Stalin regime, whole branches of science were abolished and branded bourgeois, and their leaders were persecuted. These developments caused the USSR and then the CIS, the Commonwealth of the Independent States, to lag in the fields of genetics, computers, agriculture and other.

The anti-cosmopolitan campaign also benefited by downplaying the concentrated effort of the Nazis to exterminate Jews and downplaying Jewish contributions to the war effort (in industry, government, science, the partisan movement, and directly in the Soviet Army). Although the Jews won the fourth largest number of medals in WWII (after Russians, Ukrainians, and Byelorussians), the atmosphere of the day, especially on a folksy level, presented Jews as draft-dodgers or "Tashkent partisans."

Stalin actually helped with the recognition of Israel. The USSR was the first country to officially recognize Israel's independence followed by the United States. Stalin allowed the transfer of arms from Czechoslovakia to Israel, and he also permitted a limited number of Russian Jewish pilots to join the military forces of Israel. Stalin hoped Israel would be a military base in the Middle East under the USSR command and that it would act against British and American interests. This, however, did not exactly happen.

Stalin, ever the internationalist, couldn't understand the enthusiasm of the Jewish population (at least a portion of it) for reviving Jewish culture and language, and he couldn't understand their fervent attachment to Israel. His vision of a Communist doctrine strongly opposed nationalism, even though Stalin was a Georgian who turned into a Great Russian chauvinist. Stalin even persecuted Georgians and other nationalities for the perceived expressions of their nationalism. He saw how enthusiastically the Jewish people greeted Golda Meir, the first Israeli premier, on her 1948 visit to Moscow. Polina Zhemchuzhina, the Jewish wife of the Soviet Minister of Foreign Affairs, V. Molotov, spoke in Yiddish with Meir, and as a consequence of this act, she was arrested and eventually banished from Moscow. This action was also a symbolic attack against Molotov and a reminiscence of the purges of 1930s that could be in the offing.

In this atmosphere, and as part of a newly launched official anti-Semitic campaign, the Jewish Antifascist Committee (JAC) disbanded in November 1948. The JAC was created during the Great Patriotic War by leading representatives of the Russian Jewish culture to lobby the American Jewry for financial assistance to the Soviet Union. But six months after the birth of Israel, it was gone. In the same year, the chairman of JAC, an actor and the head of the Moscow Jewish Theater, Michoels, was murdered on Stalin's orders.

Most of the JAC members were arrested. They were accused of being spies for the United States for having floated the idea of a Jewish homeland in the Crimea instead of Birobidjan. This idea was supported by Jewish agricultural communities that had existed in the Crimea since the 1920s. Another of those grisly Soviet courtroom dramas seemed in the offing.

It was almost four years before the case came to trial. In the meantime, savage interrogation, often laced with anti-Semitic abuse, elicited phantasmagorical confessions from the prisoners. After confessing, they often recanted and then, subjected to more fearsome pressure, capitulated only to again recant. The investigators failed to produce any evidence of seditious activity, however specious, and the interrogations dragged on. On August 12, 1952, some thirty Yiddish writers were executed in the cellars of the Lubyanka Prison. This secret was kept long after Stalin died in 1953.

In parallel with these events, a plot against Jewish doctors [14] was forming. It started without Jewish overtones. It was simply an outgrowth of the macabre atmosphere of intrigue in the upper echelons of government and security apparatus structures, interspersed with informants and denunciations. The immediate origin was the death in 1948 of Zhdanov, a prominent Soviet leader, in the Kremlin hospital. As a result of his death, Dr. Lidia Timashuk, who was responsible for Zhdanov's latest EKG, sent a secret letter to Stalin's chief bodyguard, Vlasic. In the letter she alleged criminal negligence in the treatment of Comrade Zhdanov by his leading physicians, who were high-ranking doctors in Soviet medicine and in the Kremlin system. None of them were Jewish.

Timashuk was an MGB informer and hoped her information would be appreciated. She hoped the professors she accused of negligence would be brought to justice and their anti-Soviet activity, which had possibly led to the earlier death of another Soviet leader, Shcherbakov, would be unmasked. Timashuk acted out of what she thought were the interests of the state. At the same time, she acted out of self-interest. If she did not denounce the other doctors, she was in danger of being denounced.

Timashuk's plans did not work out as expected. When Stalin received her letter, he sent it to the archives without further investigation. Timashuk found herself in a precarious position and sent a few more letters to the security organs, which also went unanswered. In Stalin's world of 1948, Timashuk was wrong, and the doctors were right. Due to Stalin's diabolical mind, which was bent on restoring the political climate of the Great Purges of the 1930s, and a number of other opportunistic events (particularly *Leningrdskoe delo*, the execution of Communist leaders from Leningrad and the purging of the security apparatus), the pendulum that Timashuk helped swing began gradually moving in her favor.

The *delo vrachey* (case of the doctors), as it was called by the Soviet government, was alleged to be a widespread conspiracy within the Soviet medical profession organized by Jewish physicians against Kremlin leaders. Jewish doctors were accused of murdering leaders such as A. A. Zhdanov, A. S. Shcherbakov, and others or planning their murders in league with American intelligence and corrupt Ministry of State security. They arrested hundreds of doctors over a period of five months, beginning in October 1952 and ending in February 1953. Timashuk even received the Order of Lenin. (After Stalin's death and the closure of the case, this was revoked.) "Fantastic rumors circulated that Jewish doctors were poisoning Russian children, injecting them with diphtheria, and killing newborn infants in maternity hospitals."[14]

The full power of the newly aroused Soviet state was then turned against these "criminals in white coats," as they came to be called in the press. Mass arrests began and large-scale concentration camps were built, which were supposedly for Jews deported from Soviet cities. The vicious anti-Semitic campaign already underway allegedly found evidence of "international espionage, betrayal, terrifying plots to overthrow the government and poison the nation's health."[14]

Although the doctor plot hysteria was rampaging predominantly in Moscow and Leningrad, its echo reverberated throughout the Soviet state. In the Murmansk clinic where Alla worked, a colleague of hers, a diminutive Jewish lady dentist, Dr. Kornibat, whose services I often used, was accused of infecting her patients with cancer. She was laid off and, as with many victims of denunciation, went through a sort of show trial among her colleagues before the formal charge was handed down. Fortunately the world is not without good people, and in this case the clinic director had the courage to defend Kornibat from the absurd accusations.

Typically the participants in these discussions, while they understood the absurdity of the accusations, were silent or supported them. They "unmasked" the perpetrators, being afraid for their own situations. My aunt Lyalya (the daughter of Prof. Alexander Iosifovich Dombrovsky, Grandma Lyuba's brother-in-law) wrote:

"Flourished was the atmosphere of hypocrisy from which there was no way to hide. The turn of my father came in February of 1953. I attended that Scientific Council (where my father was subject to the show trial of his colleagues). It is still too painful to recall this meeting even now. Many co-workers and students, with whom my father worked many years, stood up and denounced him.

The only one of his post-graduate students who found the courage to tell the truth was MD Vladimir Palamarchuck. He was then Chair of the X-Ray Department in the military district hospital. He said that all these accusations are a complete nonsense, and that he feels himself embarrassed to participate in this farce. He asserted that the new method of angiography that my father developed was the newest method that helps in the diagnostics of the most serious illnesses. My father was very thankful to Vladimir for his demonstrated support to the end of his life. Fortunately, in March of 1953, all this ugly campaign was over and dad was not repressed."[15]

The anti-Semitic sentiment promulgated among the grown-ups began to trickle down to the children's world. It was unsafe to play with certain children in our backyard if they knew you were Jewish. One day I went to the area of the backyard where we usually played our favorite war games. There were three boys, two of which I knew. One of them was the son of a colonel and used to go to school with me. Another, the son of a trawler captain lived in our building. The small talk I struck up with the boys turned into the officer's son asking me if I was Jewish because he saw me with my parents in the company of an officer he knew was Jewish. I knew if I admitted I was Jewish, the boys would start ridiculing me. I also suspected the new boy was from a street gang who could harass me if he shared my identity with the gang.

Since I had not yet developed strong moral scruples and convictions, to avoid trouble and mainly to participate in the game, I told the boys, to their apparent disappointment, I was not Jewish. To that, the trawler captain's son gladly informed me it had been customary to do a pogrom on the Jews, and the new boy added it was too bad Hitler did not finish all the Jews. The officer's son did not say much. However, he later became a victim of the class warfare that some schoolchildren from poorer families played out on the children of richer families.

Terrible clouds gathered on the horizon of Soviet society. As reference [14] implies, the doctor plot was not the end. It further asserts that, "Coinciding with the early phase of the Cold War…Stalin's conspiracy against the Jewish doctors…has significance far beyond specific Kremlin rivalries, Stalin's personal anti-Semitism, or the malevolence of state security underlings…whom some credit with having masterminded it (the delo vrachey). The doctor plot was a natural outgrowth of the bureaucratic, political, psychological, and moral structure of Stalin's system of government. A great public trial was rumored to have been planned for the end of March 1953."On March 5, however, Stalin died, and the *delo vrachey* almost immediately came to a halt. On March 31, 1953, the ministry of Internal Affairs (which had replaced the MGB) recommended the arrested doctors be exonerated and pardoned in full.

On April 6, 1953, *Pravda* printed an article generally accusing the security services and the former minister of state security, S.D. Ignatiev, of dereliction, putting an end to the organized madness threatening to overwhelm Soviet society. The doctors who survived the ordeal were released and pardoned in full. Meanwhile, several leading security personalities who spearheaded the doctors' case were arrested and shot.

Reference [14], however, throws out a provocative question, which it analyzes in detail. Was the group of non-Jewish Kremlin doctors who were originally accused by Timashuk completely innocent, considering that nothing in the totalitarian Soviet state happened without direct or indirect influence of its boss, Uncle Joe?

Stalin death was an epochal event. Many people cried and lamented that they would not know how to live now, acting like children who had lost their father. In Moscow, hundreds, if not thousands, perished in a stampede because of unwise logistics from authorities concerning visitation of Stalin's body lying in a governmental building in the center of Moscow. The day of Stalin's funeral, March 7, was announced as a national day of mourning. At noon all activities across the country stopped for a few minutes while sirens went off. In our class in school, the boys agreed not to laugh that day, and those who violated this rule were supposed to be beaten.

However, these rules were not enforceable, and giggles and skirmishes took place periodically as usual. In the evening, one of my schoolmates, a chubby Russian boy with freckles and red hair with the last name Yakovlev, came to our flat to play with me. When the current events were discussed over a cup of tea, he asserted that, according to his parents, all Jews were glad Stalin had died. My grandma began dissuading him from that "strange" opinion. Nobody knew yet where the political winds would blow.

After graduating from a downtown four-year junior school in 1954, several other students and I were transferred to a middle school for our residential district. It was located in a three-story brick building in the upper part of the Murmansk terrain and just above the stadium, which was fenced with closely staggered metal poles with pointed tops. A steep and long wooden staircase ran to the top of the hill where the school was situated.

One of the disadvantages of the school location was its proximity to the residential areas. This was where Murmansk's less "aristocratic" population lived. (The junior school, on the other hand, had been downtown.) Accordingly a measurable element of the student body came from families where children's upbringing occurred in the less-than-stellar conditions of communal flats, single moms, debauching sailors, and abject poverty.

Many of these children joined street gangs and were feared in school by students and teachers. "Class" warfare was rife in the school and on the streets. Children of more privileged parents who were dressed reasonably well risked being attacked, jumped on, beaten, or, in the best case, mugged and having part of their winter outfits (typically gloves or fur hats) expropriated. Seva Rudin, the son of a colonel, was frequently chased after school and beaten by a swarm of his classmates. They bitterly hated him because his father was a high-ranking officer. His complaints to his parents and his father's appearance in school to discuss the situation did not alleviate his mistreatment. Rather it made his days in school even more precarious until a year later when the group of hooligans responsible for his torments gradually outgrew their atavistic instincts or left the school.

Almost every summer we used to go to the southern parts of the country for vacation. My parents had two months paid vacation, and my school's summer break lasted three months. We traveled by railroads. Typically we went from Murmansk to Leningrad (St. Petersburg now) and then would change trains depending on the destination.

Signs of wartime destruction, in small towns and villages which were strewn along the railroads, were very visible from the passing train. The often gray sky over Karelia and Kola Peninsula (where the railroad to Leningrad ran), the war scars (many still left from the Finland campaign of 1940–1941), and the frequent rain in the dreary landscape of small lakes and swamps surrounded by small and big boulders and against a background of fir woods created a sense of abandonment and sorrowfulness. That sense was often underscored by the sad tango melodies and songs played over the train radio. One of the popular songs that was often played had these lines:

Мне бесконечно жаль
Своих несбывшихся мечтаний
И только боль воспоминаний
Гнетет меня.

I feel immense pity
For my unrealized dreams,
And only pain of recollections
Is gnawing on me.

Sometimes at small stations, bands of disabled and homeless war veterans turned beggars boarded the train. They typically were missing one or both legs. In the latter case, they moved on small self-made carts sitting on ball bearings instead of wheels. Often the beggars were blind. Despite these afflictions, one or two in the group played accordion while going through cars and soliciting money. Their melodies and songs reflected their utter despair and added to the melancholy that sometimes was present in our travels.

There was only one time our full family (parents, Grandma, and I) spent a summer together. It was in 1951 at a small resort town, Nemirov, which was near Vinnitsa, Ukraine. There were beautiful gardens. I remember a Ukrainian woman that worked in the garden. She always talked to herself. We were told she lost her mind during the war after a brutal interrogation by Germans who suspected her of collaborating with partisans. I also remember my mother expressing sorrow when coming across a monument to the young fallen soldiers of WWII. Besides everything else, these monuments reminded Alla of her brother who was killed at the liberation of Poland.

My parents usually spent their vacation separate from Grandma and me. The summers of 1950, 1952, and part of 1953 I spent with Grandma Isabella in the village of Ozerki near Leningrad. Leningrad was a convenient base for our vacation because Isabella's sister, Tamara (married to Alexander Kirillovich Shestihin, a nice Russian fellow and a construction engineer in the field of hydroelectric stations), and her brother, Grigori, lived there with their families. We often stayed with them. Most often we stayed with Tamara and Alexander Kirillowich, who was an ironic and sarcastic but friendly fellow. In his younger years, he was a sailor on Soviet freighters and traveled around the world. He knew many interesting and zany stories.

Alexander Kirillowich, or Uncle Sanya, never objected or complained that Isabella and I were staying with them, although they lived in a single room of a communal flat. It was located in the Petrograd Side District of Leningrad in a modern-style building built in the 1930s. It belonged to the GIDEP (the State Institute for Development and Planning of Hydroelectric Stations) where Alexander worked, which was located just across the street from that building. When we stayed there, I usually slept on a folding bed, Grandma slept in the wide bed with Tamara, and Alexander slept on the couch.

Grigori Solomonovich Nevelshtein and his family had a large flat with several rooms in an old building on Marat Street, which was named after the 1798 French Revolution leader Marat. It was close to the Nevsky prospect, the central avenue of Leningrad. In the early 1950s, they already had a TV set with that famous water lens in front of the screen. I sometimes stayed with the Nevelshteins but rarely together with Grandma. Isabella and Tamara had a strong bond and felt very comfortable together, even in a cramped one-room communal apartment.

Another possible reason Isabella preferred to stay with Tamara was that Rita Lazarevna, née Bromberg, wife of Grigori, and their children, Yuri and Inna, ridiculed Isabella a little for her "Red Zeal," which they saw in her support of Soviet economic and international policies. In particular, it was her support of Nikita Khrushchev's agricultural adventures promoting proliferation of corn cultivation across the USSR, justification of a foreign aid policy to USSR satellites and multiple third world countries when the Soviet population suffered from lack of bare necessities, and support of the cosmos exploration programs, which took place at the expense of the living standards of the Soviet people.

Isabella remained an idealistic person, despite the persecution of her husband. She remained also an internationalist. In the early 1950s, she wrote a play about the persecution of blacks in America. Isabella considered the Nevelshteins' attitudes simplistic and philistine, and she attributed them to Rita's upbringing in a petty-bourgeois family compared to Isabella's more affluent and intellectual family. Isabella's attitudes could be traced back to the works of the Russian revolutionary poets Eduard Bagritsky, and Vladimir Mayakovsky. Not being concerned about the ideological undercurrents in Isabella and Rita's relationship, I liked to visit the Nevelshteins. I was thrilled to spend time in Grigori's home office, which was in a separate room filled with old books in leather jackets with gilded titles and prewar and turn of the century items.

The books included encyclopedias such as the first *Big Soviet Encyclopedia* of the 1930s and *The Brockhaus and Efron Encyclopedic Dictionary*, which was a comprehensive encyclopedia published in Imperial Russia from 1890–1906. In its scope and style, it was the Russian counterpart to the 1911 Britannica. The articles in it were written by first-rate Russian scholars of the day including Dmitry Mendeleev and Vladimir Solovyov. Among other books and magazines, many were related to geography and geoeconomic and political issues. (Grigori taught these subjects.)

There were several science fiction books that aroused in me enormous interest through their intensely suspenseful atmosphere. Besides the old books, the objects of interest in Grigori's room were the old stationary and decoration items. One memorable item was a small bronze bust of Shakespeare. I had heard Shakespeare was a playwright, but I felt the name had some hidden meaning. The yellowish bronze color, which matched the color of the titles of the old books on the shelves, contributed to the mysterious aura that emanated from the small bust.

In 1950, while Grandma and I were staying in Leningrad, Alla visited us and helped oversee the recuperation of my injured finger. Tamara, the local doctor, helped arrange a consultation with a surgeon regarding the necessity of surgery on the finger. Mother and Tamara took me to the doctor, who was working in a clinic in one of the modern (constructivist style) buildings in the Petrograd District. It was a breezy sunny day. All objects cast sharp shadows. Alla was neatly dressed and wearing bright lipstick. She was very absorbed and concerned that something was not going right with the healing of my finger. I was scared to go to the doctor, and probably because of that I vividly remember the details. One of these details was Mother asking Tamara whether the doctor was *ex nostres*.

I had never heard those words before ("from us" in Latin) and was somewhat alarmed. I sensed it had something to do with the doctor's occupation as a surgeon, and that this part of his occupation could be ominous to me. As medical doctors, Alla and Tamara knew Latin from their medical school curricula. They used it in that conversation to distract me from Alla having asked whether the doctor was Jewish. Our family, in general, avoided discussing any Jewish matters in my presence. In turn, I did not like to ask adults about the meanings of various words I was not sure of. I preferred to give them my own meanings. I am not sure why Alla asked about the doctor's national identity. She was probably hoping that, in that period of anti-Semitic campaigns of the early 1950s, a Jewish doctor would be more attentive to a Jewish patient. (In the patient declaration we had disclose my nationality.)

Hearing the words *ex nostres* in relationship to various people who apparently were of "our" stock (that is, not typical northern Russians with blond hair and blue eyes), I deduced that the words referred to Jewish people who, besides being Jewish, were also mysterious "exnostresses." This was probably because of their somewhat different noses.

In 1953 my parents and I spent a month in the Black Sea resort of Sochi. We rented a room in a house and dined in one of the big restaurants at the resort overlooking the beautiful seaside. The waiting time in these restaurants, however, was prohibitively long. The echo of the anti-cosmopolite campaign was not settled yet. Here and there one would unexpectedly run into unflattering anti-Jewish remarks. Some of them bore a satirical character. For example, one street vendor who was apparently tired of being harassed by the street children, yelled to them, "Go to sleep, Joints." He was probably referring to the American Joint Distribution Committee, which provided aid for Jewish children at risk and which had organized disaster response support for Jewish people in countries worldwide. The "Joint" was an object of hatred during the anti-Semitic campaigns.

In Sochi I saw an American movie for the first time. It had funny episodes built around boxers and a monkey that had taken steroids. In the boxing matches, a lightweight boxer beat a heavyweight after taking steroids, and then a tiny, timid macaque became a horrifying monster after accidentally taking the drug. That summer, Dad, who was a superb diver and swimmer, taught me how to swim. Soon after learning to swim, he trained me how to avoid the large waves when they rushed toward the beach, and you were not yet completely out of the water. Essentially you had to undercut the wave and dive into the wall of water rising in front of you instead of waiting until it fell on you.

There was a certain bravery in this activity, which brought a feeling of audacity. This is probably familiar to those who surf. The procedure carried risk, however. If you did not use the correct diving angle, the wave might carry you along to undesirable places on the beach. That was exactly what happened on one stormy day when Father and I played in the waves. Alla nervously watched us from the beach. I somehow strayed from Dad and dived into a ten-foot-high wave at too steep an angle. As a result, I was caught by the top of the wave and thrown into a metal structure on the beach. Miraculously I survived. Alla subsequently stopped us from continuing these games.

My parents tried to keep me out of the dreary Murmansk climate as long as possible when arranging trips to the Black Sea in 1954, 1955, and 1956 during the long summer vacations. From 1954 on, I was allowed to travel alone by train from Murmansk to Rostov. It was a wonderful experience. I had traveled with Grandma Isabella in the third-class passenger cars from Murmansk to Leningrad, but for the sake of security, I was allowed to travel in the second-class cars with locked two-set bunk bed compartments called *coupé*. With the security and calm of second class came the loss of interconnection with the more colorful folks of third class. Many of those passengers were sailors wearing their romantic outfits of crewneck shirts, called *tel'nyashkas*, with horizontal blue stripes. Boys always dreamed of having *tel'nyashaks*, which were a symbol of mariners' toughness and bravery. There was even a saying, "There are few of us, but we are in *tel'nyashkas*." Large oil paintings depicting sailors and mariners in *tel'nyashaks* defending the bastions or attacking enemies in various wars were popular in Russia.

In the third-class cars were sailors from the navy bases around Murmansk or from the merchant fleet. Leaving for vacation or being transferred to other places of service, they were often accompanied by wives breast-feeding their infants. Screaming and drooling infants, the naked breasts of their mothers, and sailors playing guitars, smoking heavily, and drinking all stamped in my memory like Chagall's visionary images of his youth in Vitebsk.

Adding to the colorful picture of the third-class cars was the bouquet of body odor, cigarette smoke, alcohol, and food stuffed into suitcases. The passengers usually ate pieces of fried chicken and boiled eggs. I preferred sandwiches with melted cheese and red caviar, which was not very expensive at that time. Grandma prepared these for the one-and-a-half-day trip from Murmansk to Leningrad. As was typical in Russia, the passengers started to eat immediately after the train departed.

The long distance from Murmansk to Rostov or the North Caucasus, which essentially crossed the whole country from north to south, required three and a half to four days of train travel and justified the use of a railcar restaurant. Long-distance passenger trains were always equipped with these facilities. My parents provided me with sufficient cash for the purchase of meals, as it was impractical to take enough food because it could be spoiled during the long trip.

One could also buy food from the local peasant women who rushed to the cars with their products when the train pulled to a stop at a small, rural station. This food was typically Russian, homemade staples such as fresh boiled potatoes sprinkled with dill, cucumbers in salt brine, cheese, fresh milk, and bread. At these small stations, the trains only stopped for one to two minutes, so the money/food exchange had to happen extremely quickly like love between flying birds. If the exchange lingered longer than the train's stop time, the sellers (like aircrafts refueling midair) ran alongside the departing train while it gained speed. They stretched up their hands with small, handmade paper bags and glass and tin casserole dishes with their products. The bags were made by swirling paper to produce a cone. The folded tip of the cone became the bottom of the bag.

At the bigger stations, where the train stopped for up to thirty or forty minutes, one could go to a station restaurant. A good borscht with a hefty piece of meat was usually served in the restaurant of the log-clad station house at Monchegorsk, which was on the south side of Kola Peninsula. I only dined there one time for fear of missing the departure of my train.

I enjoyed my newly found freedom of long-distance travel and certainly abused it to the potential detriment of my own safety. One of the actions that gave me a thrill was the following. When the train was running at full speed, I used to go to the car entrance section. This was separated from the living quarters by a sturdy door, and in the absence of the car *provodnik* (the conductor), I opened the entrance door and grabbed the external vertical handles. With my legs firmly planted on the floor, I pushed my torso out of the car into a swooshing wind filled with the fresh scent of the fields, meadows, and forests sweeping by.

The romance of long-distance travel, immortalized in the songs of composer Isaak Dunaevsky, enamored many. Alla liked it too. The hallways in the first- and second-class cars were actually a strolling place where passengers could walk leisurely in their travel attire and lightly flirt while watching the landscape fly by. In all three classes, the *provodniks* provided the passengers with bed linen and served tea three times a day in thick glasses kept in metal glass holders.

Along with her vacations, Alla often used to travel to Leningrad and Moscow to attend graduate and postgraduate courses and professional seminars. On one of her trips, she met a dashing and witty military officer on the train, Major Rafael Mekinulov. He was responsible for the technical readiness of the automobiles and trucks of the Northern Army District, and he happened to be of Georgian Jewish descent. He also lived with his family in Murmansk. He and his wife, being the same age as my parents and having two young children, became close friends of our family. Rafael's Caucasian descent (not racially but in terms of the cultural heritage of the Caucasus area) was evident in his sometimes brusque treatment of his wife.

Other friends of my parents included a mild-mannered military surgeon, Captain Gershkowich, and his wife, Nadia, a nurse. They were a nice couple originally from Leningrad. They used to go with my parents and me on ski trips. Dr. Gershkowich participated in the USSR war against the Japanese Kwantung Army in Manchuria in 1945. As a trophy from the war, he brought home a Japanese military winter coat, which had the amusing capacity to be completely disassembled with only the central portion remaining as a vest.

Another family friend was a mathematician with the last name Neiding. He taught in the higher education school for ship engineers. He was an early-balding, tall, and shy fellow in glasses. The students of that marine school were known to have fights between the groups in the dorm. Neiding, who also lived in the dorm, became an object of the students' ridicule and bullying. This was because of his absentmindedness and tepidness. A common acquaintance of us and Neiding told us he saw the students attacking Neiding in the hallway, while Neiding pleaded with them, "Don't beat me. I am Neiding." Neiding frequently visited us and played chess with me when I asked. He was an excellent player, and I was certainly no match for him. I mostly played chess with Grandma Bella, who taught me the game.

I worried when Neiding stopped visiting us. We learned he did not return after a tourist trip to the Caucasian Mountains. The circumstances of his disappearance and apparent death remain unknown.

Barring coworkers, other close family friends included Mikhail Grigoriewich Guttman and his wife, Rebecca Grigorievna Guttman. Mother considered her very attractive. Mikhail Guttman was a navy colonel in the medical service and was the chairman of the X-ray department of the army hospital. They were very well-mannered, intelligent people about twenty years older than my parents. They had a neat and well-furnished one-bedroom apartment (a luxury in those days), and they always had new, interesting books. An object of my fascination was a short cutlass proudly displayed attached to a Persian rug on a wall in their bedroom. The cutlass was a status symbol for navy officer from the rank of major and higher.

When we had receptions in our flat, Isabella typically handled all the chores related to meal preparation and table service. Alla helped her. They liked exquisite china and crystal dishes. Considering the relatively high salaries my parents received in Murmansk, they could afford to buy these items periodically. Many of them were Soviet trophies brought from Germany after the war. Isabella and Alla kept the parties in a sophisticated but jolly tone.

Alla did not like ambiguous jokes. The conversations revolved around new books, movies, war, and peace. Alarmingly Isabella always asked the guests whether they thought there would be a war with America during the coming year. She was overly protective of Alla and said semiseriously that if there were a new war and Alla had to serve as a military doctor, she would go with her wherever she was sent. I don't think Mother admired this perspective. I sensed that each participant in our receptions, which were usually comprised of a relatively small group of permanent friends, had his or her own preferable topic for conversation.

Mekinulov used to joke and knew many Caucasian anecdotes. My dad kept him company and expanded the area of conversation to history, biographies of great people, and geographic explorations. Alla liked this and often offered a game. It was a sort of *Jeopardy* in which the participants had to answer questions related either to names of great people or names of countries and their capitals. The loser had to sing a song or come up with a joke. Until her last days, Alla and I used to check each other on our knowledge of all the countries in Latin America and their capitals. Being able to recall that Andorra, Liechtenstein, Monaco, San

Marino, Luxembourg, and the Vatican are the smallest countries of Europe added to our gratification.

Another type of entertainment was Ping-Pong. Dad acquired a folded Ping-Pong table, which was unfolded in Grandma Bella's and my bedroom.

Occasionally my father brought his work home. In spare time he would review blueprints of a designed fish- processing equipment or do various design tasks with it. The complicated equipment included long mechanized lines and refrigeration units. All this baffled my imagination. While he worked, he enjoyed listening to popular music on the record player. Everybody in the family liked Yves Montand, romances and various tangos.

One time father invited for dinner two of his colleagues from the Ministry of Fish Industry in Moscow who were in Murmansk on business. Isabella prepared a sumptuous dinner of meatloaf covered with green peas (these were relatively rare commodities at the time). Victor provided a good Cognac and vodka. Smoked fish was, of course, a staple snack.

At the dinner's start, Isabella declaimed her new rhymes, in which she wittingly deprecated her culinary abilities. The dinner went well until one of the guests became a little drunk, and when the conversation touched on the war with Germany, as was typical in dinner conversations, he began recalling and boasting of his war exploits. He jokingly told how, in the Red Army advance through Germany in 1945, he and a few comrades raped a German woman and what they did to her afterward, which was unspeakably cruel and sadistic. Following his revelation, the dinner fizzled, and he was never again invited to our house.

Despite summer vacations at Black Sea resorts and basking in the southern sun, life in Murmansk, with its limited sun exposure and lack of vitamins, affected my health. Concerned about my persistent cough, in May of 1957 Alla took me to her X-ray department and diagnosed me with a serious lung disease. It was urgent I leave Murmansk for a better climate in the south of Russia. There I would undergo an aggressive anti-tuberculosis treatment. By early June, I had finished the seventh grade, and Alla took me to Rostov to Victor's parents. She and Grandma Lyuba arranged for me to be seen by several lung experts. They confirmed Alla's earlier diagnosis and recommended immediate treatment.

In Russian and European medical circles, climatologic factors were traditionally given an important role in curing lung illnesses. Titans of Russian literature Anton Chekhov and Maxim Gorky suffered from full-blown tuberculosis. Chekhov convalesced in the Crimea and Gorky on the Italian island of Capri. In my case it was decided to take me to the pine forests near Kiev. Boyarka had tuberculosis sanatoriums. At the end of June, Mother and I flew to Kiev, and then we took the train to Boyarka, where we rented a room in a house near a reputed sanatorium belonging to the army. The daughter of the house's owner was a pleasant-looking girl in her late teens. She immediately informed us she had recently become a student at one of Kiev's universities and that she now lived in a university dorm, so her room would be available. She went further to describe how interesting student life was. I had already heard some intriguing stories about student life, and I was jealous I was still too young to join the daughter's crowd.

One of our relatives or friends made a call to a military doctor, which helped circumvent certain formalities in connecting me with the sanatorium. Even though I was neither a member of the military nor a family member of a serviceman, Alla arranged an appointment with the sanatorium's administration. Her occupation as a radiologist with a good record and her appealing personality were helpful in checking me in for outpatient treatment at the sanatorium. The sanatorium doctor, Philipp Moiseivich Pekurovsky, prescribed injections of a potent new drug twice daily. Fortunately this medicine had become available that year.

In July Victor joined us at Boyarka. Toward August my parents had to go back to Murmansk. To continue my treatment, I stayed in Boyarka under Dr. Pekurovsky's care. When my parents left, my supervision was arranged through my Great Aunt Polina. The sister of Grandpa Ziama, she lived with Ziama and Lyuba in Rostov, and she agreed to stay with me in Boyarka. Toward the end of the summer, my condition had dramatically improved, and there was no longer an urgent need for me to be under the constant observation of a sanatorium doctor. I was also allowed to stop the injections, but I still had to continue taking some drugs orally.

Translated from the Russian COPY

MINISTRY OF PUBLIC HEALTH USSR
STATE ORDER OF LENIN INSTITUTE
FOR QUALIFICATION OF PHYSICIANS
name after S.M. Kirov

Leningrad - 15, Saltikov-Schedrin Str. 41

October 25, 1948

Our No. 558

C E R T I F I C A T E

Issued to physician DUNAYEVSKAYA A.L., stating that from March 16 till July 15 1948 she attended the course of specialization in röntgenology.

During this period physician DUNAYEVSKAYA A.L. attended the lectures and fulfilled the practical training in accordance with the curriculum in following subjects:

1. Physics and technics of the X - ray.
2. Commom and first-aid röntgenology.
3. Röntgendiagnosis of diseases of a/ pulmones b/ heart and blood vessels c/ alimentary tract d/ bones and joints e/ scull, bones of face and teeth f/ kidneys and urogenital system.
4. Röntgendiagnosis of children diseases.
5. Röntgentherapy.

Passing the established tests physician DUNAYEVSKAYA A.L. get the mark e x c e l l e n t.

Assist. Director Manager of Studies
Assist. professor /signature/

/Seal/ Dean of the Therapeutic Facukty /signature/

On June 13, 1979, I, SIRMAIS A., State Notary of the Riga City State Notary Office No. 5, hereby authenticate the identity of this copy with the original. Collating with the original I found in it no erasures, additions, deletions or any other unauthorized corrections or distinctions.

Alla's certificate for passing a postgraduate course in radiology (1948).

Mother and me (ca. 1949).

Alla on a sunny summer day in Murmansk (1954).

Alla and Victor at the Black Sea resort, Sochi (1953).

Alla in Sochi (1953).

Alla in Sochi in the dress she said Victor liked. She brought that dress in America (1953).

Victor and our friend, Army Major Raphael Mekinulov (1954).

Our friends Michail Guttman, an army doctor,
and his wife, Rebecca (ca. 1955).

Alla with an umbrella (1955).

Alla on a ski trip near Murmansk (ca.1956).

Victor on a ski trip near Murmansk (ca. 1956, spring).

My twelfth birthhday party in Murmansk. A New Year tree is in the background. Top row: myself (middle) with school friends- Sasha Mikhailov (left), a son of a stadium director[1], and SevaRudin[2] (right), a son of a colonel. Bottom row: Alik[3] and Allochka, who were children of our friend, Rafael Mekinulov (1954).

[1] He was an unhinged and at the same time comical character of a questionable background. He was feared by anyone who attempted to be at the stadium without a proper authorization. In the town he was known as "*Hren*" that is Russian for a Horse Radish. In application to a person, *hren* is losely equivalent to Son of a bitch. He apparently knew a lot of zany and humorous profanity which he used to divulge when he was drunk, that in fact happened quite often, to those around him including his son. In turn, Sasha gleefully shared that staff with friends including me.

[2] Rudin, who was a little arrogant, was often found himself on a receiving end of the "class" hatred delivered to him by the unrestrained elements from the schoolmates of poorer families.

[3] Alik proved himself as a gifted musician and currently lives in New York City with his wife. Allochka, sadly, died early to cancer.

ГОСУДАРСТВЕННЫЙ КОМИТЕТ СОВЕТА МИНИСТРОВ СССР
ПО ВНЕДРЕНИЮ ПЕРЕДОВОЙ ТЕХНИКИ В НАРОДНОЕ ХОЗЯЙСТВО
ПАТЕНТНЫЙ ОТДЕЛ
АВТОРСКОЕ СВИДЕТЕЛЬСТВО

The certificate in authorship of one of the patents of Victor Dunaevsky. It reads, "The State Committee of the Council of Ministers of the USSR on the implementation of the advanced technology in the people's economy. The patent department. Avtorskoe svidetelstvo (author's certificate) No. 88516. The certificate is issued to the citizens Dunaevsky V. Z. and Borisov, P. A. for the invention 'A Basket for Contact Freezing of the Fish in Blocks' in accordance with the applied description per the claim No. 399338 with a priority of June 21, 1948. The certificate is valid over all the territory of the Union of the SSR. It has been introduced in the list of inventions of the Union of the SSR on August 21, 1950. Signed: Chief of the patent department (signature); Chief of the state list of inventions of the USSR (signature). Moscow, August 30, 1950."

CHAPTER VII

My Return to Rostov-on-Don: 1957

It was decided that I wouldn't return to Murmansk and will continue my education in Rostov while living with my grandparents. I stayed in Rostov with grandparents until the September of 1961 when I moved to Riga, Latvia, to join my parents who relocated there from Murmansk in 1960. One of the reasons for the relocation was a desire of my parents to be with me. However, the doctors did not recommend me go back to the polar climate, and my mother did not want to go back to Rostov because of a hot Southern sun was not good for her heart.

A climate conditions in Latvia were found to be suitable for both sides. At the same time, a decision to move to Riga, the capital of Latvia, was advanced by my father who visited Riga on a business trip in 1959 and was impressed with the ancient history of the city, its charming blend of the medieval and modern Western architecture, higher living standards, cozy cafés and restaurants and beautiful Baltic seaside. Since the beginning of the XX century Riga was called the Little Paris.

Meanwhile I was thrilled by the prospect of living in Rostov in the same flat where my father spent his youth. His athletic interests were appealing to me. I knew in his time there had been a sport implement in the flat—a crossbar hanging on ropes attached to the top doorjamb leading to the dining room. This was convenient for pull-ups. A restoration of this exercise equipment, however, was out of the question. My dad's shadow manifested itself in many other ways as well. For example, one time in 1959, two gentlemen knocked on the door and asked if Vit'ka (a diminutive for Victor) was home. These were friends of my dad from prewar time who had not seen him for eighteen or nineteen years.

While in Rostov, I went to middle school for eighth, ninth, and tenth grade. The three-story school building was just a few blocks away from our house on Gorky Street. The overwhelming majority of the students in my class were girls. There were nineteen girls and only three boys, including me. Apparently the war years favored the birth and survival of girls.

One of the boys was the son of a Rostov Medical Institute professor, Prof. Mironov. (This and the names of former students of my school are changed.) He was a tall, lanky boy with a very snubbed nose. I heard from my grandparents he was adopted by Prof. Mironov's family from an orphanage after the war. The rumor was they wanted to be assured they adopted a Russian and not a Jewish boy. The Mironovs paid strong attention to the facial features of the orphans, believing a snub nose was a good sign of non-Jewishness. I heard also the Mironovs were later disappointed in the child. He was not a prodigy as they would have hoped for, and he was rather a troublemaker.

Although we had fights sometimes, I found him a good match in the various pranks and mischief we both enjoyed. Another boy was from the family of a party functionary who recently relocated from one of the autonomous republics along the Volga River. He had dark hair, a pudgy face, and a slanted look in his eyes. He liked to play guitar. In the school year of 1958, we got a fourth boy. We heard his family moved back to Russia from the German Democratic Republic. His father later became a director of the Radiotechnic Institute in Taganrog. The boy was restrained in his behavior, had good manners, was a good student, enjoyed sports, and was decent-looking. Unfortunately he drowned while swimming in the River Don after graduation from school.

The girls wore uniforms. The boys were not allowed to wear the fashionable narrow trousers or have long hair cut in a style called *brodveika* (from New York's Broadway Avenue). This type of hairdo and trousers narrowing down from the waist were considered a sign of bourgeoisie influence and were a source of friction between the students who liked to wear them and the school administration. It was (since the mid-1950s) time for another government campaign against a "degrading" penetration of the "decadent and corrupt" Western culture into the pristine and "spiritually elevated" Soviet life. People who were wearing the fashionable Western dress, listening to jazz, rock and roll, and boogie-woogie, and sporting elaborate hairdos were derisively called *stiliaga(s)* from the Russian *stil* (style).

One time in the fall 1958, a school headmaster was surveying the students coming into the school. He measured the width of the trousers at the ankle on the arriving students. Those few unfortunate ones who had an ankle width less than 15 cm were sent home and got reprimanded. On that day I was wearing new and very narrow Czechoslovakian trousers that my parents bought me in the summer. It was not desirable to get a reprimand from the headmaster, because it could eventually affect your graduation papers, but I was able to somehow sneak into the school unnoticed.

Sometimes wearing nonstandard clothes and, as it was alleged later, not always participating enthusiastically in some *Komsomol* activities (Komsomol, *the* Young Communist league, was involved in teamwork activities with a rigid ideological undercurrent) might have had repercussions for my next steps in life. I suspect these were some of the factors two of my fellow students used as a pretext for unfriendly action against me in 1960. This was the year after graduation when I applied to college.

The students were Leonid, the aforementioned son of a party functionary, and a girl, Lena, who was the daughter of a single mother occupying a high spot in some administrative circles. Both students were the Komsomol representatives of the school, and as such they had to write me an evaluation for my application to higher education establishments. The evaluation they gave me was not sufficiently positive and somewhat eluded to the aforementioned minor infringements of the dress code and my Komsomol attitude.

The administration of the institution to which I applied (RISHM, which stands for the Rostov Institute of the Agricultural Machinery Construction) told me that with that type of evaluation, they could not admit me to the entrance exams. I felt it was a case of real treachery, as Lena and Leonid never demonstrated animosity toward me before. I was otherwise friendly with them. In addition, neither of them were the paragons of modesty and *Komsomol* zeal.

I suspected later that, besides the minor deviations of my behavior, Lena might have been jealous that I did not court her. My girlfriend was Sveta, another girl from our class. The innocent relationships we had, however, would hardly be classified as the girlfriend/boyfriend relationships of modern senior classes.

But there could have been more sinister motives in the actions of Lena and Leonid. Whatever the reason, that piece of paper was becoming the biggest impediment in my whole life. I sensed I had to take some urgent, extraordinary measures to correct the situation. Essentially I had to bend myself backward and ask Lena and Leonid to change the wording of the evaluation.

Leonid said he had no objections, but it was Lena I had to persuade. Finally the evaluation was corrected, and I was admitted to the entrance exams, which I successfully passed. Getting excellent grades in mathematics, physics, and chemistry and a good grade in literature, I was accepted to the mechanical faculty of the RISHM.

While I lived in Rostov, my parents visited me a few times. These visitations were a big joy for me. There were interesting conversations between my parents and grandparents about the recently published books of modern foreign authors and about medical issues. Alla and Lyuba debated the new research of the role fried foods play in cancer. A repetitive use of the same fried cooking oil was considered to be a possible culprit.

With my dad, Victor, we discussed the principles of semiconductors, which had begun replacing the electronic bulbs in radio equipment. The fiction books that were discussed included the novels of Feuchtwanger (*Goya*, *The Lautensack Brothers*, *Jew Suss*, *The Jewish War*, and *The Spanish Ballad*), Remarque (*All Quiet on the Western Front*, *Ark of Triumph*, and *Three Comrades*), Elsa Triolet, Stefan Zweig, Bernard Shaw, and other writers. Victor taught me the basic rules of tennis. When in a good mood, he liked to whistle and sing popular songs. He also liked to impersonate various comical characters he met through his life. When I was already in college, he provided me valuable advice about the history of various theoretical sciences I had begun to study.

The books were usually sitting on top of the big concert piano (*Royál*) situated in the big room facing Gorky Street. Except for Alla, nobody played the piano, although everyone loved music. In the summertime, my grandparents attended symphonic orchestra performances held in the open in the city park. Unfortunately I did not express a strong interest in playing musical instruments, and nobody pushed me to learn the skill. Alla later told me this was because I was very stubborn.

I recently learned there could have been another, more tragicomic reason for my not learning music, at least during my Rostov period. My Aunt Lyalya lived with her parents in the 1930s in a flat above us, and she often used to visit my father and his family on the first floor. She told me that during these visits, she was trying to learn the piano. Hitting the keys and producing a cacophony of sounds, she was asked not to do it because it irritated my grandfather, Zyama. It exacerbated his suffering from a skin disease. (He suffered from eczema on the elbows.) Despite the lack of musical education, Lyalya (a diminutive for Helen) later became a medical doctor and professor of pathology anatomy. Similar to Lyalya's experience, when I tried to learn the piano in the 1950s, it was met without enthusiasm from Zyama.

The demand for quietness complemented other rules and demands surrounding Grandpa, some of which were on the boundary of rituals. One of these rituals was the old-fashioned shaving Zyama practiced. It took place not in a bathroom but at the dinner table. Maybe it was because, in the Dunaevskys' communal apartment, the bathroom did not have the appropriate amenities such as hot water. The hot water was required to make soapy foam with which, using a brush, Zyama covered his face, neck, and head. (He shaved his head also!)

Hot water was needed, naturally, for washing up after the shaving. Zyama's sister, Polina, assisted during the shaving. She brought water from the kitchen, covered the portion of the table where the shaving occurred with a waterproof tablecloth, and installed a mirror. Grandpa Zyama wore his army style shirt (*gimnasterka*) at home, and during the shaving he kept his collar folded in. For shaving he used both a real barber blade and a safety Gillette razor. Gillette was an auxiliary tool; the main tool was the blade. Zyama sharpened his blade on a special wide and long leather belt.

The ritual of shaving, its implements, and afterward, the gleaming, bald, powerful head of Zyama, who successfully executed the tricky procedure involving two sharp tools, certainly impressed me, and it added a new dimension to the list of qualities I attributed to Grandpa. The ritual bridged him with common folks and, at the same time, gave him a swagger one could associate with the brave "heroes of our days."

Although my grandparents loved me, and Grandma Lyuba was very tender to me, my grandfather was more formal and strict. Unlike Grandma Isabella, the Dunaevskys never, or almost never, discussed our Jewish heritage or any related issues. My parents regularly sent funds to Zyama for my upkeep, from which Zyama allocated twenty-five rubles every month for my personal needs.

These allotments were certainly not enough to accommodate my burgeoning philatelist interests in acquiring postage stamps and stamp albums or to buy radiotechnic components to build a shortwave radio, scuba diving equipment and a gun for underwater hunting, sunglasses, and whatever else a teenager with healthy interests might desire.

I realized, however, some of my peers did not have even that level of support. One of these peers was a boy from another school I met through stamp collecting. He lived with his blind mother in a small, windowless dwelling in the backyard of a bigger building. They had no other income than a small pension his mother received for disability. I pitied that boy and often invited him to our apartment, which had big rooms and big windows.

With my postage stamp collecting, I found an avid supporter in no other than Moisey Filippowich (Mosya) Tsipelzon, who was the father of Tolya Tsipelzon. Tolya was a friend of my dad and the husband of Lyalya Dombrovsky.

Mosya was a colorful character. He was a very animated and enthusiastic person and a connoisseur and junkie of the latest news. He was slender and had a good suntan. Despite being bald, while walking along the long Rostov streets, he never wore a hat in the summertime. This was the case even though the southern sun was merciless, and Mosya was already in his late 60s. He knew German pretty well and helped me translate the information on the stamps from the German Democratic Republic, which I bought at a local philatelist store. His mercurial behavior was a source of light irony for the older Dunaevskys. From Mosya or Zyama I learned that sarcastic German proverb about human follies: *Morgen, morgen-nur niht heute-sagen alles faule leute.* Tomorrow, tomorrow, only not today, say all lazy people.

Zyama retired in 1958, and Lyuba continued to work until 1960. Considering the endemic food shortages in the Soviet Union, Grandpa Zyama (the chief procurer of the family's food) was spending a lot of time in long lines near and in food stores. Some food was also bought at the farmers market, but it was more expensive there and needed to be fully processed. The chickens, for example, were sold either alive or with the feathers not removed.

It always struck me that, forty years after the "Great October Socialist Revolution," the food situation was so dire that a highly educated and cultural man like my grandpa had to spend time in the food lines surrounded by semiliterate housewives. Still, along with others of my age and older, I believed things would be drastically improved as was promised by the Nikita Khrushchev's Communist Party program. I believed the Soviet people would live in Communism by 1980.

Life with my grandparents was austere. Lyuba's salary as a doctor was meager. It was less than one hundred rubles a month when the nominal living standard of a family our size was approximately one hundred fifty rubles a month. This was, in general, the salary of the white-collar workers in the USSR.

Zyama's pension was puny as well. Zyama's sister, Polina, did not have any income at all, but her contribution to the family was her assistance in the various home chores. No furniture had been bought since before the war. Among media items, we had only a small radio. In 1958 my parents bought me a simple record player. Considering the government subsidized our housing, the money was spent mainly on the electric and utility bills, food, necessary clothes, cultural entertainments (movie and theater), and summer vacations. Since Lyuba was involved with treatment of gynecological and obstetric problems, the thankful women she helped often sent her presents, as is customary in Russia. The presents were candies, cakes, caviar, etc.

The summer of 1958 I spent with Grandma Isabella near Moscow at the dacha of her Odessa friend, I. G. Shumsky, and his wife, Lidia.

They were very intellectual people involved in some literature works. They knew well the personal life and philosophies of the classic Russian authors. Considering our proximity to Moscow (one and a half hours by the electric train), I often went to the capital to visit museums. On these days I stayed overnight at the communal apartment where the family of my second cousin Natalia (see page 25) lived. Natalia was related to me through her grandmother who, like my paternal grandmother, was also called Lyuba.

She was a first cousin of Zyama. Lyuba (Lyubochka as she was called by friends and relatives) was known for preparing excellent meals, especially chicken or beef patties. I enjoyed talking with Natalia's grandfather who knew many interesting stories and humorous poems of the Soviet authors of the 1920s.

He taught me some of that stuff, and I was able to entertain my acquaintances by reciting these funny poems. One ("A Song About a Good Tone" by A. Agnivtsev) was about a British navy lieutenant who preferred to die rather than receive disapproval from his love. They disagreed over using a saber against a shark he encountered after he accidentally fell overboard from an ocean liner. The dame was so pompous and engrossed with dinner etiquette, according to which the fish is not treated with a knife, that while watching the drama from the safety of the liner deck, she remained ignorant of the danger to the lieutenant. Instead she exclaimed with indignation, "Oh no, to treat a fish…with a knife!" Upon hearing this, the lieutenant got confused, whispered pardon, and was promptly swallowed by the fish.

Another humorous poem ("Magdaliniada," which is a parody of Alexander Archangelsky on Alexander Zharov—both Soviet poets of the 1920s) was about Mary Magdalene as a sexpot.

The communal apartment where they lived reminded me of the one described in the immortal and hilarious book by Ilf and Petrov, *A Golden Calf*, which is set in 1920s USSR. In one scene, the tenants of a communal apartment with a single toilet found out someone was soiling the walls in the toilet room. Suspicion fell on an elderly and well-mannered fellow who, they observed, was the only one who washed his hands after using the toilet. Despite his protests, the tenants "avenged his transgressions" by flogging him in the kitchen.

The summer of 1959 I spent with Isabella at the dacha (summer house) on Bolshoi Fontan near Odessa. Alla also spent some time with us. It was an opportunity to meet more of Isabella's friends and many of Alla's friends from her school years. These included Alla's girlfriend, Lelya Magaziner, and her husband, Dolia Yassky, who wrote witty poems as a hobby. I also met their daughter, Lora, who later became a pianist. All three were brunets with delicate facial features.

In August of 1960, after I was accepted to the RISHM, my parents took me for a river boat cruise. It was a five-day trip on a luxury liner from Rostov to Stalingrad. It was exciting going through the sluices of the Volga-Don canal, which was built in the early 1950s, and then visiting Stalingrad, which stretched miles along the Volga River. Stalingrad was rebuilt after the devastation of the war, and it left me with a powerful impression of its vistas of the new residential and industrial complexes, a colossal statue on the Mamaev Kurgan (dedicated to the defenders of Stalingrad), and several destroyed buildings remaining as a memorial of the events of 1942–1943.

1960 was the year of the Olympic Games in Melbourne, Australia. My dad, Victor, the avid sportsman, eagerly consumed all available information about the Games and discussed it with me. He was especially interested in the boxing matches and boxers. The early cultivation Dad gave me about boxing lingo, terminology, and spirit was reinforced by watching the Games and boxing matches and by reading the catchy articles in sports magazines such as "The Blood, Sweat, and Tears of the Big Box."

After joining the technical school in September, I realized a student's life consisted of more than studying and parties. The government used the students from the higher education establishments and personnel and workers from plants, factories, and other organizations to assist in harvest collection. Decimated by the war and low living standards, the Soviet agricultural enterprises (*Kolkhozes* and *Sovkhozes,* which is Russian for collective farms and Soviet farms) suffered from the lack of manpower and machinery. In early September, before lectures started, a group of students and I were dispatched to a collective farm on the left bank of the River Don. It was not far from Rostov.

As the auxiliary workers, we had to endure several weeks on a farm while living there in very primitive conditions. We assisted the *kolkhozniks* with manual labor and all kinds of required activity. For example, we loaded by shovel the harvested grain into bags and then dumped the bags onto trucks. At the end of September, we returned to Rostov. These farm duties were repeated every school year except the last two. Despite the unenvied and very rustic lifestyle during the weeks on the farm, these were periods of some fun and camaraderie. I was surprised to find the female students, those round faced Russian girls, were very flirtatious.

It was, however, a time when those students without industrial experience had to acquire it along with their academic knowledge. To accomplish this, the lectures and studies were run in two shifts. In this way the students could match up their assigned work shifts with the lectures. The students were assigned to work in various industries, which corresponded to the profile of the higher education school they were joined to. I began working as a technician assembler on one of the assembly lines of *Krasny Aksay* (The Red Aksay). It was the same plant where nineteen years earlier my father started his engineering career. This plant produced agricultural implements. While working on three shifts, I was able to attend one of the two shifts offered by the school. Despite the early departure time for the first shift at the plant, Grandma Lyuba would already be on her feet preparing me a big mug of hot cocoa and an omelet. Interestingly enough, the arduous schedule of work and study shifts for the first two years did not affect my grades. In fact they were the best grades for the whole period of my engineering study between 1960 and 1965.

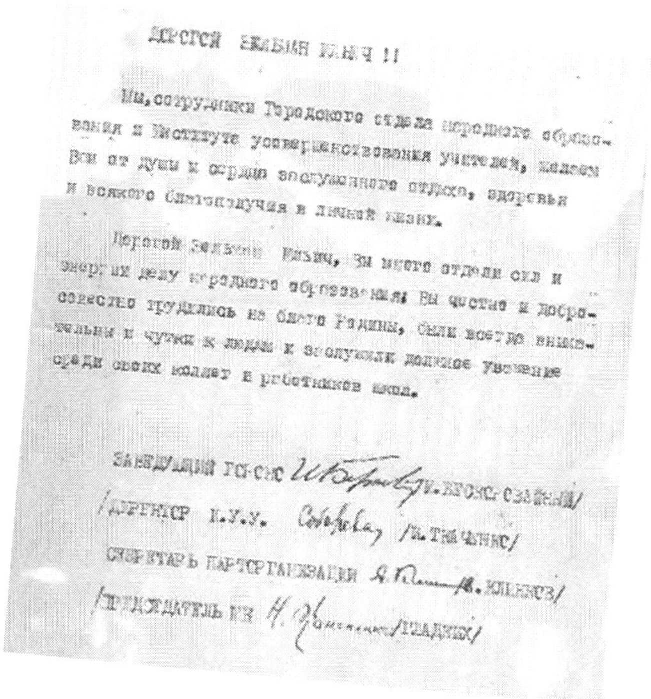

ДОРОГОЙ ЗЕЛЬМАН ИЛЬИЧ !!

Мы, сотрудники Городского отдела народного образования и Института усовершенствования учителей, желаем Вам от души и сердца заслуженного отдыха, здоровья и всякого благополучия в личной жизни.

Дорогой Зельман Ильич, Вы много отдали сил и энергии делу народного образования. Вы честно и добросовестно трудились на благо Родины, были всегда внимательны и чутки к людям и заслужили должное уважение среди своих коллег и работников школ.

ЗАВЕДУЮЩИЙ ГОРОНО /И. БЕСКОРОВАЙНЫЙ/
/ДИРЕКТОР И.У.У. /И. ТКАЧЕНКО/
СЕКРЕТАРЬ ПАРТОРГАНИЗАЦИИ /А. КЛИНКОВ/
/ПРЕДСЕДАТЕЛЬ МК /ГЛАДКИХ/

A retirement address to Zelman Dunaevsky (my paternal grandfather) from his colleagues. It reads, " Dear Zelman Ilyich, we, the workers of the City Department of the People Education and the Institute for Advancement of the Teachers, wish you from the depth of our soul and heart a well-deserved rest, health, and the best in your personal life. Dear Zelman Ilyich, you gave a lot of your strength and energy to the field of the People Education; you honestly and conscientiously worked for the benefit of the Motherland; you always were sensitive and attentive to the people, and you deserved due respect from your colleagues and workers of the schools.
Head of the GORONO (City Department of People Education), Signature/I. Beskoravainyj
Director IUU (Institute for Teachers' Advancement), Signature/I. Tkachenko
Secretary of Party Organization, Signature/A. Klinkov
Chairman of the MK (Local Committee [of the trade unions]), Signature/N. Gladkih

Me with my parents in Rostov (1959).

CHAPTER VIII

Alla and Victor Move to Riga (Latvia): 1960 I Join Them: 1961

In 1960 my parents moved to Latvia, by way of exchanging their one-bedroom flat in Murmansk for two rooms of a communal apartment in Riga. The person with whom my parents did the exchange was apparently fleeing Riga to avoid the impending penalties associated with some improprieties in the commercial activities he was involved. It was a period of another campaign in the USSR when the unusually harsh charges, up to being shot by a firing squad, were leveled against the individuals accused even in trivial corruption violations.

Victor began working as an engineer and designer in a design bureau that was involved in developing automation equipment for various industries. These were challenging assignments. However, Victor handled them well, and as a result he earned a great deal of respect from his coworkers and superiors. One of his assignments was the development of artificial heart-lungs apparatus. This was developed in collaboration with one well-reputed Latvian cardiologist. Although the work was interesting, it was demanding and stressful. The field, after all, was somewhat new for Victor, and his position was a step below the one he occupied in Murmansk. Stresses were also coming from the necessity to adapt to a new (Latvian) language and culture, which he suspected was anti-Russian and anti-Soviet. The stresses were compounded by the living conditions in a communal flat with four more tenants and by the noise coming from the street. Despite living on the fifth floor, the rumbling and squealing noise from the passing streetcars along the narrow street was sometimes unbearable, especially at night.

Alla began working as a radiologist (*roentgenolog*) for the Resort Polyclinic at Riga's seaside. She quickly gained a good reputation and was promoted in 1963 to Extraordinary Chief Radiologist for all the Latvian Republic Trade Unions' resorts. She combined the activities of that position with her clinic work. The activities required her to travel across the Latvian Republic for the inspection of the X-ray facilities. This occupation helped her learn the basics of the Latvian language for better communication with her Latvian peers and patients. This was quite appreciated by them.

After finishing the first year at RISHM, I decided to join my parents in Riga and got transferred to the Riga Polytechnical Institute (currently Riga Technical University). In Riga my parents and I lived in two rooms of a communal flat in an imposing seven-story building. It was one of many, which constituted the bulk of Riga's modern housing. It was located east of the charming Old Town and was built before WWI. My mother helped Isabella rent a small room in Yurmala at the Riga seaside.

In 1961 Russian Soviet poet Eugene Yevtushenko published in *Izvestia*, a central newspaper, his famous poem, "Babi Yar," about the massacre of the Kiev Jewish population in 1941. This had tremendous resonance as it was the first time the subject of a Jewish Holocaust was openly brought up in the Soviet press. There were repercussions. An editor of the paper responsible for the publication was fired. Rightist authors published poems denouncing Yevtushenko as unpatriotic and someone who elevated the suffering of Jews above the sacrifices and suffering of Russians. In turn, many on the Left accused him of seeking cheap popularity. Our family, however, wholeheartedly supported Yevtushenko and defended him against accusations whenever they arose among our colleagues and friends.

Meanwhile the government kept policies on suppressing Jewish cultural expression and silenced all information about Israel. One of the examples of these was the government attempt to prevent distribution of Israeli literature at a concert given, in the early 1960s, by the members of the Israeli Philharmonic Orchestra. My memory about this incident is associated with a following situation.

As college students, my peers and I were encouraged to participate in the law-and-order-supporting squads that were popular in the USSR. They were called *druzhinniki* (from the ancient Slavic word *druzhina*, a people's army). These squads were similar in their activities to the Guardian Angels in New York City. Participation in the *druzhinnik* squads was almost obligatory. Both sexes were involved in the *druzhinnik* activities by patrolling streets and neighborhood as part of the crime watch. A joke, in colloquial Russian, satirizing *druzhinnik* women would be enjoyable to those who know the language: "Хулиган забейся в щель. Девки вышли на панель." By and large, druzhinniks carried out morally-justified functions.

Meanwhile, one time our squad was instructed to attend a performance given by the Israeli orchestra. We were to oversee the overall order and prevent Israelis from distributing their literature. I thought it would be an interesting assignment, and it would allow me to familiarize myself with the literature since I had virtually no knowledge about Israel at that time. The orchestra did distribute small brochures about Israel. I don't remember that anyone, including myself, had seriously tried to prevent this distribution. Everything went very peacefully. I believe I got my brochure and was satisfied.

Few years later, however, I brought myself to a more assertive expression of my budding resistance to the anti-Jewish attitudes. Although I was not in the vanguard of the dissident or Jewish dissident movement, I always tried to cut short any anti-Semitic conversations or remarks if the opportunity presented itself.

The following is a story of these pro-Jewish actions. One time in the early 1970s, I was on a business trip in Minsk, the capital of Belorussia. On one of the days of my trip, I was standing in line at the Aeroflot agency (the only Soviet airline at the time) to buy return tickets. In front of me were two young men of approximately my age. Being in close proximity to these men, I overheard their conversation. They ridiculed a man at the front of the line for being a little bit noisy in his interaction with a sales clerk. Because that man appeared Jewish to the men, they began using flagrant anti-Semitic slurs. I felt a strong desire to react to that situation but did not know how.

Finally I made a decision. I visually estimated the physical strength of the two scoundrels and decided I could handle them if needed. I subsequently decided "to give them a lesson." After I bought my tickets, I immediately proceeded in the direction of the guys. Having just left the agency, I approached them and introduced myself. I said I was a *druzhinnik* and would like to talk about their anti-Semitic remarks in the agency. They were, evidently, surprised and didn't know what to say. I asked them to follow me and proceeded into the backyard of a nearby building. They followed with hesitation.

In the backyard I told them what I thought about their behavior and added that "we" didn't like it. They were confused with this "we" and were apparently scared. Then they apologized and brought out the standard excuse that their first friends were Jewish, so their remarks were nothing more than trash talk. I listened to them with a sullen expression on my face and demanded they never repeated the offense. They promised and immediately left.

Back to the life of our family. In the late 1960s and early 1970s, Alla began taking English courses, as it was a popular cultural activity. In 1965 she had a serious gynecological operation, which made her vulnerable to high blood pressure. In the same year, my dad unexpectedly died from complications caused by a contusion he received in his early childhood. (During the civil war in Russia, an ordinance exploded near the house where he lived.) Life stresses also took their toll. My mother told me the KGB periodically blackmailed Victor for refusing to cooperate with them. My Grandma Lyuba died in 1966, suffering apparently from excessive exposure to radiation through her medical work.

In the same year, my Grandpa Zyama with his sister Polina moved to another flat in the same building. Zyama made this move by trading his three rooms in a communal flat for a separate two-room apartment of the engineer Fridman who worked at the helicopter plant. Through this move Zyama escaped an abusive neighbor (a typical scourge in the communal apartments of the former Soviet Union). The neighbor lived with his wife in the room of the late Elena Vasilyevna, a good friend of Dunaevskys, who recently passed away from lung cancer. The wife was the niece of Elena who inherited the aunt's room. The neighbor, a former navy officer, was apparently a hooligan and sadist in disguise. He sometime used to physically attack Zyama by hitting him in the stomach whenever they ran into each other in the narrow and poorly lit passage way between the hallway and bathroom and kitchen section of the flat. Considering that the attacks went unobserved by the third party, Zyama had a hard time subduing the neighbor through the legal means. Meanwhile we learned later that there have not been physical altercations between the neighbor-hooligan and new tenant. This was possibly because the engineer Fridman was much younger and stronger than Zyama and hence did not fit the image of a potential victim for the abusive neighbor.

Grandpa Zelman died in 1968, and Grandma Isabella died in 1975. Isabella was remembered by many for her poetical work, intellectual mind, and generosity, although her income (a military pension for a son killed at war) was puny by any standards.

Considering the multitude of events during the rest of our lives in the USSR and America, only a brief description of them will be given here as fits the purpose and volume of the book.

After graduating in 1965 with a Masters in mechanical engineering I was immediately drafted for a one-year stint in the army. This was customary for graduates of the higher education establishments who did not have military training curriculum during their years of study. After serving eight months as a private (in the surface-to-air missile detachment) and four months more as a military cadet, I demobilized with the rank of junior lieutenant. One time, when I was still a private, Alla visited me. I was allowed a couple of days leave, and I spent time with my mom who stayed at the local hotel. I later learned our division was being considered for deployment to Vietnam to fight for the Vietcong. That, however, did not materialize.

The eight months as a soldier was harsh, and it was exacerbated by being surrounded and commandeered by people unequal to me in terms of age, education, and cultural upbringing. (Many of my comrades were young draftees from the rural and hinterland regions of the country, who we put up with for the time being.) The four months of cadet training, however, were the most memorable in a positive sense. The cadets were graduates from the higher education establishments from the Baltic republics. They had an equivalent educational level to me and similar cultural upbringings. The Latvian group had the majority of native Russian speakers. In that group, there were also a number of people with good musical skills, the ability to play musical instruments, and knowledge of modern songs and melodies. Our military base management took it as an opportunity to expand social contact with a local population. The base was located near the textile town Orsha in Belorussia.

The majority of the textile workers were young ladies who were glad to be associated with dashing cadets. Apparently assisted by the trade unions, the textile ladies used to throw dance parties accompanied by wine, snacks, and dance music played by our cadets. The main goal, which our military command pursued in supporting these endeavors, was to link up cadets with these girls for marriage. This would ensure the retention of the cadets in the military. They would be officers soon, and their service would continue at the same military base. Although many of the cadets (including myself) established friendly or amorous relationships with the ladies, it never resulted in marriage. At the end of the training, nobody expressed a desire to continue service.

After demobilization and working a few years in industry, particularly at the plant producing diesel electric generators for the military, I began the process of enrollment to a postgraduate program at Riga Polytechnical Institute (RPI). Entering a postgraduate school was not an easy endeavor. As a nonnative Latvian, I had additional hurdles to jump. It boiled down to the fact that my acceptance and tenure at the postgraduate program was dependent on me securing a contract with industry. After learning of the interest of one faculty member at RPI to expand their communication with the industry, I was able to persuade the management of the diesel engine plant to support my studies. The outcome was targeted on resolving several technical issues of interest to the plant. Accordingly a 50,000 ruble contract (approximately equivalent to $48,000 based on 1970 conversion rates) for one year of my program was signed. After the entrance exams, I was admitted to the first year of a three-year PhD program. The contract was renewed every year of my studies at the Chair of automation where I was surrounded by Latvian colleagues who were fine people by any measure.

I successfully completed the required scientific (and heavily mathematic) parts of my studies, and I creatively expanded my research toward resolution of the practical problems the plant was interested in. Based on implementation of some of my studies, the plant approved my dissertation, which I defended early in 1975. This was a prerequisite for a defense certificate to be submitted to the VAK (the Highest Attestation Commission at the Council of Ministers of the USSR) for confirmation of my degree (a Candidate of the Technical Sciences, which is a PhD equivalent) and the issuing of my diploma in 1976.

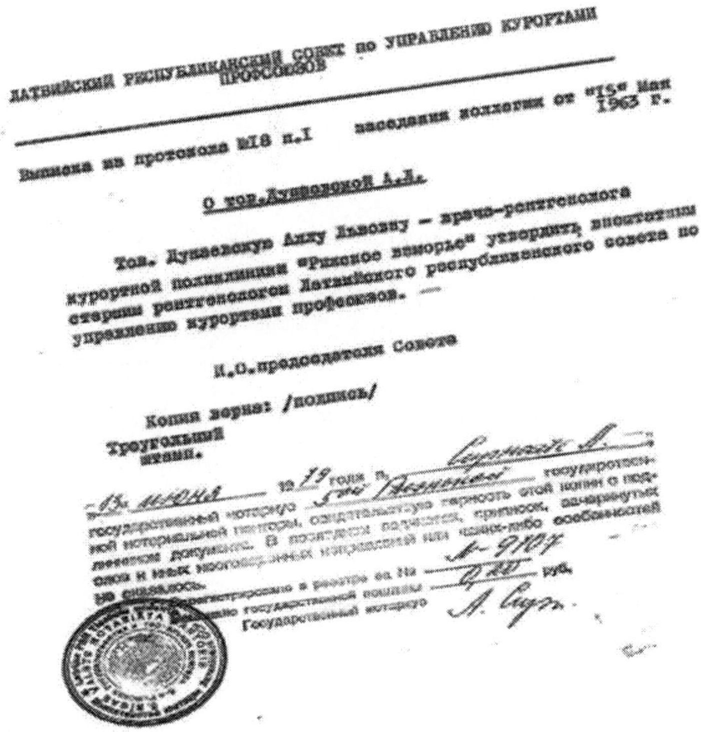
ЛАТВИЙСКИЙ РЕСПУБЛИКАНСКИЙ СОВЕТ по УПРАВЛЕНИЮ КУРОРТАМИ ПРОФСОЮЗОВ

Выписка из протокола №18 п.I заседания коллегии от "15" мая 1963 г.

О тов.Дунаевской А.Л.

Тов. Дунаевскую Аллу Львовну – врача-рентгенолога курортной поликлиники "Рижское взморье" утвердить внештатным старшим рентгенологом Латвийского республиканского совета по управлению курортами профсоюзов. –

И.О.председателя Совета

Копия верна: /подпись/

Треугольный штамп.

A statement on confirmation of Alla as chief radiologist of the Latvian resorts. It reads:
<u>A Latvian Republican Council in Charge of the Trade Unions Resorts.</u>
Excerpt from protocol eighteen, number one of the meeting on May 15, 1963.
<u>On Comr. Dunayevskaya, A. L.</u>
It is to confirm that Comr. Dunayevskaya Alla, a radiology doctor from the "Riga Seaside" clinic, is assigned to be an extraordinary senior radiologist of the Latvian Republican Council in Charge of the Trade Unions Resorts.
The acting deputy of the chairman /signature/Seal.

CHAPTER IX

Toward Emigration: 1974–1979
Emigration: 1979

At the end of 1974, at the conclusion of my PhD course, I was informed that, despite good scientific aptitudes, the Institute where I studied and worked wouldn't grant me a position. This was because of my Hebrew nationality. In addition I was told a couple of former scientists from that Institute, both Jewish, would not have been promoted if they had stayed with the Institute. They both immigrated to Israel a few years earlier.

Subsequently, instead of continuing my tenure in academia, I went back to work as an engineer at the diesel engine plant, which I associated with during my postgraduate studies and earlier. In 1976 the VAK issued me a coveted diploma. I then moved to another big enterprise, Riga Locomotive Plant. I made the transition to the locomotive plant since I was considering emigration. I understood a résumé describing recent work at the military plant might have reduced my chances of getting permission to emigrate. I also made several attempts to join other research organizations in Latvia where I could more effectively utilize my knowledge and interests, but I was not successful. For example, one research institute hired me, but my tenure lasted only two days, as the director returned from a conference where he claimed he received instructions not to hire Jewish people, as they would pollute the Latvian personnel.

The fact I did not have a membership in the Communist Party also did not help in securing a preferable position.

A joke at the time explained the unwritten policy of human resources toward Jews in the Latvian Republic and many other Soviet republics. The rule was called the "rule of three nots" (i.e., do not hire, do not lay off, and do not promote Jews.) Of course, there were numerous exceptions to the "rule," albeit of a limited scope. Alla's professional career as well as that of my father (when he lived in Murmansk) were a good example of this exception. Another exception was my father-in-law, who was director of a big construction organization. Even in Hitler's Germany there were exceptions. There is an expression attributed to Herman Goering. "In my ministry, I decide who is Jewish and who is not."

In that environment, I began seriously thinking about emigration. It was not only the Jewish or party membership problems, however, that turned me in the direction of leaving. I finally attained a position as part-time lecturer in mechanics at the Latvian Institute of Advanced Training of Engineers. My management at the locomotive plant allowed me to teach at the Institute along with continuing my activities at the plant.

However, by that time, I had matured intellectually and morally enough to see the fundamental flaws of the system. I no longer accepted its rotten ideology of pervasive campaigns of denouncements and persecution of the "politically incorrect." The persecuted include people such as academician Sakharov and writers Solzhenitsyn, Boris Pasternak, Vadim Sinyavsky, Iosif Brodsky, and others.

Suppression of various liberties and freedoms and a low living standard all contributed to my development of new interests. Leaving all this aside, the living standard was gradually improving. Many people were getting their own condos and even cars. My salary as a PhD increased by fifty rubles, which was approximately 30 percent. I suspected, along with many others, that the increasing nationalistic tendencies in Latvia and other Soviet republics and continued Jewish emigration might result in deep policy change, which could be even more unfavorable to the Jews. Thus, the time to leave (following the crowd, so to speak) had come.

That attitude was reflected in the following joke. "A Jewish person on the street approaches a group of several other Jews who were involved in a conversation. He then addresses the group by saying, 'I don't know what you are talking about, but it is time to leave.'" That mind-set was also reinforced by the heart-throbbing melodies of the Jewish songs played by the Jewish musicians in the big, fashionable restaurants.

The approaching Olympic Games in Moscow in 1980 were viewed through the prism of the 1936 Olympic Games in Berlin, after which life for Jews in Germany got much tougher. It was considered a wise decision to take advantage of a relatively lenient governmental attitude toward emigration while it lasted. Jews in the Soviet Union feared the door would shut for good, as had happened in Germany in 1939. Many of these fears were confirmed starting in the 1980s with several unfolding events. This included the dissolution of the Soviet Union, the economic collapse of its former republics, and the rise of the worst kind of nationalism, which essentially forced Jewish emigration under threats of pogroms in the early 1990s.

The Jackson-Vanik Amendment to the Trade Act of 1974 facilitated Jewish emigration. One amendment removed the requirement for emigrants to pay for their education before leaving the USSR. These were astronomical sums for regular folks, and only a few could afford them.

The only official way for Jewish people to emigrate from the USSR was to get an exit visa to Israel. The Israeli government facilitated this by providing invitations to the interested Soviet individuals. The Soviet government apparently saw in the emigration a small way to reduce the housing shortage. The emigrants typically left rooms, flats, and apartments, which the government redistributed.

Having the Israeli visa did not mean that person would be forced to go exclusively to Israel. The visa was essentially a way out of the USSR to the Free World. This peculiar situation was due to the fact the USSR did not have a diplomatic relationship with Israel at that time. With assistance from Bruno Kreisky, then Chancellor of Austria, a transit point for emigration to Israel was arranged through Vienna. Kreisky tried to use his position as a European Jewish Socialist to act as a mediator between Israel and Arabs.

The emigrants with Israeli visas were met at the Vienna airport by the representatives of the Israeli resettlement service, SOHNUT, which arranged the temporary living accommodations and a subsequent flight to Israel. The majority of Jewish emigrants were interested in going to Israel. Those who expressed a desire to move to other countries were given opportunities to meet with HIAS (the Hebrew Immigrant Aid Society) and "Joint," which were American-based organizations. The non-Jewish emigrants who managed to get to Vienna could apply for assistance with other charities. The Catholic charity "Caritas" was one example.

The details of the emigration process and many other things were little known to the potential emigrants. Lack of this information, uncertainties about getting permission to leave (and the certainties of governmental punishment for those who were refused permission to leave), a general apprehension of moving into the new economic and political system with no job secured, and little or no foreign language skills definitely slowed down the emigration.

Word of mouth was the main source of information regarding these matters. It was encouraging to me, who did not have many close friends among the emigrants that they did not dissipate into thin air after departing from the Moscow International Airport. I read their letters describing their successes in new homelands such as the United States, Canada, Australia, and South Africa.

After both my wife's cousins and one of my friends immigrated to America in 1977, and especially after my daughter Victoria (Vita) was born in 1978 (the year when the big food shortages hit Latvia), my decision to emigrate solidified further. I used a more eloquent style when I recently described the events leading to our emigration at an informal gathering (the wedding of my daughter). The three paragraphs below are an excerpt of that description.

"In December of 1979, at the age of one year and eight months, from behind the Iron Curtain, Vita arrived with her mom and dad (i.e., my wife, Ada, and me) on the American scene. Unlike the story of Abraham who led his people to the Promised Land, we actually went out of the 'promised land'—the 'workers paradise' where Nikita Khrushchev promised to build Communism by 1980.

However, with the empty shelves and suppression of various liberties, Communism was seen nowhere near the horizon by the end of the 1970s. With Vita's birth in 1978, the acute shortages of fresh fruits, vegetables, and dairy products became a source of serious concern for the healthy development of our posterity.

We, however, heard the 'voices,' and one of those was of the radio station Voice of America. That voice suggested it was time to mount our camels…and go to the country of freedom."

Meanwhile, neither my mother nor the parents of my wife were ready to leave, having held good positions in their respective fields. We did not want to separate from our parents, but had to make a gutsy decision. The time had come, and by procrastinating, we could lose opportunities in a new world. We were also confident we would be able to meet with our parents again and arrange their emigration later on. With these thoughts and with the assistance of my wife's cousins, I finally got an invitation from Israel, which was a prerequisite to applying for emigration.

Subsequently I initiated a series of necessary formalities required to get the exit visas. As I mentioned, it was not a 100 percent guarantee the visa would be granted. Approximately 5 percent of the applicants were refused permission to emigrate. The refusals were based ostensibly on matters of state security (i.e., on the pretext the applicant had access to state-protected information). Typically the refusals were groundless. Those people whose applications were turned down formed an unenviable group of *refusnieks.* Usually they were laid off from their work and had no real means of support. There weren't welfare programs in the USSR. They may have been harassed by police or arrested in some cases.

While contemplating all this, I made an educated guess about the odds of my application for the exit visa being refused. I came to the conclusion that the odds were not very high. This was based on the following. In Latvia during the time described, there had not been much impediment to emigration. In addition, I had been working at a civilian organization, a locomotive plant, since 1976. This was not a military production plant like the diesel engine factory with which I had been associated before. I considered also that a number of people from the locomotive plant had already successfully emigrated. Based on the above rationalizations, I finally decided to apply for the visa.

The first step was informing management about my decision. The plant management was supposed to be contacted later on by the OVIR (Department of Visas and Registrations of Foreigners), which was the department of the Ministry of Internal Affairs responsible for issuing visas. After I informed my boss about my intention to leave, he cautioned me to be sure I was not making the wrong decision or doing something I would be sorry about later. He was a nice and decent fellow representing the Russian portion of the enterprise *cadre*.

His warning was only a mild condemnation compared to the show trials some organizations imposed on those who applied for Israeli emigration. Following the trials, they often were ostracized by their colleagues and called traitors. In my case, however, the overall reaction at the plant was mild and in some instances (especially with my immediate Latvian supervisor) supportive. In general, the Latvians considered the decision by Jews to emigrate as a brave and right decision, and they felt sorry they did not have such an opportunity.

By applying for emigration, I had to overcome a sense of guilt that, by my actions, I was putting my boss in the spotlight. I rationalized, however, that I was not the first in his department who brought him this news, for which he could be reprimanded by his superiors for not instilling in his people a more patriotic state of mind. I also knew that with my application I might have caused Alla and my in-laws some troubles, since they had to give permission too. Alla had to give me official permission to emigrate, while my in-laws had to give the same permission to their daughter. It turned out my father-in-law did suffer some setbacks in his professional life due to our emigration. He was dismissed from a top-level position in his organization.

Besides my immediate supervisors, I had to individually inform several "bigwigs" about my decision. This included the VP of engineering, the secretary of a local chapter of the Communist Party (although I was not a party member), and a trade union leader. When I met with these people, they all stared at me with intimidation but nevertheless signed the appropriate papers, which I handed over to OVIR.

Having done this, I went on a scheduled four-week vacation, hoping the invitation to come to the OVIR would be sent saying we had been granted the visa (or to find out about the refusal, in the worst case).

Normally notification came within three to four weeks. My worries grew as, at the end of the vacation, I had not yet received the invitation to the OVIR. Upon returning to work after my vacation, I was informed that if I did not receive the approval quickly, I would have to resign to avoid being fired. The initial niceties from my management were gone, and the grim reality of an uncertain future was setting in. Fortunately, in a few days, the coveted invitation to come to the OVIR came in the mail. The meeting at the OVIR was a formality. A uniformed Latvian lady officer informed me of the decision to grant us an exit visa and gave us the appropriate papers. This outcome initiated numerous activities and formalities to prepare for the departure. Some of these steps were contradictory and plainly mutually exclusive, and this added unnecessary strife to the whole enterprise.

Arcane, Kafkasquesqe bureaucracy accompanied every step. For example, one had to resign from work, officially give up one's place of residence, and formally vacate. Because there was typically a big lag between the vacation and departure, people were often caught being emigrants in limbo. The Catch-22 of this situation was that one could not move to another residence without having a job. The paradox was usually resolved by the emigrants arranging to temporarily live with their relatives.

After getting proof of having no financial or other obligations at your work, residence, or utilities, one could proceed to other steps. Among these was the renouncement of USSR citizenship. The applicant had to pay a relatively big fee to get this renouncement approved. It was no less than six hundred dollars per individual. For a family of three, we had to pay around two thousands rubles (approximately eighteen hundred dollars). This was big money, and in order to raise it, a family heirloom had to be sold.

Large fees also had to be paid for permits to take objects of intellectual or aesthetic value abroad. Special commissions were established to estimate the value of these artifacts, which included books, postage stamp collections, vases, paintings, silver and gold utensils, furniture, etc. Even without the repayment of tuition, a policy abolished in 1974, all these fees were equivalent to highway robbery. The high cost of emigration hindered exit for many.

Along with renouncement of citizenship, one also had to return one's passports in exchange for some temporary certificates, which had only limited power. In the Soviet Union, existence without a passport, citizenship, and *propiska* (a record of your residency at a certain place) was a preposterous situation. It was asking for trouble. Life under these conditions was a life of "bird's rights." In addition, an individual leaving the country for good had to essentially leave behind all savings. The government only allowed exchanges up to ninety dollars per person.

The next step, after clearing all internal obligations, was a trip to Moscow to get approval of the visas at the Netherland embassy. The Netherland embassy represented the Israeli interests because the diplomatic relationship between the USSR and Israel was cut after the Six-Days War in 1967. With a validated visa, one could purchase tickets for air travel directly to Vienna or railroad tickets for overland transportation through Warsaw or through Chop at the Czechoslovakian border. All these steps were also not without difficulties.

Even though it sounds trivial, "a trip to Moscow" was not trivial. Staying in a hotel was out of the question, as the hotels were always overbooked and expensive. Subsequently in order to stay in Moscow for a few days, one had to have friends or relatives willing to accommodate you alone or with your family.

Some peculiar memories are associated with my visit to the Netherlands embassy. The small quarters of the embassy were overcrowded from the sheer mass of people trying to process their papers at the same time. There was only a single small window available to handle the documents in and out of the processing room. The masses of applicants from the whole Soviet Union were congregated before the embassy gates and were fragmented by the police into smaller groups.

Approaching the embassy and seeing the large crowds, I was somewhat apprehensive. I naively asked a policeman strolling by, "Who are these people?" The policeman's answer was rather unusual. It was profound and profane at the same time. He said, "These are the Jews." He added, "Now you have to live with them." I was not sure what exactly the policeman had in mind, but the experience at the Netherland embassy let me look at some of my tribesmen from a different angle.

The majority of Jews I was surrounded with my whole life were cultured, westernized people. Subsequently I extended this vision to all Jews. However, many of the applicants at the embassy were simple folks from various republics of the USSR. Among them were several big, fat women, unceremoniously pushing their way to the small window in order to handle their papers first. With their behavior and outlook, they were probably no different than the regular Russian or Ukrainian villagers. Folks are folks.

The frantic activity around and through the mentioned window was caused by the need to arrange an appointment with a Netherlands embassy representative. This appointment was required to explain your reasons for emigration to Israel. Upon acceptance of your explanation, which was usually a formality, the embassy would validate the visas. With our visa validated by the embassy stamp, we could then purchase the tickets for transportation abroad and initiate other necessary steps.

The meeting with the Dutch representative was a rather relaxing event. There were also a few other bright spots during the embassy visit. In particular, I befriended a pleasant fellow of approximately my age and background, with whom I continued the other necessary activities in Moscow.

Another bright spot was the cleanliness of the toilets at the embassy. The cleanliness was probably typical for such establishments as embassies, but it certainly surpassed the level of any in the Soviet public organizations. This was definitely a mark of *zagranitsa* (Russian for "abroad" or a symbol of the coveted foreign life). I was not wrong. The overwhelming majority of the toilets I have visited in America have been similarly hygienic and functioning.

After purchasing the air tickets, I returned to Riga and finalized activities for our final departure from the Sheremetyevo Airport in Moscow on October 21. The activities included organizing the shipment of our allowed possessions in a container to Israel. We knew, however, that when a container was in transit to its original Israel route, it could be redirected to the place of our final destination. For this to happen, we would need to contact HIAS whenever we could meet them abroad.

The seemingly smooth activities were interrupted when my daughter, Vita, got sick in the middle of September with a severe reaction to a chicken pox vaccination. She was sick for almost ten days with a high fever. No medication seemed to help her, and she spent some time in the hospital. We took her back home, though, worrying her condition might worsen at the hospital due to the opportunistic infections which exist there. A nurse visited her at home two times every day for injections of certain drugs. Fortunately and rather miraculously, at the beginning of October, Vita began to recuperate. Had her illness continued, our emigration process would have come to a screeching halt, as we could not overstay our time without running into legal hurdles. Besides we had run out of money to buy new tickets (if needed).

Along with arranging the shipments, a very important and time-consuming predeparture activity was legalizing all the documents emigrants need to take with them. For customs to allow your documents to accompany you, they had to be notarized. Understanding that Russian is not a lingua franca in the countries abroad, I (and many others) had the documents translated by the official translators and subsequently notarized.

Considering there was a relatively large volume of documents to be translated (I also had Alla's documents translated and notarized to assist her in the anticipated future emigration), I started this activity six months in advance of my emigration application. The translation and notarization was substantially complicated by the absence of free access to copy machines. There weren't public copy machines, and the government limited access to copy machines to control the population's self-expression and prevent the publication of anti-government materials.

Another hurdle for the emigrants was the absence of any travel agency or "U-Haul" type company to assist in transporting luggage to the customs facilities. Customs was officially engaged in providing a wooden crate for your goods and its packing. One had to go out on the street and "hitchhike" for a pickup truck or secure one through personal connections to find the means to deliver your stuff to customs.

The customs-prepared-and-packed crates were then shipped to the railroad yard, which handled international shipments. There, crates were put in containers for overseas travel. One had to pay substantial sums of money to arrange this transportation. Overall, the government did good business with Jewish emigration.

With all preparations finally completed, we boarded a train for Moscow on October 19 to depart on October 21. My family and Alla stayed at the flat of Alla's schoolmate, Inna. The flat was located in a big and imposing Stalin-era building, which was close to downtown Moscow. Her former husband owned the flat. I reserved a taxicab, and at 5:00 a.m. the next morning, we sped off to Sheremet'evo Airport. Nobody besides our parents came to bid us farewell. The government did not consider Jewish emigration a favorable activity for the USSR, and anyone caught openly commingling with the departing emigrants would become "fair game" for being watched and intimidated. Upon parting with our parents, we cut a couple of locks of hair from my daughter's head and gave them to her grandparents. Nobody knew for sure when we would meet again.

We were not allowed to keep more than the $270 we received per the authorized exchange, so we unloaded almost all the remaining money with our parents. Still I kept several hundred rubles to pay the baggage handlers, taking into account their role in properly processing our luggage. Knowing the precarious situation of the emigrants, the baggage handlers made fortunes on the patrons handing them their remaining cash in amounts that often exceeded their nominal rates by tenfold.

We passed customs without any hindrance. This was a big relief, as unpredictability of the customs clerks, rules, and some awkward situations were notorious for happening. It certainly helped that all our papers were notarized. We did not risk bringing any valuables, besides those listed on the custom declaration. Smuggling was severely penalized. That game was not "worth the candles." Still some emigrants managed to carry with them the "extra" stuff. They believed the sale of undeclared jewelry could provide necessary subsistence in the first months and years at their new destination. By finding the right people at the post office, I managed to send, through the mail, boxes of literature and collectible items (postage stamps) that would have been difficult to get approved in the official way. These, however, had a very limited sale value.

Finally we boarded the plane. That was another important step to freedom. During the flight, the service was of the highest level with black caviar and champagne. There were a number of emigrants on board. After approximately an hour of flying, when we had crossed the state border, the emigrants raised their glasses with champagne and cheered in elation, having achieved the coveted goal of passage to freedom.

Upon landing at the Vienna airport, the realities of a new life began immediately to materialize. Out the window I saw an Israeli plane on the tarmac, which was surrounded by several Israeli soldiers with submachine guns in the ready position. A chain of people, apparently emigrants who arrived earlier, were strolling to the plane.

After everybody departed our plane, we and the other emigrants were led to a hall where a casually dressed young man in his late twenties or early thirties with a short haircut announced he was the representative of SOHNUT, an Israeli organization involved in the absorption of emigrants. He explained it was time to decide whether we were going to immigrate to Israel or not. If we were not going there, then we would be transferred to the HIAS organization, which would resume the coordination and support of our emigration process. If we did decide to go to Israel (and he stressed it was the most reasonable way to emigrate), then the SOHNUT would provide accommodation. The next day, we could fly to Israel. He gave a little pep talk about the benefits of living in Israel and the big uncertainties we could expect in America, if we went there.

Trying to discourage us from moving to the United States, he said we would not be able to use our diplomas there, at least for a long time. In retrospect he was correct in a certain way. Foreign medical diplomas are not recognized in the United States. Considered "former" doctors, they have to pass a very serious test called the "board" to get an American MD diploma. It is easier in industry where, with rare exceptions, an employer does not ask a potential employee to show his/her diploma. I only recently found a real use for my PhD diploma in mechanical engineering (that was certified by the appropriate US agency). I got a substantial automobile insurance discount from one insurance company. They provided perks to individuals who had additional merits, and my diploma happened to be one.

Since our original intent was to go to America, our luggage was removed from the holding bin and moved to another section. We joined a group of people who were led to another room. Here, two other SOHNUT representatives requested an explanation why we were switching our emigrant route and moving to the New World. The formal answer we gave was we already had cousins living in New Jersey who were waiting for our arrival and could be our sponsors. This answer satisfied their inquiry.

I found it curious that one of the representatives was a former acquaintance from Riga. He was a red-haired, athletic fellow known to be involved in martial arts, particularly SAMBO (a Russian acronym for Self Defense Without Weapons). He immigrated to Israel ten years earlier. His companion was an attractive and intelligent-looking young lady in her mid-thirties.

Toward the evening, when more emigrants arrived from Moscow, we were put in a couple of buses and moved to a cheap hotel at the outskirts of Vienna. The hotel was somewhat run-down. The portable tools I took with us were very handy and helped fix various electrical amenities in the run-down hotel. Subsequently we could prepare a meal in our room instead of scurrying up and down the hotel stairs to get to the kitchen on the first floor. This was helpful when traveling with a child.

Vienna was actually the first stage on the way to America. The second was Rome from where the direct flights to America were organized. We were instructed that to get to Rome, we had to sign up for transportation by train and arrange other formalities in the Vienna section of HIAS. We did it within a week after arriving in Vienna. To get cash for the local transportation, we exchanged (I am not sure where) a portion of our $270. To raise the money, we sold the locals some of the items we took with us from Moscow exclusively for that purpose but that were within the limits allowed by the USSR customs. Through the years, Vienna had served as a passage to freedom for the Soviets, and the locals had established well-worn paths to the hotels where the emigrants stayed. The locals purchased the goods at a bargain rate. We sold two bottles of Stolichnaya Vodka, a can of black caviar, and an amber necklace.

Meanwhile a SOHNUT couple we met at the airport, and a few others from that organization, continued enticing us and other emigrants with the opportunities and support Israel provided to scientists. They took us several times to Vienna cafés and pizza parlors. This activity and the enchanting smell of pizza, which I never tested before, apparently worked in the direction the SOHNUT intended. An older scientist from Leningrad and I decided to switch to Israel.

Considerations of a Jewish patriotic duty, closeness to the homeland, and uncertainties of the life in America all played a role in that decision. My wife, Ada, did not have serious objections to redirecting our destination to Israel (our original official destination) and relied on my decision. Subsequently I canceled our transportation to Rome and signed up for the transportation to Israel. With these actions, our interaction with HIAS was severed.

However, having done all this, I began feeling a big uneasiness. I began thinking through all the pros and cons of moving to Israel, something I apparently did not do well in the first place. I began realizing Israel is a very small country. Hence, despite all the righteous reasons and the glorification of the country by SOHNUT I thought, it still could be difficult to find a job in my field. In this train of thoughts I, apparently, underestimated an industrial potential of Israel.

The possibility of experiencing a cultural maladjustment also went through my mind. In addition, someone from our SOHNUT friends suggested that I could be disappointed in Israel if religious freedom was not the main factor in my decision. This was the final argument that made me reverse again and return to our original plans. However, it happened to not be an easy task. My hesitations impeded a normal course of our passage to either country, Israel or America.

Despite SOHNUT promise to quickly reconnect us with HIAS, I found myself and my family in limbo. Our flight to Israel was canceled, and the HIAS link was still disengaged. With the money running short and without citizenship to any country, the situation was getting very tense. I began contemplating other opportunities to go to America or at least secure some living subsidies. There were not many. One of those opportunities was the remote possibility of getting assistance from the Catholic charity, Caritas. Based on a rumor, they supported any emigrant.

Eventually, however, we were back with HIAS and renewed our reservation for the transport to Rome. We began seeing the light at the end of a tunnel after I unintentionally sidetracked us with the possibility of going to Israel. Still, one nerve-racking incident happened on the day of our departure, November 21, 1979. It was two and half weeks after the Iran hostage crisis, in which 52 Americans were held hostage for 444 day, began. And it was exactly one month after our departure from Moscow, and we had spent an extra three anxiety-filled weeks in Vienna. (A usual stay there was seven to ten days.) The taxicab, which was scheduled to pick us up and deliver us to the proper authorities at the railroad station for our trip to Rome, did not arrive on time. Since the local transportation to the Rome-bound train was controlled by the SOHNUT, I called them to express my concerns. They promised to resolve the situation with the taxi. Nothing happened.

Taxicabs kept coming for our neighbors in the hotels, who were also moving to Rome, but not for us. Very worried, I called my SOHNUT friend and explained the situation. Semi-jokingly, I hinted I could be helpful to him if he ever wanted to move to America himself. He laughed, said he had no interest in such a move, but promised to intervene. His actions might have helped or it might have been a coincidence, but a taxicab came for us soon. Meanwhile, the taxicab brought us to the railroad station where the crowds of departing emigrants were assembling.

The train was boarded around 10:00 p.m. local time. The cars were comfortable but without sleeping accommodations. However, the train had a noticeable peculiarity. At each end of each car were guards with submachine guns. This was apparently a precaution against possible attacks by Palestinian radicals or other anti-Israeli elements, which were possible in the wake of the 1972 Munich Olympic massacre of the Israeli athletes.

We did not sleep much that night but watched the magnificent Alpine landscapes through the windows. They were seen in a dim moonlight on the sides of the train when we passed through Switzerland and northern Italy on the way to Rome. After a brief nap in the morning, we realized we were approaching Rome. At one small station before Rome, we received an announcement we had to urgently unload our luggage onto the platform.

Everybody began frantically shoving their belongings through the open windows to the suspicious-looking individuals on the platform. Were they the Mafiosi characters HIAS hired to protect us? After having our luggage (including a night pot for Vita) unloaded, we departed the train ourselves. Along with the luggage, we were put on buses that brought us to the hotel, which was located near the Rome railroad station. The bus driver called, "Termini."

The hotel was in a big building of imposing architecture with the signs of faded glory. The rooms, with an abundance of marble walls and floor, did not have heating. It was the end of November, and the evenings and nights were cold. The hotel was only a temporary shelter and was not really suitable for handling the needs of travelers. For example, there wasn't any other way to dry the washed clothes of our infant daughter, Vita, than using the heat of an electric bulb.

This was definitely a precarious operation in which we burned some of Vita's clothes. The hotel provided breakfast, which had a romantic name: continental. We soon realized the loftiness of the name did not match the content of the breakfast. It consisted mainly of toasted bread with fruit jam and a cup of tea or coffee. Fierce-looking men of Arabian (rather north African Arabian) descent served the breakfast.

Staying in the Rome hotel was an opportunity to tour the city and arrange trips to places of leisure such as Venetia, Pompey, etc. The majority of our fellow emigrants took advantage of that opportunity. However, because Vita got sick with some kind of respiratory disease, we were limited in our travel. Considering our language barrier and refugee status, it was difficult to arrange a doctor's appointment to get the necessary medication. A doctor finally arrived and ruled out Vita having pneumonia. He prescribed some medications, which we bought in a local *farmachia*.

While staying in Rome and later in the seaside town of Ladispoli, 40 km from Rome, we had to carry out a number of formalities for the transportation to America. These included registering at a local HIAS office, getting a medical checkup, visiting the US embassy, where we had a detailed conversation about reasons for our emigration and where we filled out some paperwork, securing a grant from one of the Jewish federations in America for our admission, booking the flight reservations (sponsored by HIAS), etc. Considering the unfavorable living conditions in the hotel, the majority of emigrants opted to stay, until their departure from Italy, in the rented houses of the seaside towns of Ostia or Ladispoli. These were recommended by HIAS. HIAS provided subsidies to cover living expenses for reasonable periods of time. This was justified by the specific situation of the individual emigrant family.

An Italian interlude to such countries as the United States or Canada usually did not exceed several weeks. Those few emigrants who wanted to stay longer had to provide for themselves. They would stay either to take full advantage of the once-in-a-lifetime opportunity to see Italy, or they had to wait for almost six months for a grant from countries such as Australia, New Zealand, or South Africa. We also attempted to increase our financial worthiness by continuing to sell our personal items. Unlike Vienna, the trading place was not the hotel. In Rome, it was a flea market, which was close to the city center and called Americana.

By selling some optics (a Zenith SLR photo camera and a set of long-range binoculars), several pieces of linen, some amber, and traditional Russian souvenirs such as artisan-made lacquer boxes, wooden spoons, and nested dolls (*matreshkas*), our treasury increased by a couple of hundred dollars. In the process of these sales, I learned rudimentary Italian and a few catchy words and phrases required to attract a potential buyer. One of those was "*Un regallo per un bambino!*" (A present for a child!)

The waiting time for a grant from New York City was, I believe, the shortest. I did not want to go there, however, considering it a place overcrowded with immigrants who would be pressured to take any job in order to repay the financial obligations with the sponsoring party. As we later found out, my concerns were somewhat justified. However, the New York federation provided opportunities and services on a level not available in the smaller Jewish communities.

I decided to go to Des Moines, Iowa, where Jack G., one of my friends from Riga, had already resided with his family for two years. Jack was instrumental in getting our grant approved quickly, and on December 12, 1979, we were on a plane (Boeing 747) departing to America from the Leonardo Da Vinci Airport in Rome. We arrived at Newark Airport in New Jersey. Upon arrival a HIAS representative gave the Jewish emigrants identification badges in the shape of six-pointed Stars of David colored blue. We attached the paper badges to the upper portions of our garment and were then separated from the rest of the deplaned passengers.

This reminded me of the time when Jews were obliged to wear yellow stars in Nazi Germany and were subjected to selection upon arrival to Auschwitz. The analogy was certainly unfair. After passing through customs, we were not gassed but given tickets to a plane to Des Moines and provided accommodation in one of the local hotels. A representative from HIAS assisted us in getting there. It was not a four-star hotel, but it had all the necessary amenities. It included things that were mundane for Americans but prohibitive luxuries for the Rome Termini hotel such as a functioning heater and AC. We felt our life was getting better, even though we arrived in the New World with only $470 between me and my wife, we had no guarantee of work, and we had no permanent residence.

With all this we were not any different than many others who came before us, and many of them succeeded. Favoring our situation were factors such as having good professional training, having some knowledge of the language, and being young. The very stimulating factor, however, was the absence of the opportunity to go back. With such a bouquet of qualities, we were obliged to succeed.

The reader of this edition of the book will be spared from the various intriguing details of our progress and challenges in the New World, as they would deflect from the main topic of the book: my mother's image woven into the Old and New World tapestry. A detailed account of the emigration process has been given because my mother went through similar steps a few years later. I will say only that my engineering aspirations, the fulfillment of which was one of the chief motives of our emigration, were realized to a sufficient degree. Some of my engineering developments have been implemented in various industries and are appreciated in academia.

My wife has been employed for many years in her construction engineering profession. What is more important, however, is that my daughter grew up in a tolerant atmosphere, got a good education, and became a practicing physician with an MD diploma. In this she followed in the footsteps of her Grandma Alla who, compared to other immigrants of her age, achieved a higher status in terms of her adjustment to the new home. This was due to her abilities, interests, and persistence.

With this I would like to express gratitude to SOHNUT and HIAS for their assistance during my and my mother's emigration. Also, I would like to express an appreciation to those Israelis who helped us to secure the invitation that resulted for us in getting an exit visa from the USSR.

Things would be somewhat different for us had we decided not to emigrate. First of all, I am sure I wouldn't have been able to realize my engineering interests, as the economy in Latvia collapsed like in many post-Soviet republics. Besides it is likely we would have immigrated to Israel after Latvia became independent, and the ethnic issues there came to a head. Israel is a wonderful country (with its own host of the problems of cause), and it became a powerhouse especially after the mass exodus from the former Soviet republics in the early 1990s. A number of US high-tech companies moved to Israel too. We could have succeeded there as well. Many of my friends and relatives who made an *aliyah* to Israel have done well, and their children have become real patriots of the country. However, there has been a percentage that did not end up well.

The middle-aged physicist researcher from Leningrad who I befriended in Vienna and who switched to Israel later wrote us tearful letters about how he was disappointed in what was in store for him in Israel. An acquaintance of mine, a reputed medical professor from Baku (Azerbaijan) who immigrated to Israel in the early 1990s, was so upset with the opportunities offered to him he committed suicide. The mass Jewish exodus to Israel from the USSR certainly exacerbated an employment problem in the small Jewish state. That situation painfully touched the people with medical backgrounds, some of whom had to work as street sweepers in the early part of their Israeli emigration. Not knowing exactly what were the problems of two aforementioned individuals, one can speculate that besides anything else they might have an enlarged sense of self entitlement.

However, not every immigrant felt him/herself "hunky-dory" on this side of the "pond" either. Reagan's recession of the early 1980s, which in some ways was worse than the recent one, hit hard. Some Russian immigrants I knew, especially those over fifty, lost their jobs, and chances of them securing gainful employment in their respective fields were slim. I remember one engineer from Leningrad who was laid off from the nuclear division of Westinghouse in 1982. As a way to raise cash and partially compensate for the loss of income, he began delivering flowers during the holidays. It was always a frantic game of chance for him to find even that kind of menial work.

Tragic was the story of one family from Moscow who settled in Pittsburgh in the mid-1970s. They lived in the same apartment complex we did, and their daughter, Zhenya, was just two years older than my daughter. They were in the process of buying a new house, and by all standards they appeared to be very successful. By the mid-1980s, however, they ran out of luck. First Zhenya's mother was killed in a car accident. Then, in a typical American twist of events, her father, VP in a high-tech company and a proud owner of the 1977 Corvette, was unexpectedly demoted. He couldn't cope with this and died from a massive heart attack. Thus Zhenya become an orphan. Her situation was further complicated because she did not speak Russian. At that time, in some affluent Russian families, there was a curious fashion of speaking only English and not teaching children Russian. Ostensibly it was done to ensure a flawless transition of the Russian children to American life and prevent the children from being corrupted by the Russian culture, which was considered in decline at the time. Hence it would have hardly made sense to send Zhenya back to Russia to her grandparents. She was eventually adopted by her parents' English-speaking friends.

Also the situation with employing scientists was not very smooth. Several older professors from Leningrad, who arrived in Pittsburgh at approximately the same time we did, couldn't get jobs in the universities. They finally were hired by various divisions of Westinghouse for some secondary roles.

This was certainly a source of frustration for these professors. In addition to job status, another source of frustration for them was the means of transportation to and from work. In suburban America driving one's own car is a way of life. However, many expats including the aforementioned Leningraders, had no previous driving experience. Worse, they had an aversion to learning how to drive. Subsequently, they became dependent on their relatives bringing them in and picking them up after work.

However, their reaction to these limitations and aggravations was much milder than that of their peers in Israel. This was probably because nobody invited them here. Hence there was a smaller sense of entitlement, and their financial compensation and living standards were sufficiently high.

Meanwhile, all other conditions being the same, having the right set of skills was critical for gaining and retaining the employment. I know a number of successful employment stories for immigrant scientists and engineers of all ages.

Some even managed to retrain themselves by going back to school and getting additional PhD degrees. This facilitated their entrance into the job market.

For understandable reasons, the percentage of successful immigrant stories is probably higher in the United States than anywhere in the world, and the modest achievements of my family are a part of those statistics.

CHAPTER X

My Mother's Arrival to Pittsburgh, USA and Her Life There: 1982–2009

After we had settled in the routine of life and work, a sense of separation from my mother became stronger, and a desire grew to arrange her move here. In our phone conversations and correspondence, however, she did not express an interest in leaving right away, and I did not push her. Still I considered it prudent to arrange an invitation for my mother. This way she could use it when she felt ready. I couldn't invite her to come directly to America because we were not yet citizens. The invitation had to be, as it was in my case, from Israel. In order to increase the odds of getting this invitation in the shortest time, I found American-Israeli contacts in New York City, and with my payment of $2000, Alla's invitation was issued in mid-1981. At the end of the year, she decided to make good on this invitation.

We later learned one of the factors which influenced Alla's decision to emigrate, besides her desire to be with us, was her feeling of personal insecurity. That feeling grew out of the fact her apartment in Yúrmala (on the Riga seaside) was burglarized.

To enter the apartment, thieves cut out a wooden plank near the lock on the front door. Then they opened the lock and entered the flat.

So as not to make me worry, my mother did not tell us anything about this event in our correspondence. The thieves were later caught, but none of the high-value silverware, which had been collected through the years, could be retrieved. In addition, the court proceedings were very lenient.

Fortunately Alla's application for emigration was quickly approved, and she began preparations to leave the country. In all these many activities, she relied on assistance from friends, relatives, and in-laws. Still it was more than a handful for Alla, a single person, to carry out in a limited time, even with assistance, all the activities associated with emigration.

Something had to give. The weak link was the preparation for shipment of all the items approved to be taken out of the country. In the turmoil of preparation, several important things were left behind. Among those were many good books from our home library and some valuables. Also Isabella's handwritten notebooks, which were kept in the apartment, were regretfully mishandled. Their whereabouts are unknown. At the beginning of April 1982, my mother departed Moscow Sheremetyevo Airport. It was not, however, without a friendly "farewell" from the customs people who subjected Alla to a humiliating body cavity search for potentially smuggled valuables.

The remaining portion of travel to America through Vienna and Rome went smoothly overall. Mother told how she followed one friendly emigrant couple who helped her carrying luggage and performing other activities requiring appreciable strength. Thanks to HIAS, which provided emigrants with temporary housing, living expenses, and transportation and because of my acceptance of all financial responsibilities for her medical and living expenses in America, Alla actually was able to enjoy her trip.

On April 28, 1982, my mother finally arrived in Pittsburgh. I went to the airport to pick up my mother with my family. My four-year-old daughter, Vita, was shy about meeting Grandma, who she did not remember much. When Grandma Alla, a red-haired lady in a dark beret and winter coat with a serious expression in her eyes and a straight bearing showed up on the Jet way, Vita covered her eyes with her hands. She admitted later she still was able to peek at Grandma between her fingers.

What a joyful day it was for me and my mother! We took her to our apartment in Monroeville. Upon waking up the next day, she told us how relaxed she felt with us in America compared to the anxiety she experienced back in Latvia.

Unlike my mother, who arrived in America in good condition, albeit tired, the wooden crate she shipped from Latvia and which arrived a few months later, was tampered with. In particular her winter coat and some fur items were absent. For a number of reasons, we suspected the tampering took place on our side of "the pond," and we felt the party at fault could be associated with the trucking company that delivered the crate.

Alla lived with us for approximately one and a half years. Within that time her medical and SSSI (Supplemental Social Security Income) coverage were approved, and she received the opportunity to rent her own apartment in a government-subsidized building for low-income people.

Soon after my mother's arrival, I signed her up for the yearlong English course for foreigners, which was held in a school in Monroeville. I drove her to and from the school. I continued to drive Alla everywhere she needed to go until 1987. This was when she received her driver's license and bought her first car.

Through the English course and by becoming a member of the International Women's Club and the University Women's Association, Alla forged friendships with a number of ladies from various countries. Many of them came to America with their husbands, who relocated to work in the nuclear industry. At that time, Monroeville housed the Westinghouse Nuclear Research Center and its associated enterprises. This was where the husbands of these ladies worked. Alla continued corresponding with many of these friends to the end of her life. I was always pleasantly surprised to see postcards from some of these ladies, even though Alla had not seen them for many years after they left America when their husbands' contracts expired.

My mother left a lasting impression on people, and this was not only in her mature years. In one of the Pittsburgh Orchestra performances we attended in 1983, she was recognized by a much younger Russian lady. With her husband, they were also recent émigrés from the USSR. That attractive lady, Lyuba Model, was a clothing and leather goods designer from Moscow. She happened to live in Murmansk in the mid-1950s in the same building where Alla and the rest of our family lived. Lyuba was a few years older than me. We did not know her in Murmansk, but she vividly remembered Alla. She had admired her for her looks and style even then, decades earlier. In America, Alla and Lyuba became close friends.

Alla also made many friends among the members of the Reform Synagogue Temple David in Monroeville. At the same time, in the 1990s, she became acquainted with several families of Christian emigrants from the FSU (countries of the former Soviet Union) who settled in her apartment building. Many of them belonged to non-favored Christian denominations in the USSR such as Pentecostal (Lyuda and Pavel Shulikovs from Rostov-on-Don) and Baptists (Valentina and Vladimir Ulyanuk from western Ukraine). These people were disillusioned by post-Soviet life and saw more opportunities in the New World.

Already proficient in English, Alla was a substantial help for these emigrants. She translated, filled out various critical documents, arranged medical appointments, and assisted with translation during life-threatening operations and labor. These people valued her assistance and became lifelong friends. In turn they helped Alla with various car problems and other home chores.

The good word about my mother's deeds had spread. Newcomers from the Ukraine and Russia heard that a Jewish Russian-speaking doctor was helping Christians, and they called her looking for assistance. Recently, after visiting Alla's gravesite with Lyuda Shulikov and Natasha (the daughter of Alla's friend, Yuri Umilyanovsky), we went for a cup of coffee in a Panera Bread in Monroeville. Sitting at the table, the ladies began recollecting various moments they shared with Alla. Lyuda recalled that Alla liked that restaurant and frequented it, sometimes having a tuna salad lunch.

Lyuda recalled also that when Alla was already ill, she asked Luda to pray for her in church. Alla liked to talk to Luda's husband, Pavel, who reminded her a little of her late husband, Victor. Pavel also liked to strike up conversations with Alla. These often had pleasantly humorous overtones. Alla also liked Lyuda and Pavel's children, especially the youngest, Yurochka, who was delivered by C-section. During the procedure, Alla was present as Lyuda's interpreter and confidant, providing a human touch by holding Lyuda's hand and helping to diminish Lyuda's anxiety.

With her ability to carry on a calming, quieting style of conversation, Alla provided a beneficial influence on many people, from those who needed psychological support to someone who just wanted a casual conversation. These people included members of Temple David, our family friends, acquaintances, and unfamiliar people who, in one way or another, came into contact with my mother. The driver of the bus Alla used to take to work and shopping (after losing her driving privileges in 2009 from hearing problems) expressed his condolences after he learned about Alla's departure. He talked at length about the positive feelings he had about "that old lady." He could not always understand her (her voice became very weak in her last years), but she was always cheerful and friendly.

After completing two hundred hours of the English as a second language course in 1983, Alla got a volunteer job in the pharmacy of a division of Forbes Hospital in Monroeville. She also began preparing to pass her boards to get certified as an American MD. However, on the day of the exam in the spring of 1984, she had a strong allergic reaction to a medication she took for blood pressure. The trip to the board examination was canceled, and Alla never again attempted to pass the test because the preparation required too much time and effort. Nevertheless she gradually progressed to the level of an honorary staff member of the radiology department at Forbes (which had been associated with Almar Radiology), where she was involved in quality-assurance work. Dr. Meyrowitz from Forbes originally sponsored Alla's admission to the X-ray department.

In preparation for her naturalization test, Alla completed two more sets of English courses, comprising more than five hundred hours. Alla received her naturalization in 1987, two years after I and my family did. That achievement was the source of great pride for her.

Alla's work at the radiology department was a part-time job, for which she received a token fee of less than $2000 per year. But more than a paltry addition to her modest Supplemental Social Security income, the work gave my mother a sense of self-worth and dignity. Alla worked until July 23, 2009, which was the day she fell down in her apartment and broke her shoulder. This situation put her in the rehabilitation/nursing home where her condition gradually deteriorated. The rehabilitation facility (A Golden Living Center in Monroeville) was actually across the street from the high-rise apartment building where she had moved at the end of 2004.

Along with the volunteering and semi-volunteering activities Alla conducted at Forbes, Alla helped with my daughter's supervision when Vita was out of kindergarten or school. Alla's arrival at the end of April 1982 was quite timely. Vita developed an ear infection and had to stay home to recuperate. It was difficult to find a babysitter for Vita because she was very choosy. For whatever reason, Vita did not like one pleasant lady, who babysat a few times. That lady was the mother of one of our friends and another emigrant. Instead of being under her command, four-year-old Vita actually dominated that babysitter.

With her arrival, Grandma Alla replaced that lady and was able to mend fences with Vita and quickly win her confidence. She sung Vita the songs she heard in childhood, recited children's poems and verses, some of which Isabella wrote, and told her the family stories. Vita liked these. In summer Alla accompanied Vita to the playground and swimming pool, which were on the premises of our Fox Hill apartment complex. It was located in a picturesque, hilly area above a four-lane highway. Adding to the beauty of the area was a pure white Indian temple. The largest in North America, it was situated on a hill a few miles down the road and was at the level of our apartment complex.

When Vita was attending elementary school, I used to bring her before school to Grandma's on my way to work, and I'd pick her up after school. Alla fed her and took her to the school bus before departing for work herself. The seemingly mundane activities of seeing off and meeting a granddaughter were not without risk in wintertime. The yard around the building where Alla lived was not always cleared of ice and snow. One chilly morning in 1983, when Alla returned home after getting Vita to the school bus, she slid on the ice, fell, and broke her left hand. She couldn't get up and lie on the snow for forty minutes until a passerby saw her and brought her to Forbes Hospital. I was called at work and rushed to the hospital to assist my mother.

Another precarious situation developed one winter evening in 1985. A blizzard was slowing all traffic, and the return of Vita's school bus was delayed. Meanwhile Alla waited at the bus stop. When the bus arrived and Vita came out, a strong snow squall with winds of 70 mph, as it was later reported, hit the area. It was a miracle Alla was able to catch Vita's hand and pull her out of a snowdrift, which had begun to drag Vita downhill. With this Alla literally saved Vita.

My mother provided a positive cultural influence on Vita, adding to what she received from her parents. Alla familiarized Vita with quotes of wisdom and instructions on proper manners and behaviors. When Vita was ten years old and attended musical school, Alla also arranged additional piano lessons with a teacher who happened to be Russian American and played the bassoon in the Pittsburgh Philharmonic Orchestra. Alla also served as a role model, and it was probably not accidental that Vita elected to be a doctor.

Alla's first apartment was located in a three-story, garden-style apartment building on Cambridge Square Drive in Monroeville. The apartment had good views of the surrounding areas. During the first ten or fifteen years of her life there, the apartment complex housed mainly common folks. They were not very wealthy. However, starting from the mid-1990s, a rent increase forced many of these folks to move out of the complex. The new tenants replacing them consisted of young, welfare-supported male and female characters living in subsidized flats with their infants.

Observing the behavior of these tenants, one could sense the area had become infiltrated with drugs and was ripe for crime. I asked my mother to move to another apartment complex. I wanted her to live in the so-called Borough Building, which was built originally by and for Jewish WWII veterans. However, at the time there was not an available and suitable apartment for her. The available apartments did not have good views like her Cambridge Square apartment. She cherished those views as a sort of compensation for her bygone youth and respectable past life.

Alla's nostalgia was augmented by watching TV serials depicting broken dreams. Featuring beautiful actresses, handsome heroes, and delicate music, these serials worked as a nostalgia feeder, but they also instilled in Alla a sense of belonging to a different and more exquisite culture. She enjoyed the freedoms of a new home country. She often shared with me how unusual and liberating it was to see commentators, during election campaigns, asking presidential candidates questions in a free setting. This was not heard of in our former motherland.

The names of American cities such as Cincinnati, Detroit, and Chicago and our shared trip to the Midwest in 1988 reawakened in Alla memories of the renowned American writer Theodore Dreiser (*Sister Carrie*, *The Financier*, *The Titan*, and *An American Tragedy*), which she read in the 1930s. The books of Dreiser, who is almost forgotten in America, evidently impressed Alla's generation of Russian readers with the American spirit and the panoply of American life the author wrote about.

Alla also managed to make a few trips abroad independently. These were to Saint-Petersburg, Russia and Riga, Latvia (Latvia was then part of the USSR) in the winter of 1989, to Karlovy Vary and the Czech Republic in 1995, and to Israel in 1999. Israel left a very strong impression on her.

As the years passed, Alla's outlook became less rosy regarding the events occurring around her. One day in the spring of 2004, my worries about unsafe living at Cambridge Square came true. An officer from the Monroeville Police Department, Mr. Fischer, called me and said my mother had been attacked near her apartment building, and her purse had been snatched. Fortunately she survived the attack. Alla later told me she was returning home after work and was coming up the porch stairs to the building when a black youngster, one among a group standing on the porch, grabbed her purse and tried to wrench it out of her hands. She could not keep her balance, fell down, and rolled down the stairs from the porch.

She was in winter clothing, and her head was covered with a scarf. That scarf possibly helped cushion Alla's head as she tumbled down the steps. A tomography scan Alla underwent following the attack did not register any appreciable head or brain injuries, but Alla felt the traumatic experience affected her memory. The perpetrators of the attack were quickly apprehended thanks to a call to the police by a neighbor who saw the events through the windows of his first-floor apartment. Before they were apprehended, the vandals emptied Alla's purse and threw it into one of the refuse containers sitting in the backyard.

The juveniles that participated in the attack were put in a detention center. The court proceedings took place several weeks later in a Pittsburgh courthouse in an area adjacent to the jail where the defendants were held. The courtroom was filled with the relatives of the perpetrators, and they threw sullen glances toward Alla and me. The main perpetrator, a youth of fourteen years, explained his actions by saying he had been bullied by his older peers. They told him he would be a coward if he could not snatch a purse from the fragile old lady.

For the speech Alla made at the court hearing, she was prized by the judge, an African American lady. In Alla's speech she tried to persuade the relatives of the defendants that she was not after them to recoup the money they stole from her. She focused her speech on the defendants' need to seriously review their behavior, make something of themselves, and stop blemishing their reputations and their relatives'. Alla was proud of the appreciation she received from the judge and other people in the court system, and she told them she acted following the principles of her father, an attorney from Odessa. The court provided an interpreter for Alla, a young lady and recent emigrant from Moldova (one of the former Soviet republics). However, Alla delivered her speech by herself with elegance, eloquence, and clarity. She also wrote the speech mostly by herself with only minor corrections from me.

This accident heightened the urgency of transferring Alla to the Borough Building. The move fell on New Year's Day, 2005. She enjoyed the upscale accommodations (compared to her former dwelling). It was a new apartment with a balcony and good views. She was, however, a bit upset that the few Jewish WWII veterans who lived in the building, or were its sponsors, were not interested in communicating with her as she expected from former comrades-in-arms. I suspected the veterans' attitude might have had something to do with Alla's strong Russian accent. To be honest, though, she and I had pleasant chats with them on a few occasions.

While working in the radiology department, Alla engaged in freelance activities. She became a photographer and historiographer of the department. The new directors of the department and hospital were always pleased to set a picture-taking appointment with Alla, after having heard good words from the staff about her capacity. One of these appointments, I remember, was as recent as 2008. She was already getting frail, but she was still very active and enjoying the feeling of being purposeful.

In order to be on time for the appointment, which was set up quite early at 8:00 a.m., Alla had to wake up much earlier than normal, especially considering that at her age she moved somewhat slower in her preparations. We agreed I would call around 5:30 a.m. to wake her up in case she missed her alarm. When I did she was already on her feet. She did not sleep much that night. Alla explained she felt heartaches and kept her hands around a bottle of warm water, which was a technique she used to mitigate her heart conditions. For a long time, she suffered from heart ailments and high blood pressure. However, only after arriving in America was she able to actively monitor her blood pressure using over-the-counter devices. She regularly took her blood pressure readings and also assisted her neighbors with that procedure.

During her more than twenty-year tenure in the radiology department, she made several photographic albums in which the history of the department was well presented. These albums were cherished by the department staff. The photographs not only registered the events and faces, but they also showed a touch of the photographer's personality, and they often reflected Alla's mood and thoughts. At the end of the album, she usually placed her own picture, taken by a colleague. She appears in these pictures with an expression of light sadness against the background of early autumn.

Photography was not Alla's only interest. She enjoyed collecting and memorizing interesting quotes, a couple of which are shown in her handwriting at the end of the chapter. Below I present a couple more of the expressions of wisdom that Alla enjoyed.

By W. Churchill: "If you are not a rebel in your twenties, then you have no heart, and if you are not a conservator at forty, then you have no brain."

By W. M. Thackeray in *Vanity Fair*" "Ah! *Vanitas Vanitatum!* Which of us is happy in this world? Or, having it, is satisfied?"

She liked to attend musicals, the ballet, opera performances, and art exhibitions. She liked to participate in social gatherings such as the parties that Almar Radiology used to hold for its staff a couple of times a year at a country club. Almar appreciated Alla's contribution, enjoyed her presence at the parties, and often presented her with winter holiday gifts of big baskets of various goodies. These were usually sent on behalf of Dr. Bartoletty or his colleagues. Alla kept up a good tradition of sophisticated toasts at the dinner table in celebration or commemoration of various events.

Despite her relatively upbeat lifestyle (unusual for a low-income Russian immigrant), Alla always longed for her late husband, Victor. She told me that among the many fine male colleagues and acquaintances she met through her life, she felt Victor fared the best, judging from his moral, intellectual, and physical traits.

Alla became good friends with the director of Pittsburgh's Opera, and I believe she even somewhat influenced the staging of the opera *Eugene Onegin*, which premiered in the fall of 2009 at Carnegie Hall of Pittsburgh. I know the director visited Alla one time and often sent her personal invitations to the performances.

Alla liked to invite her friends and colleagues to her apartment for "Russian tea," which was code for lunches or dinners she prepared herself and served with exquisite tableware. The invitees always enjoyed these parties and reciprocated with their own invitations to Alla.

Although Alla was already in a rehabilitation/nursing facility when *Eugene Onegin* premiered, I managed to take her to the performance, which she enjoyed. In the facility, Alla continued her *kultuträger* (German for someone promoting culture) activities. At her request, I made several paper signs with slogans written in Latin such as "*Dum Spiro Spero*" (Hope Until You Breath). We placed the signs in the facility hallways.

The director of the Pittsburgh Opera did not know about Alla's condition, and long after she was placed in the nursing home, he kept leaving messages on her answering machine with invitations to performances.

In respect for Alla and in appreciation of her activities, the radiology department of Forbes Health Center in Monroeville posthumously dedicated a golden leaf with her name on it for the "Golden tree," which Forbes arranges for their most esteemed colleagues. The Temple David of Monroeville also dedicated a golden leaf for Alla on their tree.

My mother was not religious in a traditional sense, but she enjoyed attending services at the reform temple in Monroeville. The opportunity to freely socialize with people of the same religion and/ or ethnic origin was perhaps the main reason Alla attended the services. In the Soviet Union, we were essentially deprived of this opportunity. She also appreciated the profound role religion played in peoples' lives and the philosophical significance of monotheism. She was always puzzled about the reasons for enmity among people of different religions. Her thoughts about it could be expressed as, "Why hate each other when the Almighty God is one and the same for all?"

"She was a real lady," said the manager of the Borough Building where Alla rented her last apartment.

Alla in the United States

Alla's first Thanksgiving dinner.
On the left of her is daughter-in-law Ada
and four-year-old granddaughter Vita (1982).

**Alla with Lyuba Model, a clothing and leather designer from Moscow and a former neighbor.
She recognized Alla after twenty-five years (1982).**

Alla worked on a computer at the Forbes pharmacy during her first volunteering assignment.

FORBES REGIONAL HEALTH CENTER

2570 Haymaker Road • Monroeville, Pennsylvania 15146 • 412/858-2000

COPY

April 20, 1993

University of Pittsburgh
Medical Center
DeSoto at O'Hara Street
Pittsburgh, PA 15213

Attn: Lynette Taylor-Griego

RE: DR. ALLA DUNAYEVSKAYA

Dear Ms. Taylor-Griego:

I am writing on behalf of Dr. Alla Dunayevskaya. I understand that she is applying as an interpreter for Russian-speaking patients.

Dr. Dunayevskaya works at Forbes Regional Hospital. She was instrumental in providng care for a pregnant patient, a recent immigrant from Russia and a large Russian family consisting of eight children, also recent immigrants from Russia. Dr. Dunayevskaya not only helped bridge the communication gap between our physicians and the Russian-speaking patients but provided invaluable interpretations of the childrens' medical immunization records. This interpretation allowed the physicians to complete the pre-school examinations and enter the children into the appropriate grades without interruption.

I have utmost confidence in Dr. Dunayevskaya's abilities and willingness to help provide appropriate medical care. I believe she will be a valuable addition to your medical service.

Thank you very much.

Sincerely,

Carey T. Vinson, MD, MPM
Medical Utilization Director

CTV/dd
cc: Alla Dunayevskaya

Member of Forbes Health System

A support letter for Alla to enter the medical service staff of the Forbes Hospital (1993).

Alla near her apartment on Cambridge Square Drive (ca. 1985).

Alla with her first car, a Chevrolet Vega (1987).

DUNAYEVSKAYA, ALLA, radiologist; b. Odessa, USSR, July 25, 1920; came to U.S., 1982; d. Leo and Isabella (Feldman) Shmulyan; m. Victor Dunayevsky, (dec. 1965); 1 child, Valery Dunnevsky. MD, Med. Inst. Rostov-Don, Russia, 1947. Resident in radiology Inst. for Qualification fo Physicians, Leningrad, 1948; resident in roentgen diagnosis Roentgeno Radiol. Inst., Moskow, 1951, 53, 64; resident in radiol. diagnoses of cardi- ovascular diseases Acad. Med. Sci. of Surgery of Cardiovascular Diseases, Moscow, 1969; resident in radiol. diagnosis of bone and joint diseases Radiol. Inst. for Qualification of Physicians, Kiev, 1977; mgr. radiology Dist. Polyclinic, Murmansk, Russia, 1948-60; chief radiologist Council of Trade Union of Health Resorts of Latvien Rep., Russia, 1961-81; vol. Forbes Reg. Health Ctr., Pitts., 1982-85; researcher in med. statistics and quality as- surance Forbes Health Sys., Pitts., 1985—; cons. in field. Contbr. articles to profl. jours. Mem. AAUW, Internat. Womens Club. Jewish. Office: Forbes Health Systems 2570 Haymaker Rd Monroeville PA 15146

Alla was a biographee of Marquis's Who's Who of American Women, seventeenth edition (1991–1992).

Alla is serving a dinner for her Russian emigrant friends, Pavel Shulikov (with mustache) and his wife, Lyuda (on left with son), Natasha (daughter of Alla's friend, Yuri Umilyanovsky), and her ex-husband on a visit from Moscow (ca. 1998).

Alla's childhood friend, Yuri Umilyanovsky, who lived in Moscow (ca. 1955).

Alla in her apartment (ca. 1998).

Alla in her apartment with the artwork from Riga:
two wood inlay boards depicting the famous Riga Cathedral (ca. 2002).

A section of Alla's apartment with portraits of Einstein, Witold Shmulian, and Conrad Röntgen.

Alla with her Monroeville friends at one of her birthday parties. These were usually held in the Italian restaurant on Mosside Boulevard in Monroeville (ca. 2003).

Alla in one of the Forbes radiology offices where she worked sometimes (ca. 2000).

Alla in the radiology department hallway near the wall with posters of radiology pioneers Conrad Röntgen and Marie Skladovska with her husband, Pierre Curie. Alla was the initiator for displaying these posters (ca. 1999).

Dr. Stephan Bartoletty, a radiology chairman at Forbes, and Alla's supervisor for many years (ca. 1998).

Alla in the company of the Forbes and Almar Radiology directors (ca. 2007).

Alla's at her seventy-fifth birthday.

Alla at her eightieth birthday. On the right from her are me, my wife Ada, and in-laws Lena and Karl Shalit (2000). Karl is a decorated WWII veteran.

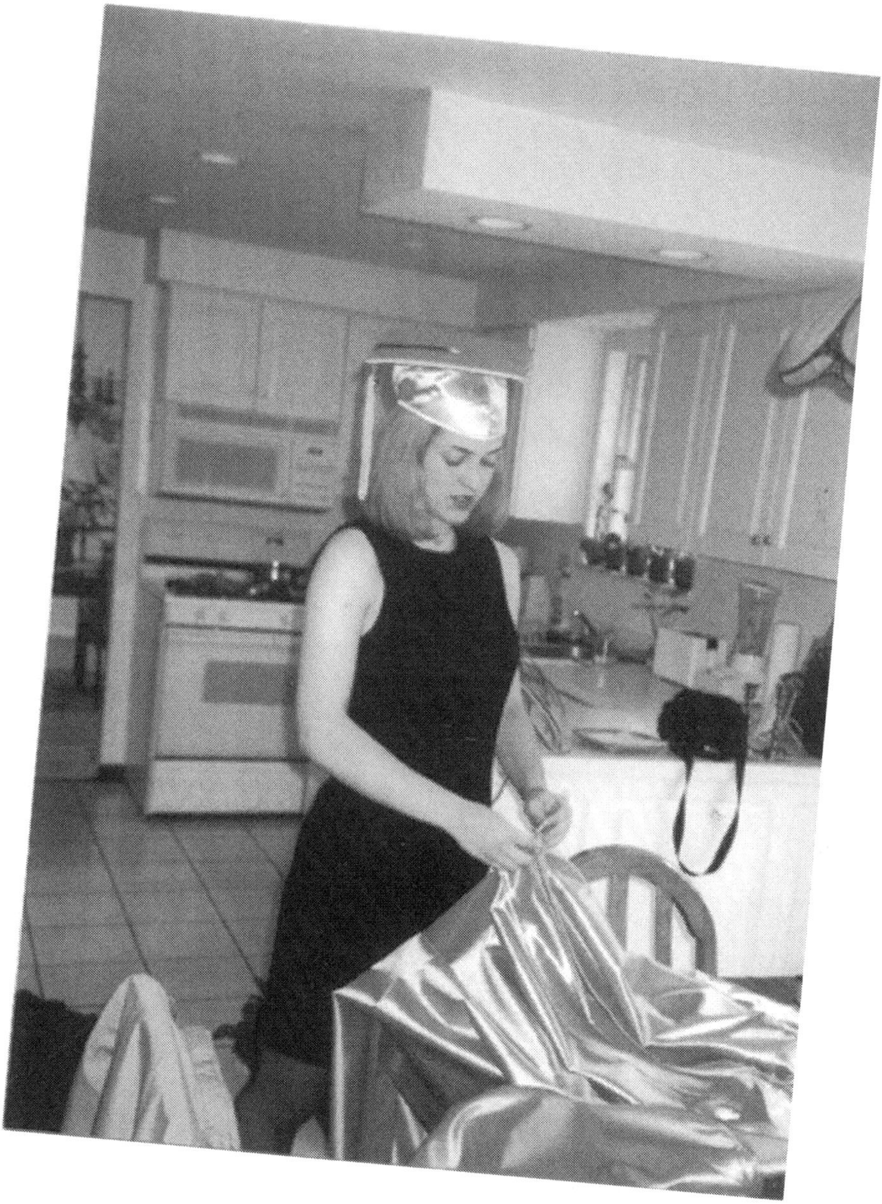

My daughter, Victoria, preparing to her high school graduation ceremony (1996).

„65 ЛЕТ ПОБЕДЫ
В ВЕЛИКОЙ ОТЕЧЕСТВЕННОЙ ВОЙНЕ
1941 – 1945 гг."

А № 0041659

Дунаевская
Алла
Львовна

Указом
Президента Российской Федерации
от 4 марта 2009 г.
награжден(а) юбилейной медалью
„65 ЛЕТ ПОБЕДЫ
В ВЕЛИКОЙ ОТЕЧЕСТВЕННОЙ
ВОЙНЕ 1941 – 1945 гг."

От имени
Президента Российской Федерации
медаль вручена
16 февраля 2010
Генеральный консул
России в Нью-Йорке
М.П.

A medal in commemoration of the sixtieth anniversary
of the victory in the Great Patriotic War, issued to Alla.

It reads: Dunayevskaya Alla Lvovna. By the order of the President of Russian Federation from February 28, 2004, awarded by the jubilee medal "60 Years of Victory in the Great Patriotic War, 1941–1944." From the President of the Russian Federation the medal is handled on April 15, 2005. General Consul of Russia in New York. Signed: S.V. Garmonin.

A photo album (left) with the pictures of Alla's Forbes colleagues. They presented it to her while she was in the nursing home. On right: the photo of Alla's supervisors, Dr. Maureen Bidula and Dr. Ted Molnar proudly exhibiting a portrait of K. Röntgen, which Alla brought to the radiology department (2009).

Mother and me (ca. 1997)

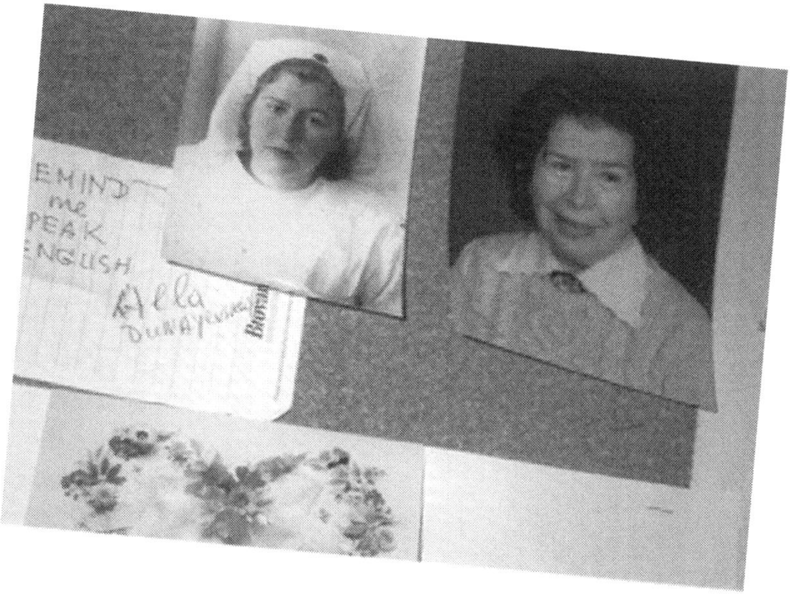

A bulletin board with Alla's pictures near her bed in the nursing home. Seen also is a note requesting people in attendance remind Alla to speak English. After her illness, she began relapsing to Russian, which made communication with her difficult.

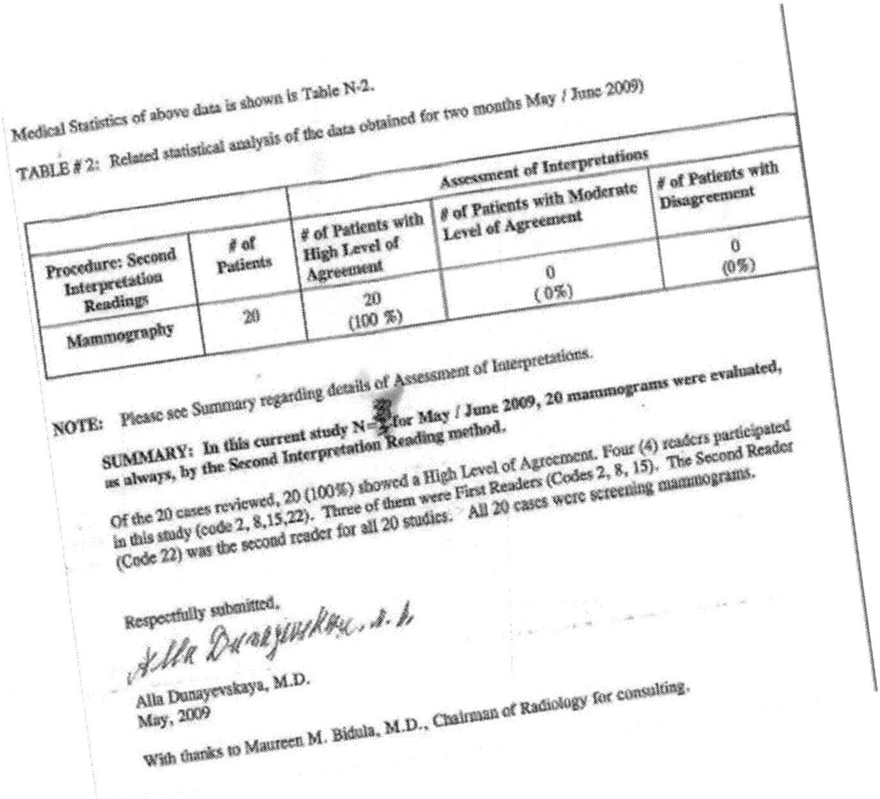

Medical Statistics of above data is shown is Table N-2.

TABLE # 2: Related statistical analysis of the data obtained for two months May / June 2009)

Procedure: Second Interpretation Readings	# of Patients	Assessment of Interpretations		
		# of Patients with High Level of Agreement	# of Patients with Moderate Level of Agreement	# of Patients with Disagreement
Mammography	20	20 (100 %)	0 (0%)	0 (0%)

NOTE: Please see Summary regarding details of Assessment of Interpretations.

SUMMARY: In this current study N=[illegible] for May / June 2009, 20 mammograms were evaluated, as always, by the Second Interpretation Reading method.

Of the 20 cases reviewed, 20 (100%) showed a High Level of Agreement. Four (4) readers participated in this study (code 2, 8,15,22). Three of them were First Readers (Codes 2, 8, 15). The Second Reader (Code 22) was the second reader for all 20 studies. All 20 cases were screening mammograms.

Respectfully submitted,

Alla Dunayevskaya, M.D.

Alla Dunayevskaya, M.D.
May, 2009

With thanks to Maureen M. Bidula, M.D., Chairman of Radiology for consulting.

Excerpts from Alla's last work in quality assurance (May, 2009).

In Memoriam Dr. Alla Dunayevskaya, z"l
July 20, 1920—March 29, 2010

Dr. Alla Dunayevskaya, z"l, was born Alla Shmulian in Odessa (Ukraine), the youngest of three children. Her parents were lawyers and, despite the hardships of post-revolutionary Russia, they were able to provide her with an "aristocratic" childhood, i.e. Alla had a governess and was taught French and how to play the piano. Alla's family was part of the Russian-Jewish intelligentsia. Her maternal grandfather, Solomon Nevelstein was a prominent lawyer in Ukraine. Alla's father Lev Shmulian practiced law and lectured on the subject. He was arrested during the Stalinist purges and died in a gulag. Her mother Isabella achieved a law degree but never practiced. Rather Isabella was a playwright and poet. Isabella's maiden name was Feldman. One of Alla's cousins, Valentin Feldman was prominent in the French resistance during WWII. Alla's oldest brother Vitold was a prominent mathematician who died during WWII in the battle liberating Warsaw in 1944. Alla's younger brother Theodor was an engineer who died in 1998.

Alla became a physician and practiced Radiology in the USSR. After immigrating to the USA, Alla worked for many years in the Medical Director's office at Forbes Regional Hospital. Alla was married to Viktor Dunaevsky and they had one son named Valery. He and his wife have one daughter, named Victoria after her grandfather. Victoria is a physician practicing in Pittsburgh.

Valery Dunayevsky thinks of his mother as a star in the motion picture entitled "The Life of Alla". He will remember her as one of the stars that light up the night and that will shine for everyone forever.

Zichrona l'vrakhah, may her memory be as a blessing.

(*Editor's note*: Thank you to Dr. Richard Myerowitz for producing this excerpt from the eulogy delivered by Valery. The full text is available at www.tdnow.org/watts/Alla.pdf.)

Excerpts from Temple David bulletin article in memoriam of Alla.

A thoughtful contribution has been made by

Joan Paul

201 Curtis Street

Pittsburgh PA 15235

to the Rabbi's Mitzvah fund of

Temple David

In memory of the shining life and blessed memory

of

Dr. Alla Dunayevskaya

Temple David of Monroeville, PA, announced a donation in the memory of Alla.

Rabbi Barbara Simons from Temple David in Monroeville, PA, officiated at Alla's funeral (2010).

Alla's grave marker in the Jewish section of Homewood Cemetery in Pittsburgh, PA (2010). A lower portion of the inscription reads, "Your loving image, kindness and inspiration will always live in our hearts."

Page 1 of 1

Cemetery Visit

From: krgesuale <krgesuale@comcast.net>
To: valdunay <valdunay@aol.com>
Subject: Cemetery Visit
Date: Fri, Aug 12, 2011 12:20 pm

Hello Val

I wanted to let you know that Jeanne, my wife Robin, and I went to the cemetery to visit your mom. I was a nice day and we had a great visit discussing the impact that your mom had on our lives. It is truly these things that make life eternal!

One of the things that we discussed was just how proud your mom was when she earned her American Citizenship. She took me to her apartment to show me her documents, and the American Flags on her TV set. I noticed that one of the graves near her had a small flag waving in the breeze. I thought that perhaps your mom would like that, and I wanted to return and place a small flag there. I would not do this without your permission so I am asking you what your feelings are about this.

Thanks again for sharing your mother's memories with us. She was truly special!

Warmest Regards
Ken Gesuale (Director, Forbes)

A message from the Forbes director to me upon visiting Alla's gravesite (2010).

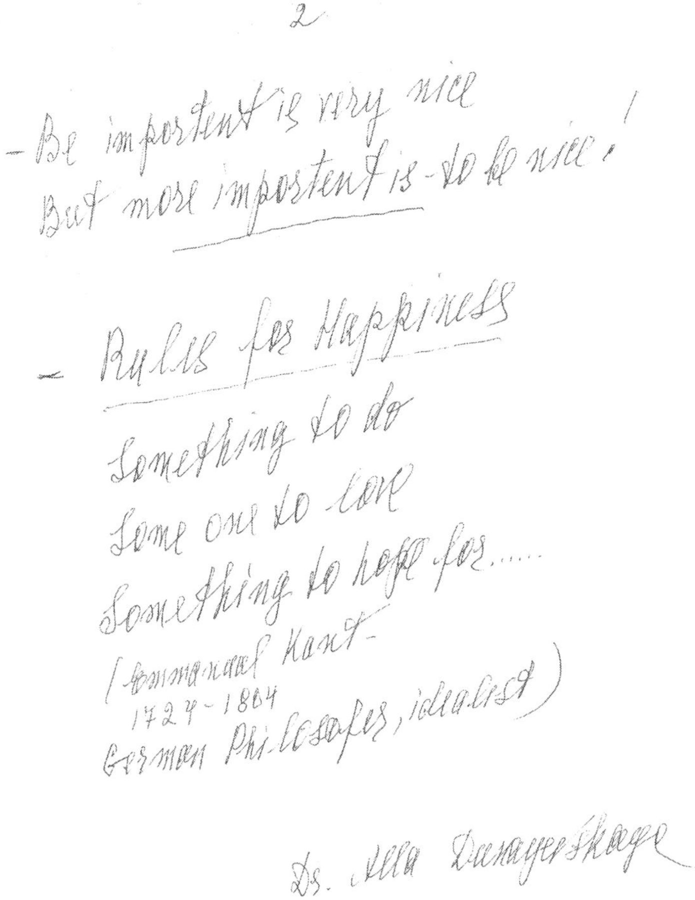

2

- Be importent is very nice
But more impostent is - to be nice!

- Rules for Happiness

Something to do
Some one to love
Something to hope for.....
(Emmanuel Kant-
1724-1804
German Philosofer, idealist)

Dr. Alla Danayevskaya

Several favorable quotations of Alla.

Trees for Israel
כי תבאו אל הארץ ונטעתם
"When you shall come to the land you shall plant trees."— Leviticus 19:23
Three Trees Planted Through Hadassah In Memory of
Alla Dunayevskaya

Alla in the Pittsburgh Carnegie Hall.

APPENDIX A

Alla's brother, Witold Shmulian, was a renowned mathematician and a Soviet Army officer. He was killed at the liberation of Warsaw during WWII.

Translation from: Krein, M.G. [22]

During the difficult time of the Great Patriotic War, many Soviet scientists and mathematicians joined the army. Here is what one of them, Witold L. Shmulian, wrote to me in the summer of 1942:

"I am writing this letter at the top of the church. Here I conduct an observation of a disposition of the German troops. In the morning I was at another observation position and also was involved in detection of the coordinates of the targets…"

The letter ended unconventionally.

"I will send you soon a letter reporting on my latest research."

It is evident Shmulian meant the results of mathematical research he conducted continuously, even on the front during periods of relative calm.

On June 16, 1943, during a radio transmission about the scientists serving on the front, A. N. Kolmogorov[13] highlighted the uninterrupted scientific activity of Shmulian. It was also Kolmogorov who went on to present for posthumous publication the last of Shmulian's written work. A *doctorant* of the Steklov Institute of Mathematics, Shmulian and a group of his coworkers joined the military service at the beginning of the war and went a long way from Moscow to the walls of Warsaw. On August 29, 1944, he would have turned thirty, but a few days prior, he fell heroically and was buried in a common grave in Prague, a Warsaw suburb.

In the battles for the city of Sevsk in 1943, Shmulian was awarded a medal for bravery, and in 1944, for his participation in a Kovel operation, he received an Order of the Great Patriotic War. In the papers accompanying the awards, it was reported that "despite the fire and bombing from the enemy aircraft, Lieutenant Shmulian has always timely located the targets." Again, "During the battles for Kovel, started on July 7, Lieutenant Shmulian enabled a precision setting of the firepower systems of the artillery regiment. Based on his data, there were two anti-tank guns and seven machine guns eliminated, one observation position and two bunkers destroyed, and fire from two mortar batteries of the enemy was suppressed."

From the letters Shmulian wrote from the front and from the memories of his regiment's fellow colonel, G. P. Tarasov, emerges a vibrant image of a patriot and warrior-mathematician. A boundless thirst for knowledge that always distinguished him grew even deeper and more profound in the army. Before the army his passion for mathematics gave the impression he was a person who stayed far from the realities of life.

Meanwhile artillerist Shmulian, after becoming a commander of the artillery regiment, very soon won the confidence of his superiors and his charges. He studied special geodetic literature (his letters from the front show multiple requests for more new literature in that field) and put all topological reconnaissance on serious scientific footing. As an officer and mentor, he also taught his charges that discipline. At the front he gave lectures on probability theory to his fellow officers. Shmulian

[13] A. N. Kolmogorov, an academician of the USSR Academy of Sciences, was a preeminent mathematician of the twentieth century.

introduced and his superiors accepted a number of valuable proposals related to camouflage, setting false fire positions, etc.

Throughout a considerable mail exchange Shmulian conducted with his friends, relatives, and colleagues, he always reminded them what a joy the books delivered to him on the front gave him and what a hunger he had for them. He reread all the works of Turgenev, the novels of Chekhov and Gorky, and the poems of Lermontov and Nekrasov. He swallowed books on the history of the Middle Ages and the history of the First World War on the Middle East. Although he was proficient in reading German and English scientific literature, he thoroughly studied a self-tutoring book on French, which accidentally came into his hands. Nevertheless he always retained a passion for mathematics.

In the letters to me, W. L. Shmulian kept asking about new results from his colleagues and requested I send him new books on mathematics. In the spring of 1942, I sent him a recently published book, authored by me and F. R. Gantmacher, *The Oscillating Matrices and Small Oscillations of the Mechanical Systems.* It is doubtful Shmulian would have spent time on a book so far removed from his scientific interests in peacetime, but we later found out he studied it in detail. Moreover he sent a long list of necessary corrections and improvements that were utilized in the second edition of that book in 1950.

The student years of W. L. Shmulian coincided with the restoration of the Odessa State University, which was based on the former Institute of People Education and the Physics-Chemical-Mathematics' Institute. When I met W. L. Shmulian in 1934, he was already the strongest student at his faculty. He was interested in the fields of theory of measure and integral that far exceeded the boundaries of the official program. Upon applying to the graduate school in 1936, he presented a treatise on the abstract integral of Freshet. In this treatise he provided a detailed proof of one of the results of the theory that Freshet himself lacked.

In the 1936–37 school year I began a lecture course on the theory of the linear operators in Banach spaces. For the first time the elements of a theory of cones were presented. At the same time I switched my seminar on the theory of integral equations toward the study of the geometry of the Banach spaces. One of the most active participants of that seminar was Shmulian. He immediately became interested first in the problems of a Banach sphere and then in the general questions of the geometry of the convex and ordinary convex pluralities in the Banach and associated spaces. In that area he devised a number of elegant solutions that continue to be studied and generalized by Soviet and foreign mathematicians.

Of all the participants from our seminar, Shmulian was the only one who understood the new opportunities of the general theory of linear topological spaces. He alone devoted to this subject a lot of important studies. During the very short time from 1937 to 1941, he published nearly twenty papers. Even on the front, Shmulian did not stop his studies, which he presented in the form of papers and letters sent to the Steklov Institute. A portion of these was published during the war years in the *Doklades (Treatises) of the AN USSR* and in the *Mathematics' Collection.* Another portion remained in the manuscripts (twelve papers and several letters). Still it is quite possible Shmulian had no time to reflect in these journals all his ideas and intentions. One can judge this from a note in one of his letters to me. "Have you paid any attention that, although my latest results have their former abstract character, they already have been targeted toward the study of the concrete things (a theorem of Bochner, theorems of Tauber)?" Unfortunately one could not establish what Shmulian had in mind.

In a photograph from the front, the face of a young man filled with vigor and twinkling eyes looks at us. There are no doubts, however, he understood the whole enormity of the ongoing historical battle and considered he might not be able "to have the opportunity to continue his mathematical work...One would have desired that somebody continue these studies. It would be pitiful if my undertakings were stopped in their tracks."

The undertakings of Witold did not stop. They developed in the works of a new generation of mathematicians. Meanwhile the memory about a talented mathematician and wonderful person lives in the hearts of his friends.

M. G. Krein

Google Translate

12/29/10 3:08 PM

Witold Lvovich Schmulian

From Wikipedia, the free encyclopedia

Witold Lvovich Schmulian (Russian Витольд Львович Шмульян, in other transliteration also Šmulian, * August 29 1914 , † 1944 in Prague (Warsaw)) was a Russian mathematician .

Schmulian achieved in 1936 his first degree in mathematics at the State University of Odessa and continued his studies with Mark Grigorievich Krein gone, his interest in the functional analysis , especially for the geometry in Banach spaces , aroused. In the period from 1937 to 1941, he has published 20 works.

Schmulian then entered the military service, but continued his research, as far as possible away, and shared his findings and articles, in letters to the Steklov Institute with. The pressure of his last work was supported by Andrei Nikolaevich Kolmogorov prepared more than he already did not live. Schmulian fell in 1944, a few days before his thirtieth birthday in Prague, where he was buried.

The set of Eberlein-Šmulian and the set of Krein-Šmulian have his name associated with.

Sources

- MG Krein: *Vitol'd L'vovich Shmul'yan* Russian Mathematical Surveys, Volume XX (2), pages 127-129 (in Russian version in the Успехи математических наук found a picture of Schmulian)
- DA Raikov: *The work of VL Shmul'yan on topological vector spaces*, Russian Mathematical Surveys, Volume XX (2), pages 130-141

Retrieved from " http://de.wikipedia.org/wiki/Witold_Lwowitsch_Schmulian "
Categories : men | Russian | Mathematicians (20th century) | Born 1914 | Died in 1944

- This page was last updated on 31 December 2009 at 18:57 clock changed.
- Text is available under the license "Creative Commons Attribution / Share Alike available, additional conditions may be applicable. Details are included in the terms of use described.
Wikipedia ® is a registered trademark of the Wikimedia Foundation, Inc.

- Privacy Policy
- About Wikipedia
- Imprint

Some information about Witold Shmulian gleaned from the web.

Математический Институт им. В. А. СТЕКЛОВА

Москва 5, ... 2-46-00

15 „ Октября 1940 г.

№ 41/М-13/33

СПРАВКА

Выдана Математическим Институтом Академии ...

Ученый секретарь
Математ. ин-та АН СССР

Отв. исполнитель

The certificate confirming acceptance of Witold Shmulian as doctorant of the Steklovs's Mathematics Institute at the USSR Academy of Sciences. Moscow, USSR, October 15, 1940.

(воинское звание)

(фамилия, имя и отчество)

Вам, участнику боев за освобождение города КОВЕЛЬ, за отличные боевые действия приказом Верховного Главнокомандующего Маршала Советского Союза товарища СТАЛИНА объявлена благодарность.

Командир части

The certificate of appreciation to W. Shmulian for his combat successes. It reads, "To Lieutenant Witold Lvovich Shmulian. To you, the participant of the battles for liberation of the city of Kovel, for excellent fighting operations, an appreciation is announced by the Supreme Commander Marshal of the Soviet Union comrade Stalin.
Signed: Commander of the detachment (signature).

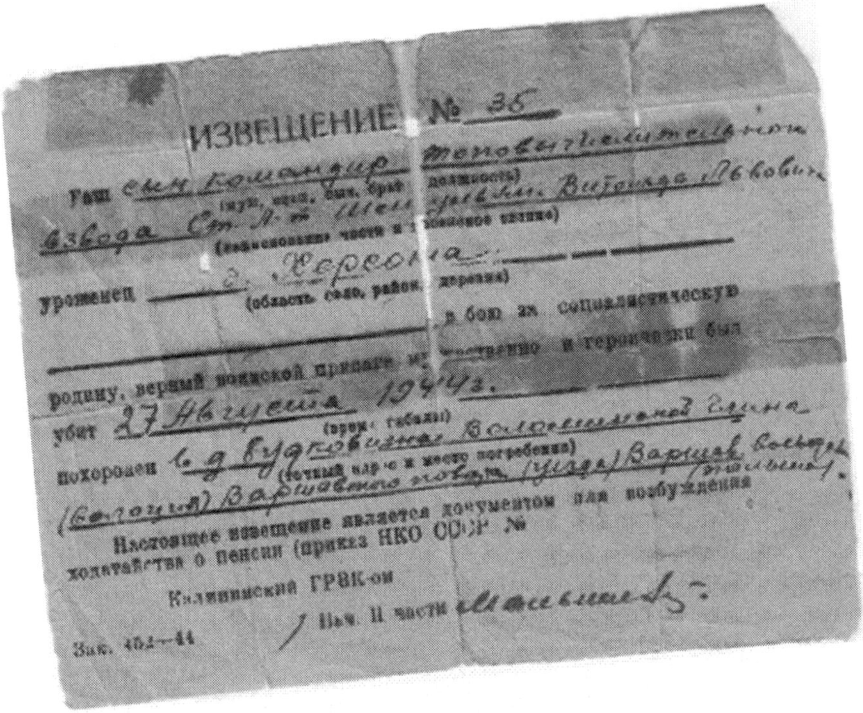

ИЗВЕЩЕНИЕ № 35

Ваш сын командир топовычислительного
(чин, звание, должность)
взвода Ст. л-т Шмульян Витольд Львович
(наименование части и воинское звание)
г. Херсона
уроженец (область, село, район, деревня)
в бою за социалистическую родину, верный воинской присяге, мужественно и героически был убит 27 Августа 1944 г.
(время гибели)
похоронен в д. Будковизна Волошинской Глина (Волошия) Варшавского повята (уезда) Варшав. воеводства (Польша).
(точный адрес и место погребения)

Настоящее извещение является документом для возбуждения ходатайства о пенсии (приказ НКО СССР №

Калининский ГРВК-ом

Нач. II части Малышев

Зак. [illegible]—44

The notice of death of W. Shmulian. It reads, "Notification #35. Your son, the commander of a recognizance platoon, Sr. Lieutenant Shmulian Witold Lvovich, born in the city of Kherson, in the fight for the socialistic motherland, faithful to the military oath, was courageously and heroically killed on August 27, 1944. He was buried in the village Budkovizna of Voloshinskaja Glina (Voloshia), Warsaw District, Poland. This notification is a basis to apply for a pension (by the order of NKO , Peoples' Commissar of Defense, of the USSR #). Kalinin's GRVK (district military commissariat).
Signed: Chief of II department, Malyshev.

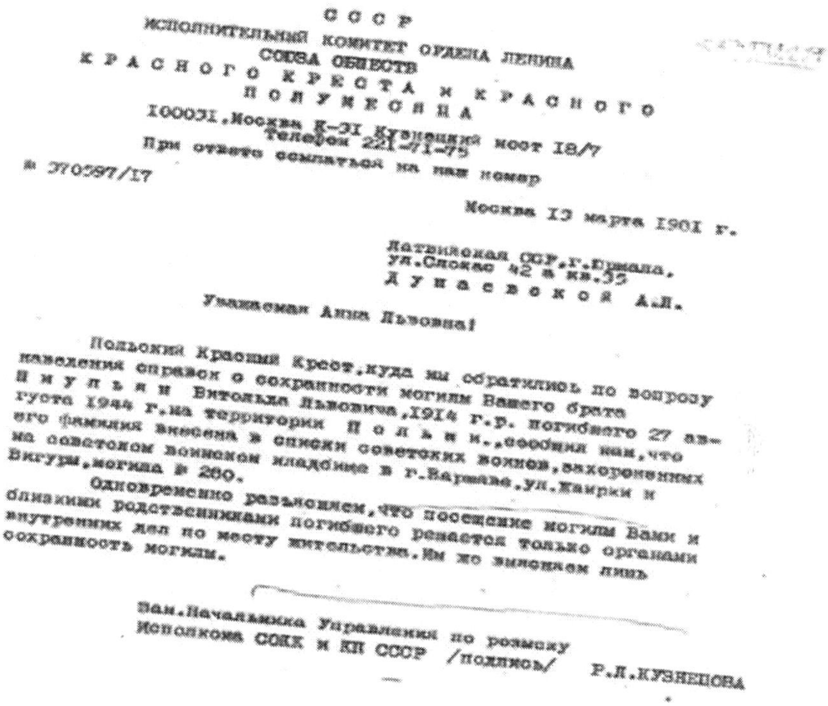

СССР
ИСПОЛНИТЕЛЬНЫЙ КОМИТЕТ ОРДЕНА ЛЕНИНА
СОЮЗА ОБЩЕСТВ
КРАСНОГО КРЕСТА И КРАСНОГО
ПОЛУМЕСЯЦА
I0003I, Москва К-3I Кузнецкий мост I8/7
Телефон 22I-7I-75
При ответе ссылаться на наш номер
№ 370597/I7

Москва I3 марта I98I г.

Латвийская ССР, г. Юрмала,
ул. Слокас 42 а кв. 35
Дунаевской А.Л.

Уважаемая Анна Львовна!

Польский Красный Крест, куда мы обратились по вопросу наведения справок о сохранности могилы Вашего брата Шмульяна Витольда Львовича, I9I4 г.р. погибшего 27 августа I944 г. на территории Польши, сообщил нам, что его фамилия внесена в списки советских воинов, захороненных на советском воинском кладбище в г. Варшаве, ул. Жвирки и Вигуры, могила № 280.

Одновременно разъясняем, что посещение могилы Вами и близкими родственниками погибшего решается только органами внутренних дел по месту жительства. Мы же выясняем лишь сохранность могилы.

Зам. Начальника Управления по розыску
Исполкома СОКК и КП СССР /подпись/ Р.Л. КУЗНЕЦОВА

A statement of the USSR's Red Cross reads, "The Polish Red Cross states that the name of Witold Shmulian, who was killed in the territory of Poland on August 27, 1944, is retained in the list of the Soviet soldiers buried in the Soviet military cemetery in Warsaw, Zhvirki Str., grave site #280."

Witold Shmulian in a soldier coat.

Witold Shmulian promoted to the rank of officer in November of 1941. Last rank was senior lieutenant (1944).

Vera Gantmacher, wife of Witold Shmulian, and also a mathematician. Right: a note from Isabella on the back side of the photograph. It reads: "During the war, Vera perished in Odessa in 1942."

APPENDIX B

On anti-Semitism

This section is not intended to provide a comprehensive review of the subject. It compiles comments on the related subjects as they were highlighted throughout the book.

The fact Yagoda and many other workers of the USSR security apparatus were of Jewish descent has been used by anti-Semites to identify Jews with Bolshevism and, based on this canard, to promote an anti-Jewish agenda. This thinking led to the genocide of Jews during WWII, and it continues to be the justification today.

The falseness of this canard can be exposed on several levels. First of all, the majority of Jews were certainly not Bolsheviks[14]. "In 1922,

[14] In 1903 the Russian Social Democratic Labor Party split into two factions: the Bolsheviks and the Mensheviks. Bolsheviks, meaning "belonging to the majority," were led by Vladimir Lenin, while Julius Martov took control of the Mensheviks, meaning "belonging to the minority." Party membership was the main cause of the original divide between the Bolsheviks and the Mensheviks. The Mensheviks wanted to build a party modeling it on Western European social democratic parties with the inclusion of anyone sharing Marxist ideals in the party. Lenin and the Bolsheviks on the other hand believed in an organization of professional revolutionaries characterized by a rigid adherence to the leadership of the central committee and based on the principles of democratic centralism. Lenin believed the only way for communism to succeed in Russia was by revolution. Martov disagreed. Instead he wanted to keep the ruling party in power and bring communism into the country slowly through democratic elections.

they (Jews) reached their maximum representation in the party (not that they found a coherent group) when, at 15 percent, they were second only to ethnic Russians with 65 percent." [16] These were nominal, non-religious Jews who were ideologically equal to other Bolsheviks of various ethnicities. They built their drive based on a platform of Marxism that, toward the end of the nineteenth century, was well entrenched in the ethnically Russian revolutionary circles. For example, Leon Trotsky was introduced to Marxism by his Russian girlfriend. Also some Jews served in the anti-Bolshevik White Guard.

The October Revolution brought about a tremendous upheaval in Russian Jewry. Consisting mainly of the urban middle class, it was ruined economically; naturally majority of it could not be sympathetic to communism. Sometime in 1918, while Ukraine was under German occupation, the rabbis of Odessa ceremonially anathematized (pronounced herem against) against Trotsky, Zinoviev, and other Jewish Bolshevik.[37]

Even though many Jews reached high ranks in the Communist Party after the revolution, it was only a small minority. In his own locale where he was born, he (Trotsky) was hated intensely and accused of robbing and plundering the Jews. It is related that the chief Rabbi of Moscow, Rabbi Jacob Maze, once appeared before Trotsky to plead on the behalf of the Russian Jews. Trotsky answered him, as he had done on various occasions, that he was a Communist and did not consider himself a Jew. To this Rabbi Maze replied: "*Trotsky makes the revolutions, and the Bronsteins pay the bills.*" [38]

It is very questionable to assert, as many (not only anti-Semites) do, that Marx was a Jew, and thus Marxism is a Jewish enterprise. Although his parental lineage is Jewish, he is a scion of a Protestant family (albeit converted), and in the ideology of his early work *Zur Judenfrage* (*On the Jewish Question*) he espouses anti-Jewish sentiment by declaring the Jewish religion as a spiritual reflection of Jewish economic life. He said money "is the jealous god of Israel, in face of which no other god may exist." Having thus figuratively equated "practical Judaism" with "hucksterism," Marx concludes that "the Christians have become Jews" and that ultimately it is humankind (both Christians and Jews) that needs to emancipate itself from ("practical") Judaism. Some researchers see *Zur Judenfrage* as a precursor to *Mein Kampf*, while others find some redeemable qualities in it. The proverb "With such a friend who needs an enemy?" is very suitable in this case. Through Marx, Jews suffered from both the Left and Right.

The Bolsheviks represented a radical branch of Russian revolutionary movements (including antimonarchist and anarchist) whose associates through the entire nineteenth century, beginning with the Decembrist Mutiny in 1825, were overwhelmingly pure Russian (at least not Jews) and included many from the privileged classes. Also the Russian Savely Morozov, grandson of a serf and one of Russia's richest industrialists, and Russian writer Maxim Gorky (*Aleksey Peshkov*) financially supported the Bolsheviks. Their donations, however, were not the only source of the Bolsheviks' treasury. In his fund-raising efforts, Lenin relied also on armed robberies conducted by a flamboyant revolutionary named Koba (an early party pseudonym of Josef Djugashvili/J. Stalin) and his Caucasian bandit revolutionaries.

Georgy Plekhanov, a leader of the Mensheviks, which also had a strong Jewish presence, was outraged knowing the Bolsheviks sanctioned holdups. (One raid on the Tiflis Post Office raised 250,000 rubles; the gang used bombs during the robbery, and several people were killed.) Plekhanov threatened to cut off all relations with the Bolsheviks. It was only later, in the revolutionary period of 1917, the Bolsheviks got alleged financing from Germans and New York bankers.

The anti-Semites tried to assert Jews' unprecedented notoriety by referring to the killing of Tsar Nicholas II and his family. Although it is not proven Lenin and Sverdlov gave orders to kill the tsar family, it is known that a leader of the execution squad, Yurovsky, was Jewish (who in fact converted to Lutheranism). Although certainly not condoning this event from either point of view, one should be reminded that not the Jews but the Russians were the first tsar killers in Russia, even in the considered time period.

In 1881, after several attempts, ethnically Russian members of a revolutionary organization called *Narodnaya Volya* (The People Will) finally managed to mortally wound the liberal monarch Alexander II, who in 1861 instituted the emancipation of serfs and introduced other reforms. At the time this event set off anti-Jewish pogroms and suppression of liberties. The Jews, as always, suffered for the ills of society.

During WWI Russia experienced tremendous losses of fighting men and a decline in the economy. Fearing a violent revolution, on February 28, 1917, the army command demanded the abdication of Tsar Nicolas II. This event would be considered a second Russian revolution—the February Revolution—after the revolution of 1905. With their slogans of the immediate peace (by a recognition of the defeat of Russia) and the distribution of land to the peasants, which appealed more to the masses than the slogans of the other parties, and with their better organization, the Bolsheviks were able on October 25, 1917 to wrestle power from the lawyer Alexander Kerensky's Provisional Government, which was formed after the abdication of the tsar. With this act Russia was plunged in a brutal and murderous four years of civil war during which both sides, Reds representing the revolutionary forces and Whites representing the defenders of the old regime, committed horrible atrocities. In his poem about the revolution, Vladimir Mayakovsky wrote, "The exploded Petersburg went to the bottom as a submarine."

There was a high percentage of Jews among the Bolsheviks' security apparatus, Cheka (an acronym for *chrezvychaynaya komissiya*, Extraordinary Commission, was the first of a succession of Soviet state security organizations), which was formed in the few days after the October Uprising. This is evidenced by:

a) Upward mobility of the Jews in the first postrevolutionary years in all spheres of public life due to a number of factors, not the least of which was a release of pent up energy.[1]

b) An act of redressing the balance after centuries of tsarist oppression. [1]

c) Stalin's use of Jews as pawns in the newly established Soviet republics, considering they would not share the nationalistic inclinations endemic for a given republic. Stalin is attributed with an anecdotal expression about his manipulation of people. "They are my jackasses. I put them wherever I want."

For an anti-Semite, reality has no meaning when it comes to Jews. Under Yagoda, and other Stalin-era Jewish and non-Jewish satraps alike, the Jews suffered not much less than other ethnicities. For example, those poor Bolsheviks, Kamenev, Zinoviev, and many others persecuted by Yagoda, were Jews themselves.

Some historians even consider Stalin's purges leading to a decimation of the old revolutionary guard as a wholly anti-Semitic campaign. The anti-Semites downplay that a real bloodbath started when Ezhov was at the NKVD helm, and Yagoda was the last top-level Jew in the security apparatus. After him all leading positions were occupied by Russians and Mengrel Beria, although a sizable amount of Jewish high- and mid-level officers still remained in the security organs until the early 1950s when they were purged by Stalin.

Along with Jews, other Russian minorities also represented a high percentage of the chekists. In fact the feared first head of the Cheka (a predecessor of NKVD), Felix Dzerzhinsky (the "Iron Felix" as he was called for the uncompromising attitude toward the "enemies" of Revolution), and his first deputy, Vyacheslav Menzhinsky, were from the impoverished Polish nobility, and many other leading chekists were Latvians or Caucasians. The pathology of anti-Semitism as well as other racist ideologies is well-illustrated by Maxim Gorky, who wrote in the early twentieth century that when a Russian thief is caught, people say a thief was caught, but when a Jewish Russian thief is caught, people say a Jew was caught. The unfortunate truth has been that, for an anti-Semite, a Jew is fair game even if he/she is not a thief, rich, a Communist, a Socialist, or even ultraorthodox in strange garb. An example from my experience supports a pervasive alogism of an insidious anti-Semitic malady.

In 1967 I was working at a technologically advanced plant in Riga, Latvia. On one particular June day, which happened to coincide with the Six-Days Arab-Israeli War, a group of other engineers and I went through a model shop. A middle-aged machinist, who happened to be Jewish and was known as an excellent specialist, was working on a lathe. While passing by that machinist, I overheard one of our peers, a Latvian engineer who was always talkative and smart-alecky. He whispered to another engineer, a Russian lady, that it would be good to kill this Jewish machinist now while a war was going on. That way it could easily be written off as the war. A few colleagues giggled uneasily at his suggestion, which they probably mistook for a bad joke.

This example is not to single out Latvians or any other nationality as harboring hatred for Jews. In fact during WWII, despite the mass extermination of Jews in Latvia, there were a number of heroic Latvians who, despite the tremendous risk for their lives, saved Jews as much as they could.

As D. Rayfield writes,

"A few of Dzerzhinsky's formidable henchmen were Russian: Ivan Ksenofontov, a former factory worker and army corporal, chaired revolutionary tribunals and organized mass shootings of hostages...

Dzerzhinsky surrounded himself with fellow Poles, notably a trusted friend from the Warsaw underground in the 1900s, Josef Unshlicht...

Poland that snatched independence in 1917 was a nationalistic country, led by its landed gentry. The Polish Left and Polish Jews who wanted political equality were marginalized by Marshal Pilsudski's state and saw their best chance of power as a Soviet-inspired revolution—hence the prominent role they played in the Cheka.

Latvians were an even more effective ethnic group at both the highest and lowest levels of the Red Army and Cheka....

The motivation of those Jews who worked for the Cheka was not Zionist or ethnic." [16]

Their motivation was the success of a proletarian revolution for all nationalities. The malevolent actions of Cheka were often depicted as a result equivalent to the alien invasion onto the Russian nation and which could not be possible without the Jewish domination in the organization. However, as was showed, not only Jews were running the Cheka/GPU/NKVD. The overwhelming majority of those running day-to-day life in the Gulag camps and who carried out the orders of their superiors were not Jews. In Solzhenitsyn's *One Day in the Life of Ivan Denisowitch*, a brutal guard was immortalized in the novel. This was Russian Lieutenant Volkovoy. Fittingly, the name's root is *volk*, or "wolf" in Russian.

Furthermore one shouldn't forget that in many countries at various times, zealous revolutionaries or secret police from elements within the indigenous population terrorized their own brethren. Recall also what the Frenchman Robespierre did to his countrymen during the bloody French Revolution. If it could happen in a predominantly mono-national, mono-religious, and supposedly enlightened country like France, then what could one expect from the revolution in the immense and "backward" Russia with multiple fault lines, which the eighteenth-century Russian writer Radishchev called a monster[15]?

The anti-Semites only too easily forget how Russia was changed during the time of Ivan the Terrible at the hands of the *oprichina* (his secret police), or in the time of Peter the Great, who built Saint Petersburg by methods not much different than Yagoda employed in the construction of the Belomor Canal. The subject matter of the renowned Russian poet Nikolay Nekrasov's major poems was a verse portrayal of the plight of the Russian peasant during the time of the tsar. One of his poems addressed the suffering of the Russian peasant workers during construction of a Moscow-St. Petersburg Railroad, which according to the poem, was built literally on the bones of Russians.

This is not intended to whitewash the excesses of a Soviet security apparatus whose numerous elements at one time included Jewish extracts. The socioeconomic upheaval into which WWI and the Bolsheviks thrust Russia favored people who found their calling in service to the proletarian revolution (or at least it offered the opportunity to stay in power in the new political order). This justified lowering the moral bar (toward the "enemy" of the revolution or the socialist motherland) and elevated ends over means. Complicity of the security organs in the malevolent actions described here is only one part of the equation. Another part was rooted in the fact that, as described earlier, top leaders of the party and government condoned and sanctioned these abuses, while emulating the will of their master I. Stalin. In particular, it is

[15] The Journey from St. Petersburg to Moscow (in Russian: Путешествие из Петербурга в Москву), published in 1790, was the most famous work by Aleksandr Nikolayevich Radishchev. The book starts with an epigraph about the Beast who is "enormous, disgusting, a hundred maws and barking," meaning the Russian Empire.

known that Lazar Kaganovich (who built the magnificent Moscow metro and introduced the state pension system) and Nikita Khrushchev were among the leading enforcers and perpetrators of the harsh Stalin policies and purges. In turn, Lenin's violent "Red Terror" of the Civil War period set stage for the purges. However, in his testament Lenin warned against Stalin and suggested his removal from leadership.

See page one hundred eighteen. Addressing someone as Jew–face did not mean he or she had some outstanding or stereotypically Jewish facial features. My Uncle Theodor, many members of our family, and many other Jews I knew did not have remarkably Jewish features. That type of address was just an insult and a way to express a scornful attitude toward someone's ethnicity.

One can look into anti-Semitism or racism as a sort of mental health issue because many of the beliefs are not based in reality. Persons infected with this disease become impervious to a realistic perception of and an adequate response to the individual or the fact or object associated with anything Jewish. For example, some Palestinian, Iranian, and Arab leaders have facial features considered stereotypically Jewish. Still Muslim radicals who fit perfectly into the aforementioned images are not called Jew-faces by their brethren or non-Muslim anti-Semites.

That ambiguity and double standard is well played out in the Arthur Miller novel *Focus,* which was written in the mid-1940s when anti-Semitism was common in America. The novel presents a narrative of the travails of two non-Jewish individuals, an insurance company clerk and his female customer. Both assume the other is Jewish, as do their respective employers. The aforementioned ambiguity about the perception of typically Jewish looks and deeds is further exemplified in the plight of German people of mixed racial descent. They are called *Mischlinge* in German. In Nazi Germany one was considered a Jew if he had no fewer than three Jewish grandparents. These people were deprived of their citizenship and the right to serve in government positions or the army. People with one or two Jewish grandparents, under the racial Nuremberg Laws of 1935, fell into the category of the half-Jew (Jewish *Mischling* first degree) and the quarter-Jew (Jewish *Mischling* second degree). A *Mischlinge* status temporarily protected these people from persecution.

Some even received exemptions (*Deutschblütigkeitserclärung*) equating them to full-blooded Germans.[17]

Ironically, a photograph in a Nazi propaganda newspaper depicting the ideal German soldier (blond with blue eyes) was of Werner Goldberg, a man whose father was Jewish. As the war dragged on, though, Nazi politics came to trump military logic, even in the face of the growing *Wehrmacht*'s manpower needs, making it virtually impossible for the *Mischlinge* soldiers to escape the fate of millions of other victims of the Third Reich. This subject of how a Jewish outlook does not match a stereotype is artfully shown in the German-French movie *Europa, Europa*.

Upon finalizing this section one can recall an ironical quote from Einstein: "If my theory of relativity is proven successful, Germany will claim me as a German and France will declare that I am a citizen of the world. Should my theory prove untrue, France will say that I am a German and Germany will declare that I am a Jew."

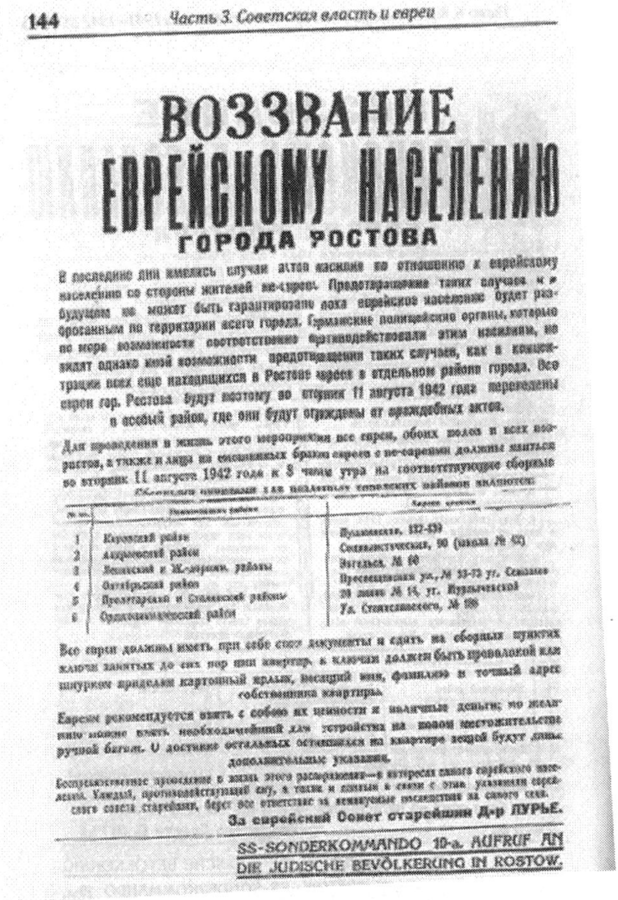

144 Часть 3. Советская власть и евреи

ВОЗЗВАНИЕ
ЕВРЕЙСКОМУ НАСЕЛЕНИЮ
ГОРОДА РОСТОВА

[illegible] ... во вторник 11 августа 1942 года переведены
в особый район, где они будут ограждены от враждебных актов.

[illegible] ... во вторник 11 августа 1942 года к 8 часам утра на соответствующие сборные [illegible]

№	[illegible]	[illegible]
1	Кировский район	[illegible]
2	[illegible] район	[illegible]
3	[illegible] районы	[illegible] № 60
4	Октябрьский район	[illegible]
5	Пролетарский и Сталинский районы	[illegible]
6	[illegible] район	[illegible]

[illegible]

За еврейский Совет старейшин Д-р ЛУРЬЕ.

SS-SONDERKOMMANDO 10-a. AUFRUF AN DIE JUDISCHE BEVÖLKERUNG IN ROSTOW.

<u>To chapter IV (regarding the massacre of Jews in Rostov).</u> **Shown above is the announcement of the German Occupation Authorities to Rostov Jews. It demands they gather on August 11, 1942 in the designated places for resettlement into a special district of the city. (This was under the pretext of protecting them against hostile actions of non-Jewish citizens.) The thousands of assembled Jews (men, women, and children) were then marched and/or brought to the places of execution on the outskirts of Rostov. [4] Police, former Soviet citizens collaborating with Germans, shot the adults with machine guns. The victims were forced to undress before being shot. Some were killed in the "gas vans." The children were poisoned by smearing their lips with strong cyanide. The victims were laid on top of each other in the trenches or pits dug in advance by the captured Red Army prisoners (several hundreds) who were then shot or killed in gas vans.**

APPENDIX C

R. Burns' Epigrams and Epitaphs

Robert Burns [12] Title Introduction Original text	Marshak's [13] Russian adaptation. (Excellent rhyme and substantial retention of the original)	V. Dunaevsky's English adaptation of Marshak's. Copyright © 2012 Valery Victorovich Dunaevsky
On Commissary Goldie's Brains Lord, to account who does Thee call, Or e'er dispute Thy pleasure? Else why within so thick a wall Enclose so poor a treasure.	Господь во всем конечно прав, Но кажется непостижимым , Зачем он создал прочный шкаф С таким убогим содержимым	Lord, your wisdom is beyond dispute. But I can't fathom your intent Of enclosing in a sturdy safe Such a miserable content.

On Wee Johnee Whoe'er thou art, O reader, know, That Death has murdere'd Johnee, Au'here his *body* lies fu'low- For *saul* he ne'er had onie.	Здесь Джон покоится в глуши. Конечно только тело, Но, говорят, оно души И прежде не имело.	Our John, or rather his *body* Is resting here. But it has been said that even in life He had no *soul*, my dear.
Epitaph on a Hen-pecked Squire As father Adam first was fool'd, A case that's still too common, Here lies a man a woman rul'd: The Devil ruled the woman.	С времен Адама все напасти Проистекают от жены. Та, у кого ты был во власти, Была во власти сатаны.	It has been known that All troubles in life Since the time of Adam Come from the wife. Things happened for reason That is clear and level. Your wife, who ruled you, Was ruled by Devil.
To the Portrait of a Religious Person No original text was found in the reviewed Sources. [12, 18]	Нет у него не лживый взгляд. Его глаза не лгут. Они правдиво говорят, Что их хозяин плут.	No, he has not a deceitful gaze. His eyes don't lie or jitter. They are expressing truthfully: Their owner is a cheater.

APPENDIX D

Documents

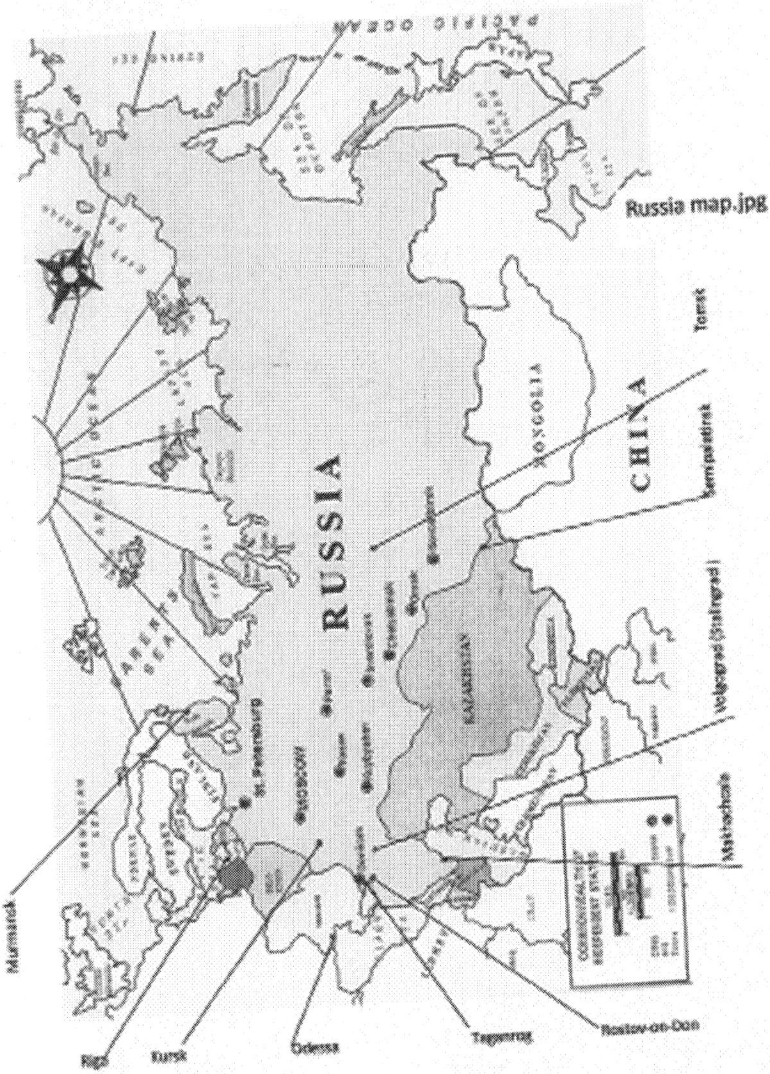

Map of the USSR, which pinpoints the places highlighted in the book.

CURRICULUM VITAE

Name: **Alla Dunayevskaya, M.D.**
Home Address: 112 Cambridge Square Dr., Apt. C
Monroeville, PA 15146
Home telephone: (412) 372-0861
Business Telephone: (412) 856-2350

Birthplace: Odessa, USSR
Citizenship: USA - 1987
Come to America: 1982
Social Security: 184-62-3305

EDUCATION AND TRAINING

Undergraduate Dates Attended	Name and Location of Institution	Degree Received and Year	Major Subject
1938 -1947	Rostov/Don State Medical Institute USSR	Physician - 1947	Medical Treatment - Prophylactic

Graduate Dates Attended	Name and Location of Institution	Degree Received Program	Major Subject
1948 (4 months)	Ministry of Public Health USSR, State Institute for Qualification of physicians Leningrad, USSR	Specialization in radiology	- Physics and technics of x-ray - General and urgent radiology - Roentgendiagnosis of diseases: (pulmonary, heart, and blood vessels, alimentary tract, joints, bones, teeth, kidney, and urogenital system) - Roentgenodiagnosis of children's diseases - Roentgenotherapy

Alla's CV, p.1

Alla Dunaevskaya, M.D.
- 2 -

Post Graduate Dates Attended	Name and location of Institution	Name of Program Director and Discipline
1951 (one month)	Ministry of Public Health RSFSR State Scientific-Research Roentgen-Radiology Institute Moscow, USSR	S. Rainberg, M.D., Professor Fluororoentgenography
1953 (two months)	Ministry of Public Health RSFSR State Scientific-Research Roentgen-Radiology Institute Moscow, USSR	T. Shehter, M.D., Professor Roentgenodiagnosis gastro-intestinal diseases
1963 (one month)	Academy of Medical Science of USSR Institute of Rheumatism Moscow, USSR	V. Zodiev, M.D., Professor Collagen Disease and pathology of bone & joint
1964 (one month)	Ministry of Public Health RSFSR State Scientific-Research Roentgen-Radiology Institute Moscow, USSR	L. Rosenstrorch, M.D., Professor Cholecystography, bronchography
1967 (2.5 months)	Central Institute for Qualification of Physicians Moscow, USSR	U. Socolov, M.D., Professor Qualification in Roentgenology for manager of Roentgen department of regional, district, and city hospitals
1969 (3 weeks)	Academy of Medical Science of USSR, Institute of Surgery of cardiovascular diseases Moscow, USSR	N. Ivanitskaya, M.D., Professor Roentgenodiagnosis of heart diseases
1977 (2.5 months)	Roentgeno-radiology Institute for Qualification of Physicians Kiev, USSR	L. Koval, M.D., Professor Roentgenodiagnosis of bones and joints diseases

Alla's CV, p.2

Alla Dunaevskaya, M.D.
- 3 -

APPOINTMENTS AND POSITIONS

Years Inclusive	Name of Organization	Title
1948 - 1960	District Polyclinic Murmansk, USSR	Head of roentgen department
1961 - 1981	Latvian Republic Council of Trade Union Health Resorts Riga, USSR	Chief Roentgenologist of Latvian Health Resorts

MEMBERSHIPS IN PROFESSIONAL AND SCIENTIFIC SOCIETIES

Years	Organization
1948 - 1960	Roentgeno-Radiology Societies of Murmansk and All-Soviet
1961 - 1982	Roentgeno-Radiology Societies of Latvian Republic and All-Soviet

PROFESSIONAL ACTIVITIES

In the position of chief roentgenologist of Health Resorts of Latvian Republic (USSR), I supervised the medical activity of all radiology departments in the resort's policlinics and sanatoriums. My responsibilities included: control over the professional levels of the medical staff and its upgrading; control over the occupational radiology safety; control over the accuracy of diagnoses; implementation of the new methods of the x-ray examinations; delivery of the related lectures; annual review in all aspects of radiological activities in the resorts of Latvian Republic.

RESEARCH ACTIVITIES

- Scientific-practical work in bones and joints system (roentgenodiagnosis of painful heel)

- Scientific-practical work in cardiovascular pathology (significant contrastless roentgenology examination in diagnosis of the acquired heard defects)

- At the present time, I'm conducting research in medical statistics and quality assurance in Radiology Department of the Forbes Regional Hospital.

LANGUAGE FLUENCY

Russian (mother language)
English

Alla's CV, p.3

Alla Dunaevskaya, M.D.
- 4 -

REFERENCE

Copies of the diplomas translated into English with signature of the state notary

PAPERS (PUBLISHED)

Dunaevskaya A.: Roentgenodiagnosis of painful heel. Vestnik Kurortology of the Latvian Republic Council of Trade Union Health Resort Administration, Riga 1969, USSR.

Dunaevskaya A.: Notes regarding preparations of the roentgenology examinations:
- cholecystography
- gastrointestinal tract
- lumbar and sacral spine

Latvian Republic Council of Trade Union Resort Administration, Riga 1967, 1969, 1975, USSR.

LECTURES

The lectures delivered on the Latvian Republic Health Resorts meetings and the meetings of the Latvian Republic Roentgeno-radiology Society (1963-1981).

1. Roentgenodiagnosis of painful heel.
2. Significant contrastless radiology examination in diagnosis of the acquired heart defects.
3. Roentgenoanatomy and roentgenodiagnosis of the degenerative changes in the spine.
4. Roentgenodiagnosis of the diseases of the larynx.
5. Roentenodiagnosis and methods of examinations of appendicitis.
6. Roentgenodiagnosis and methods of examination of the intestine.
7. Significance of the contrast examination of sinusitis.
8. Professional responsibility of medical staff of the Radiology Department.
9. The problems of the medical deontology (ethics).
10. The rules of preparations to the some complex and contrast examinations.

Along with the above, I updated the medical staff with rhe information about participation tn the All-Soviet and Republics Congresses.

Alla's CV, p.4

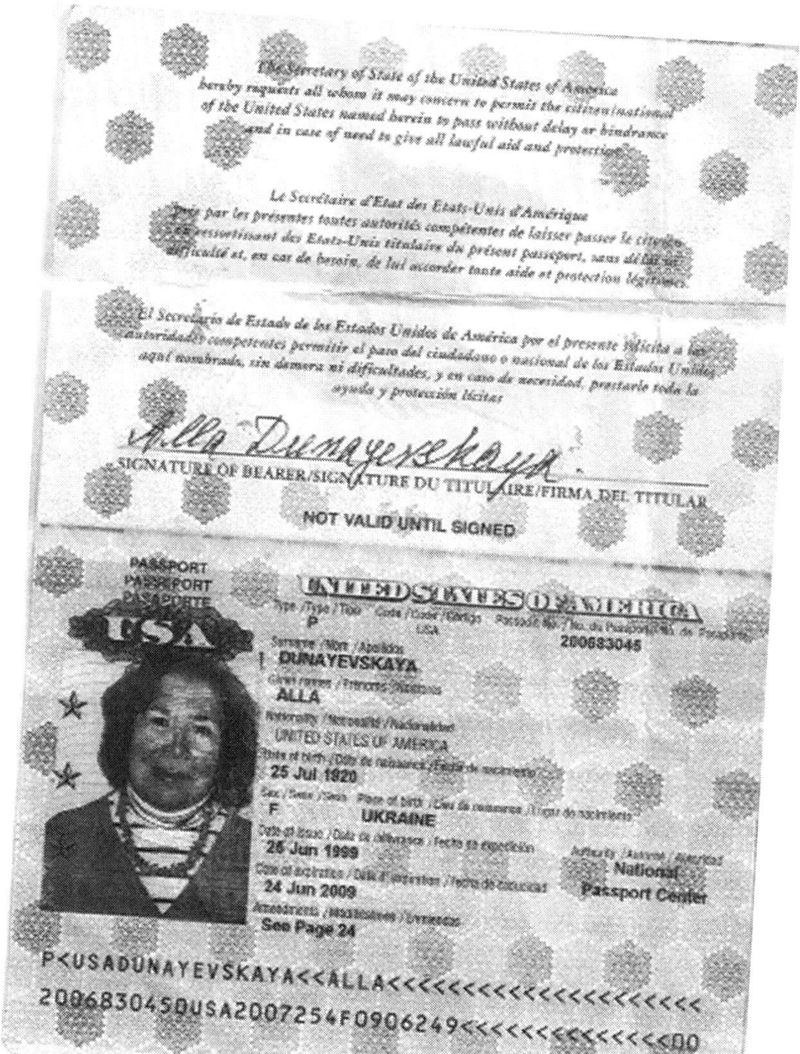
The Secretary of State of the United States of America hereby requests all whom it may concern to permit the citizen/national of the United States named herein to pass without delay or hindrance and in case of need to give all lawful aid and protection.

Le Secrétaire d'Etat des Etats-Unis d'Amérique prie par les présentes toutes autorités compétentes de laisser passer le citoyen ou ressortissant des Etats-Unis titulaire du présent passeport, sans délai ni difficulté et, en cas de besoin, de lui accorder toute aide et protection légitimes.

El Secretario de Estado de los Estados Unidos de América por el presente solicita a las autoridades competentes permitir el paso del ciudadano o nacional de los Estados Unidos aquí nombrado, sin demora ni dificultades, y en caso de necesidad, prestarle toda la ayuda y protección lícitas

Alla Dunayevskaya

SIGNATURE OF BEARER/SIGNATURE DU TITULAIRE/FIRMA DEL TITULAR

NOT VALID UNTIL SIGNED

PASSPORT
PASSEPORT
PASAPORTE
USA
UNITED STATES OF AMERICA
P
USA
200683045
DUNAYEVSKAYA
ALLA
UNITED STATES OF AMERICA
25 Jul 1920
F
UKRAINE
25 Jun 1999
24 Jun 2009
National Passport Center
See Page 24

P<USADUNAYEVSKAYA<<ALLA<<<<<<<<<<<<<<<<<<<<<<<<
2006830450USA2007254F0906249<<<<<<<<<<<<<<00

The last passport of Alla (2009).

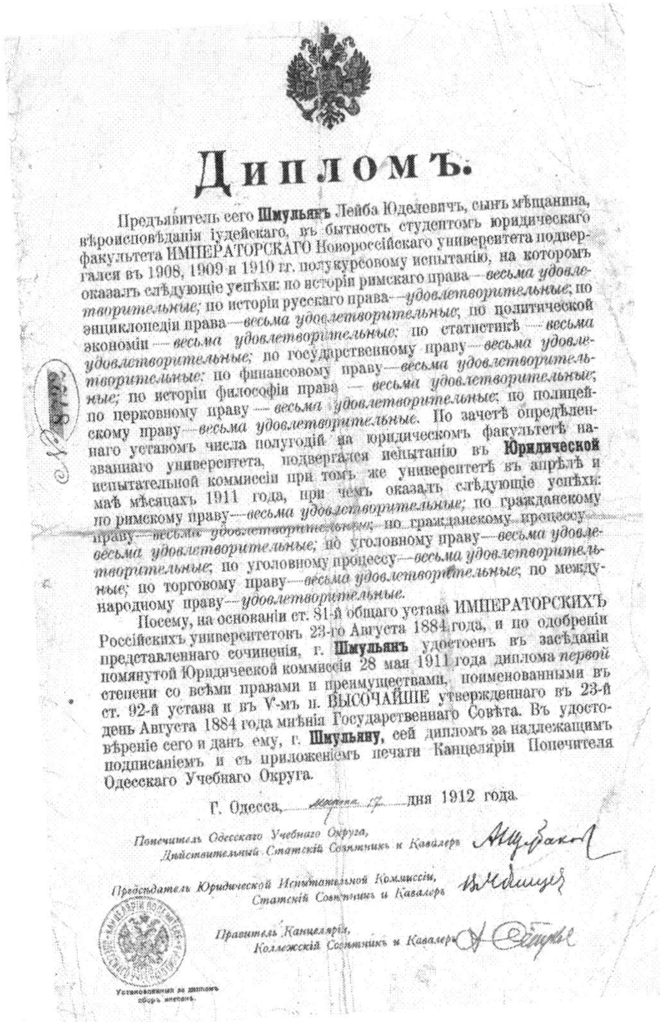

ДИПЛОМЪ.

Предъявитель сего **Шмульянъ** Лейба Юделевичъ, сынъ мѣщанина,
вѣроисповѣданія іудейскаго, въ бытность студентомъ юридическаго
факультета ИМПЕРАТОРСКАГО Новороссійскаго университета подвергался въ 1908, 1909 и 1910 гг. полукурсовому испытанію, на которомъ
оказалъ слѣдующіе успѣхи: по исторіи римскаго права—*весьма удовлетворительные;* по исторіи русскаго права—*удовлетворительные;* по
энциклопедіи права—*весьма удовлетворительные;* по политической
экономіи—*весьма удовлетворительные;* по статистикѣ—*весьма
удовлетворительные;* по государственному праву—*весьма удовлетворительные;* по финансовому праву—*весьма удовлетворительные;* по исторіи философіи права—*весьма удовлетворительные;*
по церковному праву—*весьма удовлетворительные;* по полицей-
скому праву—*весьма удовлетворительные.* По зачетѣ опредѣлен-
наго уставомъ числа полугодій на юридическомъ факультетѣ названнаго университета, подвергался испытанію въ **Юридической**
испытательной коммиссіи при томъ же университетѣ въ апрѣлѣ и
маѣ мѣсяцахъ 1911 года, при чемъ оказалъ слѣдующіе успѣхи:
по римскому праву—*весьма удовлетворительные;* по гражданскому
праву—*весьма удовлетворительные;* по гражданскому процессу—
весьма удовлетворительные; по уголовному праву—*весьма удовлетворительные;* по уголовному процессу—*весьма удовлетворительные;* по торговому праву—*весьма удовлетворительные;* по между-
народному праву—*удовлетворительные.*

Посему, на основаніи ст. 81-й общаго устава ИМПЕРАТОРСКИХЪ
Россійскихъ университетовъ 23-го Августа 1884 года, и по одобреніи
представленнаго сочиненія, г. **Шмульянъ** удостоенъ въ засѣданіи
помянутой Юридической коммиссіи 28 мая 1911 года диплома *первой*
степени со всѣми правами и преимуществами, поименованными въ
ст. 92-й устава и въ V-мъ п. ВЫСОЧАЙШЕ утвержденнаго въ 23-й
день Августа 1884 года мнѣнія Государственнаго Совѣта. Въ удосто-
вѣреніе сего и данъ ему, г. **Шмульяну,** сей дипломъ за надлежащимъ
подписаніемъ и съ приложеніемъ печати Канцеляріи Попечителя
Одесскаго Учебнаго Округа.

Г. Одесса, ... 17 дня 1912 года.

Попечитель Одесскаго Учебнаго Округа,
Дѣйствительный Статскій Совѣтникъ и Кавалеръ

Предсѣдатель Юридической Испытательной Коммиссіи,
Статскій Совѣтникъ и Кавалеръ

Правитель Канцеляріи,
Коллежскій Совѣтникъ и Кавалеръ

Установленный за дипломъ
сборъ внесенъ.

Jurisprudence Diploma of Lev Shmulian (Alla's father)

Diploma's Content:

It reads, "Diploma. The bearer of this, Shmulian Leiba Yudelevich*, a son of a *meschanin,*† of a Jewish confession, while being a student of a jurisprudence faculty of the IMPERIAL Novorossiysk University was subject in 1908, 1909, and 1910 to a semi-annual examination at which he demonstrated the following successes: in the history of Roman law—very satisfactory; in the history of Russian law—satisfactory; in the encyclopedia of law—very satisfactory; in the political economy—very satisfactory; in statistics—very satisfactory; in state law—very satisfactory; in financial law—very satisfactory; in the history of the philosophy of law—very satisfactory; in church law—very satisfactory; in police law—very satisfactory...In April and May of 1911 he was subject to examination by the jurisprudence commission at the same university, and he demonstrated the following successes: in Roman law—very satisfactory; in civil law—very satisfactory; in civil procedures—very satisfactory; in criminal law—very satisfactory; in criminal procedures—very satisfactory; in commercial law—very satisfactory; in international law—very satisfactory. Subsequently, based on article 81 of the general charter of the IMPERIAL Russian universities, on August 23, 1884, and based on approval of a presented essay, Mr. Shmulian is conferred at a session of the aforementioned jurisprudence commission, on May 28, 1911, a first degree diploma with all the rights and advantages...In the confirmation of this, is given to him, Mr. Shmulian, this diploma with the appropriate signatures and seal of the secretariat of the sponsor of the Odessa Educational District. Odessa, March 12, 1912. Signed: Sponsor of the Odessa Educational District, *Statsky* Assessor and Cavalier (signature), Representative of the Jurisprudence Examination Commission, *Statsky* Assessor and Cavalier (signature), Chairman of the secretariat, Collegian Assessor (signature)."

---

* A formal transcription of a Russian name or formal salutation includes a family name (Shmulian in this case), given name (Leiba or Lev in the particular case), and a second (patronymic) name. Each of these may have different endings depending on gender. Lev's father was Yudel. Accordingly Lev's patronymic name is Yudelevich or Yulyevich. Alla's patronymic name became Lvovna.

† Meschanin - a representative of a lower - middle class

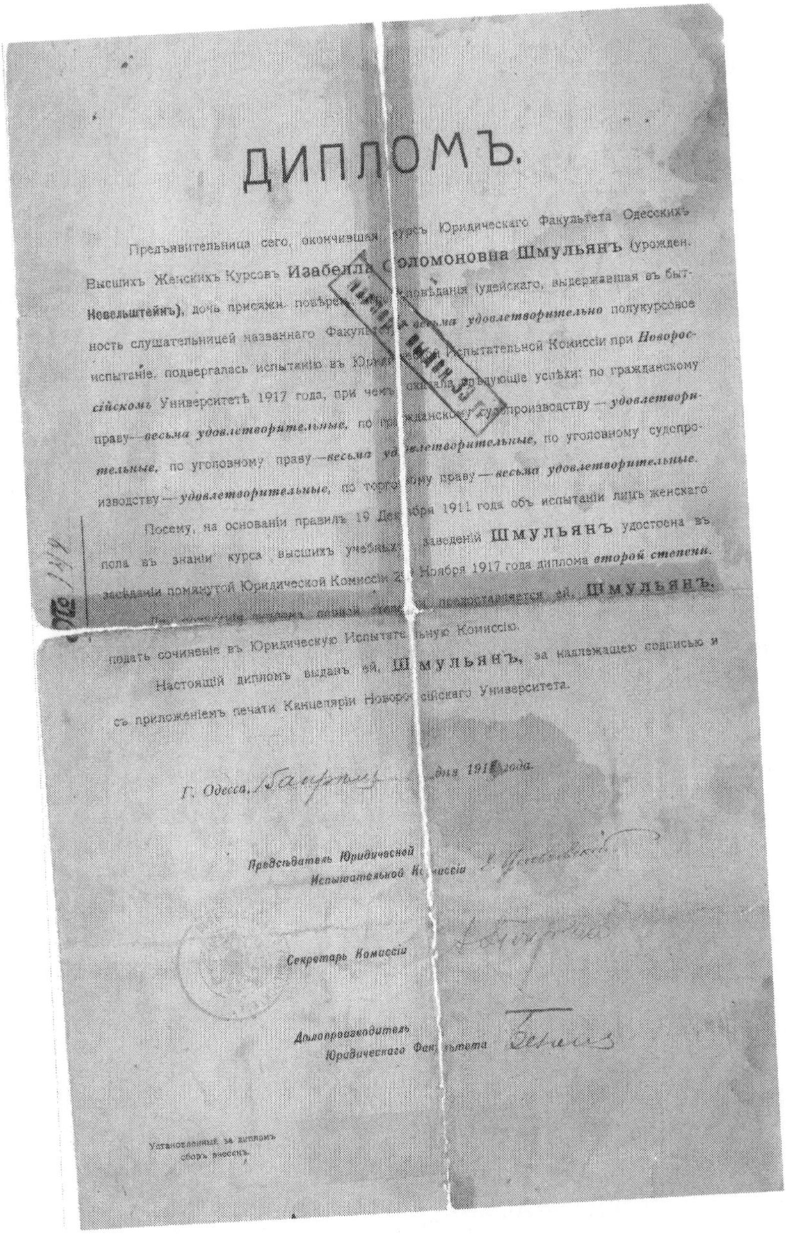

ДИПЛОМЪ.

Предъявительница сего, окончившая [illegible] курсъ Юридическаго Факультета Одесскихъ
Высшихъ Женскихъ Курсовъ Изабелла [illegible]оломоновна Шмульянъ (урожден.
Невельштейнъ), дочь присяжн. повѣре[illegible] [illegible]повѣданія іудейскаго, выдержавшая въ бытность слушательницей названнаго Факуль[illegible] [illegible] весьма удовлетворительно полукурсовое
испытаніе, подвергалась испытанію въ Юри[illegible] [illegible] Испытательной Комиссіи при Новорос-
сійскомъ Университетѣ 1917 года, при чемъ [illegible] [illegible] слѣдующіе успѣхи: по гражданскому
праву—весьма удовлетворительные, по гр[illegible]жданскому судопроизводству—удовлетворительные, по уголовному праву—весьма уд[illegible]влетворительные, по уголовному судопроизводству—удовлетворительные, по торго[illegible]ому праву—весьма удовлетворительные.

Посему, на основаніи правилъ 19 Дек[illegible]бря 1911 года объ испытаніи лицъ женскаго
пола въ знаніи курса высшихъ учебныхъ [illegible] заведеній ШМУЛЬЯНЪ удостоена въ
засѣданіи помянутой Юридической Комиссіи 2[illegible] Ноября 1917 года диплома второй степени.
[illegible] [illegible] предоставляется ей, ШМУЛЬЯНЪ,
[illegible]
подать сочиненіе въ Юридическую Испытате[illegible]ьную Комиссію.

Настоящій дипломъ выданъ ей, Ш[illegible]МУЛЬЯНЪ, за надлежащею подписью и
съ приложеніемъ печати Канцеляріи Новоро[illegible]сійскаго Университета.

Г. Одесса, [illegible] дня 191[illegible] года.

Предсѣдатель Юридической
Испытательной К[illegible]миссіи

Секретарь Комиссіи

Дѣлопроизводитель
Юридическаго Фак[illegible]льтета

Установленный за дипломъ
сборъ внесенъ.

Jurisprudence Diploma of Isabella Shmulian (Alla's mother)

Diploma's Content

It reads, "A bearer of this, having completed a course of the jurisprudence faculty of the Odessa Highest Female Courses, Isabella Solomonovna Shmulian (née Nevelshtein), a daughter of a *prisiazhnoporeverennogo**, of a Jewish confession, having passed very successfully the semi-annual tests while being a listener in the aforementioned faculty, was subject to the additional test in 1917 at the Jurisprudence Examination Commission at the Novorossiysk University, and she demonstrated the following successes: in civil law—very satisfactory; in civil court procedures—satisfactory; in criminal law—very satisfactory; in criminal court procedures—satisfactory; in commercial law—very satisfactory. Subsequently, based on the rules of December 1911 of the Highest Education Establishments about examination of females in the knowledge of the course, Shmulian is conferred, upon the session of the aforementioned Jurisprudence Commission on November 20, 1917, a diploma of a second degree. To receive a diploma of the first degree it is allowed to her, Shmulian, to present an essay to the Jurisprudence Test Commission. A present diploma is given to her, Shmulian, with the appropriate signature and seal of a Secretariat of the Novorossiysk University. Odessa, April 15, 1918. Signed: Chairman of the Jurisprudence Test Commission (signature); Secretary of the Commission (signature); Secretary of the Jurisprudence Faculty (signature)."

---

* Prisiazhny poverenny - A Russian jurisprudence term referring to attorney at government service who took the oath. It was extremely rare in the tsarist Russia for a Jewish person to hold this honorable position

UNITED STATES PATENT

The United States of America

Granted on January 3, 1995

Valery V. Dunaevsky

INVENTOR

5,378,129

ELASTIC UNLOADER FOR SCROLL MACHINES

1. A scroll machine comprising:
a first scroll member and a second scroll member mounted for orbital movement with respect to one another in an inter-meshed relationship;
a powered drive shaft having a generally flat driving surface for causing said relative orbital movement;
a drive bushing drivingly connected to one of said scroll members;
a driven surface on said drive bushing, said driving surface driving said driven surface to cause said one scroll member to orbit with respect to the other of said scroll members.

The Commissioner of Patents and Trademarks has received an application for a patent for a new and useful invention. The requirements of law have been complied with, and it has been determined that a patent on the invention shall be granted under the law. Therefore, this

UNITED STATES PATENT

Grants to the person or persons having title to this patent the right to exclude others from making, using or selling the invention throughout the United States of America for the term of seventeen years from the date of this patent, subject to the payment of maintenance fees as provided by law.

PATENT AND TRADEMARK OFFICE UNITED STATES OF AMERICA

Bruce Lehman Marcia S. Campsey

A commemorative plaque for one of the patents of Valery Dunaevsky. U.S. Patent No. 5, 378, 129 was issued to him on January 3, 1995.

ДИПЛОМ
КАНДИДАТА НАУК
ТН № 008907
Решением
присуждена ученая степень
КАНДИДАТА
ТЕХНИЧЕСКИХ НАУК

PHD Equivalent Diploma of Valery Dunaevsky conferred upon him by the Riga Polytechnical Institute on March 31, 1975, and issued to him on July 21, 1976 (by VAK, The Highest Attestation Commission at the Council of Ministries of the USSR).

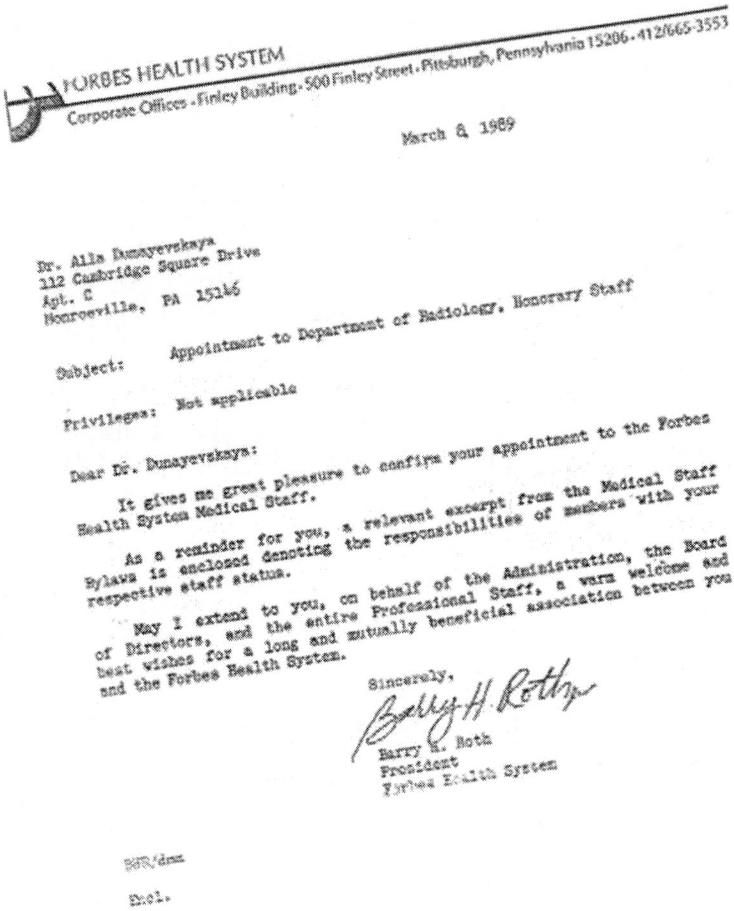

FORBES HEALTH SYSTEM
Corporate Offices - Finley Building - 500 Finley Street - Pittsburgh, Pennsylvania 15206 - 412/665-3553

March 8, 1989

Dr. Alla Dunayevskaya
112 Cambridge Square Drive
Apt. C
Monroeville, PA 15146

Subject: Appointment to Department of Radiology, Honorary Staff

Privileges: Not applicable

Dear Dr. Dunayevskaya:

It gives me great pleasure to confirm your appointment to the Forbes Health System Medical Staff.

As a reminder for you, a relevant excerpt from the Medical Staff Bylaws is enclosed denoting the responsibilities of members with your respective staff status.

May I extend to you, on behalf of the Administration, the Board of Directors, and the entire Professional Staff, a warm welcome and best wishes for a long and mutually beneficial association between you and the Forbes Health System.

Sincerely,

Barry H. Roth
Barry H. Roth
President
Forbes Health System

BHR/dms

Encl.

The letter of the president of Forbes Health System to appoint Alla into the Honorary Staff of the Department of Radiology.

Myself (on the left) with my German colleagues at a business meeting (ca. 2002)

ALLA'S FAMILY TREE

Alla's Grandparents
Solomon Nevelshtein
Tatyana Feldman

Their children
Isabella Nevelshtein, 1891-1975
Tamara Nevelshtein, 1899 -1983
Grigori Nevelshtein, 1895-1966

Alla's parents
Isabella Shmulian (née Nevelshtein), mother
Lev Shmulian, 1878-1945, father

Their children:
Alla Dunayevskaya (née Shmulian), 1920-2010
Witold Shmulian, 1914 -1944
Theodor Shmulian, 1912-1998
Theodor's son George Shmulian, 1939 - 2012

Alla's husband
Victor Dunaevsky (Valery's father), 1918 -1965

Victor parents
Zelman Dunaevsky, father, 1891-1968
Lyuba Dunaevsky (née Osherovsky), 1891-1966

Alla and Victor's son
Valery Dunaevsky, 1942 –
Valery and Ada Dunaevsky's (née Shalyt) daughter Victoria Dunaevsky, 1978 -
Victoria and Michael Bane's son Eric Bane, 2013 -

ADDITIONAL NOTES

8, 4.3	**Industrialization.** The firm of an American architect Albert Kahn built 521 industrial plants in the USSR between 1930 and 1932.*
27, 1.2	**Beria.** Beria was imprisoned and executed late in 1953. His former comrades, Khrushchev and Malenkov, resented Beria liberalization reforms (that were introduced after the death of Stalin), especially his intent to unite Germany. They also feared that Beria planned a military coup and "sharpened his knives" to use against them.
58, 1.2	**Sorge.** A crucial piece of information that Sorge supplied to Russians was that the Japanese Army did not procure a winter uniform. The obvious implication of the message was that the threat of a Japan winter attack has gone. However, for a number of selfish reasons Stalin did not return favor to Sorge. He even refused to trade him on one of the Japanese spies when offered by Japan. Sorge wife was arrested and thrown to Gulag.

65, 5.1	**...resistance offered by Soviet troops...** The burden of the initial defense of the city (with general V. Chuikov commanding the 62nd Army) fell on the 1077th Anti-Aircraft Regiment, a unit made up mainly of young female volunteers who had no training for engaging ground targets. Despite this, and with no support available from other units, the AA gunners stayed at their posts and took on the advancing panzers. The German 16th Panzer Division reportedly had to fight the 1077th's gunners "shot for shot" until all 37 anti-aircraft guns were destroyed or overrun. The German 16th Panzer Division was shocked to find that, due to Soviet manpower shortages, it had been fighting female soldiers. In the beginning, the Soviets relied extensively on "Workers' militias" composed of workers not directly involved in war production. For a short time, tanks continued to be produced and then manned by volunteer crews of factory workers. They were driven directly from the factory floor to the front line, often without paint or even gunfights. [9]

NOTES

66, 3.2	**Rokossovsky.** He later took part in the suppression of the Polish independence movement and Stalinization and sovietization of Poland in general and the Polish Army in particular. In June 1956 during Poznań protests against poverty of working class, and Soviet occupation of Poland, Rokossovsky approved the order to send military units against protesters. As a result of the action of over 10,000 soldiers and 360 tanks, at least 74 civilians were killed. [39]
75, 5.1	**Italy in the War.** This excurse was also prompted by the memory of Alla often singing one prewar song with a catchy and carefree melody and with lyrics satirizing life in Italy under Fascists.

*Stalin calculated that Soviet Union only had 10 years to catch up with the Western World in terms of industrial grows before Germany invaded, which was highly plausible. The Soviet Union industry was weak and in the decline, obviously lacking the capacity to produce enough metal and heavy machinery for the imminent war. So, "tightening the screws" and exploiting thousands of Gulag prisoners at construction sites and at plants became a part of his sinister industrialization plan. <http://russiapedia.rt.com/of-russian-origin/stalins-purges/.

BIBLIOGRAPHY

[1] Montefiore, S.S. *Stalin: The Court of the Red Tsar*, New York: Alfred A. Knopf, 2003. Print.

[2] Feuchtwanger, l. *Moscow, 1937: My Visit Described for My Friends*. London: Victor Gollancz, 1937. Print.

[3] Anderson, D., L. Clark, and S. Welsh. *The Eastern Front: Barbarossa, Stalingrad, Kursk and Berlin, 1941–1945*. USA: MBI Publishing Company, 2001. Print.

[4] Movshowitz, E.V. *History of Jews on Don*. Rostov n/D, Russia: Kniga, 2011.Print.

[5] Klee, Ernst, Willi Dressen, and Volke Riess, eds. "*The Good Old Days*": *The Holocaust as Seen by Its Perpetrators and Bystanders*. New York: Konecky & Konecky, 1991. Print.

[6] *The Secret History of World War II: The Ultra-Secret Wartime Cables and Letters of Roosevelt, Churchill and Stalin*. USA: Konecky & Konecky LLC, 2008. Print.

[7] Ryan, C. The Longest Day. New York: Simon & Shuster, 1984. Print.

[8] "Stalingrad Battle 1942-1943." *BSE (Big Soviet Encyclopedia)*. 1976, 401-404. Print.

[9] "Battle of Stalingrad." Wikipedia, The Free Encyclopedia. Wikimedia Foundation, Inc.. n.d. Web. 19 Nov 2012. <http://en.wikipedia.org/wiki/Battle of Stalingrad>.

[10] Clark, L. *Kursk: World War II.* USA: Wieder History Group, 2011. Print.

[11] "Military History of Italy During WWII." Wikipedia, The Free Encyclopedia. Wikimedia Foundation, Inc.. n.d. Web. 6 Nov 2012. <http://en.wikipedia.org/wiki/Military_history_of_Italy_during_World_War_II>.

[12] *The Complete Poetical Works of Burns.* USA: Houghton, Mifflin and Co., the Cambridge Press, 1964. Print.

[13] Marshack, S. *Collection of Works in Four Volumes, Selected Translations.* Moscow: Goslitizdat, 1957. Print.

[14] Brent, J., and V. Naumov. *Stalin's Last Crime: The Plot Against the Jewish Doctors, 1948–1953.* New York: Perennial, 2003. Print.

[15] *Professor A. I. Dombrovsky, 1889–1972.* Rostov n/D, Russia: RNIOI (Rostov-on-Don Oncological Research Institute), 1998. Print.

[16] Rayfield, D. *Stalin and His Hangmen: The Tyrant and Those Who Killed for Him.* New York: Random House, 2004. Print.

[17] Rigg, B. M. *Hitler's Jewish Soldiers: The Untold Story of Nazi Racial Laws and Men of Jewish Descent in the German Military.* USA: University Press of Kansas, 2002. Print.

[18] *Robert Burns: The Poems, Epistles, Songs, Epigrams and Epitaphs.* Edited by Charles S. Dougall. London: A & C Black, Ltd., 1927. Print.

[19] Ehrenburg, I., and V. Grossman. *The Complete Black Book of Russian Jewry.* New Brunswick and New Jersey: Transaction Publishers, 2011. Print

[20] Clarton, D. *Churchill and the Soviet Union.* Manchester: Manchester University Press, 2000. Print.

[21] Dallek, R. *Franklin D. Roosevelt and American Foreign Policy, 1932–1945.* New York: Oxford University Press, 1979. Print.

[22] Krein, M.G. "Witold Lvovich Shmulian (Toward the 50th birthday and 20th anniversary of death)," *Successes of Mathematical Sciences*, XX, **122**, Publishing House "NAUKA", Moscow, 1965. Print.

[23] Reid, A. "Death of Army." *World War II.* USA: Wieder History Group, 2012. Print.

[24] Hind, A. "Operation Carnivore: The Destruction of Second Shock Army." *World at War.* USA: Decision Games, 2012. Print.

[25] "Odessa." Wikipedia, The Free Encyclopedia. Wikimedia Foundation, Inc.. n.d. Web. 20 Dec 2011. <http://en.wikipedia.org./wiki/Odessa>.

[26] "Genrikh Yagoda." Wikipedia, The Free Encyclopedia. Wikimedia Foundation, Inc.. n.d. Web. 20 Dec 2011. <http://en.wikipedia.org/wiki/Genrikh_Yagoda>.

[27] "Nikolai Ezhov." Wikipedia, The Free Encyclopedia. Wikimedia Foundation, Inc.. n.d. Web. 20 Dec 2011. <http://en.wikipedia.org/wiki/Nikolai_Ezhov>.

[28] "Moscow Trials." Wikipedia, The Free Encyclopedia. Wikimedia Foundation, Inc.. n.d. Web. 20 Dec 2011. <http://en.wikipedia.org/wiki/Moscow_Trials>.

[29] "Vasili Blokhin." Wikipedia, The Free Encyclopedia. Wikimedia Foundation, Inc.. n.d. Web. 20 Dec 2011. <http://en.wikipedia.org/wiki/Vasili_Blokhin>.

[30] Stites, Richard. *Russian Popular Culture: Entertainment and Society Since 1900.* England: Cambridge University Press, 1992. Print.

[31] "Lyrical Song of Sormovo." Web. 16 Aug 2012. < http://sovmusic.ru/ text.php?fname= sormovsl>.

[32] "Great Terror." Web. 16 Aug 2012. <www.hoover press.org/ product detail.cfm/ PC=947>.

[33] "The Sacred War Song." YouTube. n.p., n.d.Web. 20 Dec 2011. < www.youtube.com/watch?v=BSaimLTQafg >.

[34] "The Dark Night Song." Web. 17 Aug 2012. <http:// www.youtube.com/watch?v=IJS7M3J2Xos >

[35] "Odessa Song." Web. 17 Aug 2012. <http://www.youtube.com/watch?v=Uv3tjDvuhqY >.

[36] "Taganrog during WWII." Wikipedia, The Free Encyclopedia, Wikimedia Foundation, Inc.. n.d. Web. 19 Aug 2012. < http://en.wikipedia.org/wiki/Taganrog_during_World_War_II>.

[37] "Herem (censure)." Wikipedia, The Free Encyclopedia. Wikimedia Foundation, Inc.. n.d. Web. 24 April 2012. <http://en.wikipedia.org/wiki/Herem_(censure)>

[38] "Trotsky and the Jews." Web. November 2007. <http://jewishmag.com/118mag/trotsky/trotsky.htm>

[39] "Konstantin Rokossovsky." Wikipedia, The Free Encyclopedia. Wikimedia Foundation, Inc.. n.d. Web. 16 March 2013. <httm://en.wikipedia.org/wiki/Rokossovsky>

[40] Adamovich, A., and Granin D. *The Book of Blockade*. Saint-Petersburg: Pechatny Dvor, 1994.

ACKNOWLEDGMENTS

I would like to thank my daughter, Victoria Dunaevsky, and my friends, Linda Day, Terry Nadler, and Lane Rosenthal with assistance in proofreading the book.

I would like to thank also my friend from Riga, Latvia, Eduard Aivazian, for assisting with the adaptation of M. Svetlov "The Italian Cross."

V. Dunaevsky
2012

INDEX

Abraham, 72, 180
USSR Academy of Sciences, VII, 51, 242, 246
Agatov, 84
Airport:
  Leonardo Da Vinci, 193
  Moscow International; Sheremetyevo, 180, 187, 200
  Newark, 193
  Vienna, 179, 187
Africa (n); South Africa, 60, 73, 76, 180, 192, 193, 207
Agfa photo paper, 19
Agnivtsev, 164
Aivazian, 68, 291
Akhmatova, 7
Al Alamein, 73
Alaska, 59
Albanians, 6,
Alexander I, 17
Alexander II, 255
Alexandrov, 53
aliyah (immigration to Israel), 195
Allied commanders:
  Eisenhower (USA), 61, 62
  Montgomery (UK), 73
  Malinovsky, 7
  Chuikov, 284
  Rokossovsky, 66, 285
  Timoshenko, 54
  Vasilevsky, 75
  Vatutin, 75
  Zhukov, 66, 74
Allied leaders:
  Churchill, 59, 60, 208
  Roosevelt, 59, 94
  Stalin, (see Stalin, Josef)
Allies, title page, 59 - 63, 65, 67, 73, 76 -78
Almar radiology, 203, 208, 224
America(n), title page, VII, 19, 23 - 25, 30, 40, 41, 54, 59 - 61, 63, 73, 76, 83, 94, 109, 110, 123, 124, 129 - 131, 137, 139, 143, 144, 150, 173, 180, 181, 185, 188 - 193, 195, 196, 199 - 208, 216, 260, 283
Andorra, 144

Annam, 115
Anti-Semitism, anti-Semite(s), anti-Semitic, 45, 46, 70, 71, 128, 130, 132, 133, 139, 171, 172, 253 - 261
Apuli, 77
Arab(ian), 179, 192, 257, 260
Aralsk, 117
Arkhangelsk Oblast, 3
Archangelsky, 164
Archive of Ministry of Defense of the USSR, 87
Arctic, 59, 105, 106, 124
Armenians, 6
Army (ies):
Allied, 77
Axis, 53, 65
Catherine's, 6
German, 54, 65, 69
German Alpine, 69
German Group Don, 66
German Panzer, 54
German Sixth, 66, 73
German Seventh, 62
Italian, 65, 76
Japanese, 7, 142, 283
Kwantung, 94
People's, 51, 171
Red, 7, 26, 40, 46, 48, 51, 53, 55, 57- 59, 62, 64, 65, 69, 70, 74, 75, 144, 258, 262
Romanian, 65
Russian Liberation (ROA), 64
Soviet, 54, 57, 63, 66, 67, 69, 83, 94
62nd, 284
64th, and Soviet Don Front, 66
2nd Shock, 63
White, 24
Ashgabat, 117
Atlantic Coast, 62, 106
aul (Turkmen village), 117
Auschwitz, 77, 193
Australia, 73, 165, 180, 193
Austria, 179
Axis leaders:
Hitler, VIII, 28, 40, 45, 46, 48, 53, 54, 57, 61, 62, 66, 67, 69 - 71, 76, 133, 178
Mussolini, 76 - 78
Axis Powers, 58, 59, 76
Azeris, 6
Azerbaijan, 53, 195

Babel, Isaac, 7, 27
Babi Yar, 170
Badoglio, 76
Bagritsky, Eduard, 138
Baku, 53, 69, 195
Balkans, 77
Baltic, 25, 63, 157, 174
Banach Spaces, Banach Sphere, 243
Bartoletty, Stephan, 209, 223
Bauman Engineering School, Moscow, 85
BBC code, title page, 61
Belgian, 17
Belorussia, 20, 39, 174
Belovalova, Zhanna (and her relatives), 107, 108, 121, 122, 124, 127
Beria, Lavrenty, 27, 28, 257, 283
Bidula, Maureen, 229
Big Soviet Encyclopedia, 112
Birobidjan, 130
Black Sea resort, 21, 22, 139, 144, 148
Blokhin, 26, 27

Blyukher, 24
Bogoslovsky, 84
Bolsheviks, 24, 26, 27, 253 - 257, 259
Boyarka, 145
British, title page, 20, 46, 58, 61, 62, 73, 76, 83, 84, 110, 129, 164
Brockhaus and Efron Encyclopedic Dictionary, 138
Brodsky, 178
Bron, 7
Brunacci, Aldo, 77
Bruno, Djiordano, 113
Bucephalus, 111
Bukharin, 24, 26
Budapest, 64
Bulgaria(ns), 6, 129
Burns, Robert, R., 84, 114, 263

Calabria, 77
Cambodia, 115
Canada, Canadian, title page, 180, 192
Canal:
Moscow-Volga, 26
Suez, 73
Volga-Don, 165
White Sea-Baltic, Belomor, 25, 259
Capri, 145
"Case of the doctors," *(Delo vrachey)*, 131 - 134
Catholic Charity "Caritas," 180, 190
Caucasian Mountains, 48, 69, 143
Caucasus, 18, 22, 40, 46, 48, 53, 64, 65, 69, 73, 141, 142
Cemetery, 55, 235, 249
Chagall, 140
Channel, 60 - 62
Chaplin, Charlie, 41
Chardzhou, 117
Cheka/GPU/NKVD, 1, 2, 3, 24 - 27, 31, 40, 49, 50, 70, 74, 123, 256, 257, 258;
MGB, 123, 131, 134; MVD, 123; KGB, 172
All Commissariats and Ministries of Internal Affairs and State Securitiy
Chernykh, 29
China, 59
Chelyabinsk Oblast, 49
Cherdyn, 29
Chop, 184
CIS (Commonwealth of the Independent States), 129
Cincinnati, 206
City Lights, 41
Chicago, 206
Christmas tree, 85
Cleveland, 67
Collectivization, 5, 8, 28, 29, 31
Commissars, 27, 45, 64
Communism, Communist(s), Communist party, 20, 21, 25 - 27, 31, 40, 43, 45, 48, 55, 61, 64, 108, 119, 127, 130, 131, 159, 163, 178, 180, 182, 253, 254, 257
Corsica, 76
Cossacks, 47
Craig, Daniel, 19
Crimea, 29, 130, 145
Crimean Peninsula, 64
Crimean Tatars, 6

Dagestan, 48, 70
D-Day, 60, 61
De Langeron, Andrault, 6
de Pachmann, Vladimir, 7
De Ribas, Jose, 6
De Richelieu, Duc, 6
Decembrist Mutiny, 255
Derbent, 49
Des Moines, 193
Detroit, 206
Dix, Otto, 19, 38
DNA, 22
Doctor Zhivago, 5, 29
Dolmatovsky, 110
Dom otdykha (Rest house), 22
Dombrovsky, Elena Alexandrovna (Lyalya), 79, 90, 132, 161, 162
Dombrovsky, Alexander Iosifovich, 21, 79, 96, 132
Don Institute of the People Economy, 19
Don Quixote, 111
Dreiser, 206
Dulcenea, 111
Duma, 6
Dunayevskaya, Alla (Shmulian, Alla, A.L.), Alla Lvovna, A.L., Mother, my mother, title page, VII, VIII, 1- 15, 17 - 19, 21–24, 32, 33, 35, 40 - 42, 46, 47, 48, 50 - 52, 56, 60 - 62, 67, 70 -72, 78 - 81, 83, 84, 86 - 91, 95, 96, 100, 101, 102, 103, 107 -110, 113, 114, 122 - 126, 128, 132, 136, 138 - 140, 143 - 149, 150, 152, 160, 161, 165, 168, 170, 171 - 173, 176, 178, 181, 182, 186, 187, 194, 199 - 239, 267 - 272, 274, 278, 281, 285
Dunaevsky, Ada, 180, 189, 211, 226
Dunaevsky, Valery, Valery Victorovich, V., Valerick, front page, VIII, 78, 79, 80, 100, 102, 147, 168, 230, 263, 276, 277, 279, 281, 291
Dunaevsky, Victoria (Vita), 180, 181, 185, 186, 191, 192, 200, 204, 205, 211, 227, 281, 291
Dunaevsky, Isaak, 41, 69, 142
Dunaevsky, Victor, 18, 19, 21 - 23, 32, 34, 36, 37, 40, 41, 44, 46 - 48, 50, 52, 72, 79, 85, 89, 90, 95 - 97, 100, 102, 103, 106, 107, 128, 144, 145, 148, 150, 151, 153, 155, 158, 160, 165, 168 - 170, 172, 202, 209, 281
Dunaevsky, Zelman (Zyama) and his wife Lyuba
(see Osherovsky Lyuba);
Dunaevskys, 19, 20, 23, 37, 38, 41, 45 - 47, 49 - 52, 56, 73, 74, 78, 95, 96, 161 - 164, 167, 170, 172, 173, 281
Duranty, 31, 44
Dutch representative, 185
Dylan, Bob, 19
Dzerzhinsky, 257, 258

Einstein, 83, 220
Elbrus, 69
Emilia, 3
Emigration, 177 - 197, 200
Elena Vasilyevna, 95, 173
Enemy of the people, 2, 18, 23,

42, 43
Engels Street, 40, 96
England, 59
Esenin, Sergei, 114
Esentuki, 69
Estonia, 39
Eugene Onegin, 24, 209
Europe, *Europa*, European, 2, 7, 9, 22, 23, 42, 44, 57, 58, 60, 61, 62, 64, 69, 110, 122, 144, 145, 179, 253, 261
Evacuation, 44 - 50, 72, 87
Ezhov, 25 - 27, 257
Ezhovshchina, 25

Fallada, Hans, 61
False Helendjik, 22
Famine, 6, 29, 31
Fascists, 46, 52, 284
Feldman, Valentin, 2
Feltsman, 7
Feuchtwanger, 31, 160
Filatov, 8
Florence, 77
Fonvizin, 42
Forbes (hospital), 203, 204, 209, 213, 214, 222 - 224, 229, 236, 278
France, title page, 2, 20, 59, 60 - 62, 76, 77, 129, 259, 261
French, title page, 2, 5, 6, 7, 20, 46, 61, 62, 73, 74, 76, 110, 115, 121, 137, 243, 259, 261
Freshet, 5, 243
Front:
African, 60
Eastern, 54, 60, 65, 74, 75
Moscow, 57
North Atlantic, 60
Pacific, 60
Second, 59, 60, 62, 63
Southwestern, 54
Volkhov, 63, 64
Western, 160
Führer, 54, 74

Gamarnik, 24
Gamow, 8
Gašek, 112
Georgia(n), 24, 25, 27, 130, 142
German Democratic Republic, 69, 158, 163
Germany, Nazi Germany, German (s), 2, 3, 6, 17, 19, 22, 27, 28, 38 - 41, 44 - 48, 53 - 67, 69, 71, 73 - 78, 83, 84, 92, 94, 95, 98 - 100, 105, 122, 125, 136, 143, 144, 162, 163, 178, 179, 193, 209, 241, 243, 254, 255, 260 - 262, 279, 283, 284, 285
German generals:
Kleist, 54
Manstein, 66, 74, 75
Model, 75
Paulus, 66, 67
Reichenau, 54
Rommel, 62, 73, 76
Rundstedt, 54
Gershkowich, 94, 142
Gilels, 7
Gillette razor, 161
Glushko, 8
Goering, 178
Golaya Pristan' (Naked Haven), 13
Golden Calf, 7, 164
Golden Living Center,

Monroeville, PA, 204
Goldstein, Boris, 7
Goldshtein (Victor's acquaintance), 123, 128
Gorbachev, 29
Gorbachev's perestroika, 23
Gorky, Maxim, 145, 255, 257
Gorky Street, 41, 98, 158, 161
Grand Council of Fascism, 76
Great Britain, 59, 63, 106
Great Depression, 31
Great Purge, 25, 26, 131
Great Terror, 25
Greek(s), 6, 17, 21, 77, 109, 111, 114
Grozny, 53
GTO, BGTO, 125
Gulag, 2, 3, 10, 25, 26, 28, 29, 30, 42, 121, 258, 283, 284
Gulf Stream, 105
Guttman, 143, 151

Haffkine, Waldemar, 8, 113
Hebrew, 45, 112, 177, 180
HIAS (The Hebrew Immigrant Aid Society), 180, 185, 188 - 194, 200
Holocaust, VIII, 52, 56, 70, 76, 77, 170
House of Culture, 121
Humanité Dimánsh, 20
Hungarians, 66

Ibsen, 114
Ilf and Petrov, 7, 164
Indochina, 115
Industrialization, 8, 25, 26, 40, 42, 71, 283, 285
Intelligentsia, 6, 114
Iran(ian), 59, 190, 260
Israel (i), 129, 130, 171, 177, 179 - 182, 184, 185, 187 - 191, 194 -196, 199, 206, 254, 257
Israeli Philharmonic Orchestra, 171
Italy, Italian(s), 6, 58, 65 - 68, 75 -78, 113, 145, 191 - 193, 221, 285, 291
Ivan the Terrible, 259

Jabotinsky, Ze'ev, 7
Jackson - Vanik Amendment, 179
Japan(ese), 3, 7, 58, 73, 94, 112, 142, 283
Jewish Antifascist Committee (JAC), 130
Jewish Heritage, 113, 162
Jewish question, 76
Jews, 6, 22, 45, 46, 48, 53 - 56, 69 -71, 76 - 77, 113, 118, 120, 129, 132 - 134, 170, 178, 179, 182, 184, 193, 253 - 258, 260, 262
Joint (The American Joint Distribution Committee), 139, 180
Judaism, 113, 254

Kahn, Albert, 283
Kalinina, 127
Kamenev, 24, 26, 257
Kandror, 25
Kant, Immanuel, 114
Karelia, 135
Kartsev, 7
Katyn, 40

Kazakhstan, 50, 56
Kazbek, 69
Kerensky, 256
Khadjibey, 6
Kherson, 5, 6, 13, 113, 248
Khronovsky, 122
Khrushchev, Nikita, 29, 137, 163, 180, 259, 283
Kiev, 23, 118, 128, 145, 170
Kirov, 44
Kishinev, 64
Kislowodsk, 69
Kola Bay, 103, 108
Kola Peninsula, 135, 141
Kolmogorov, A.N., 82, 242
Komsomol (the Young Communist League), 45, 159, 160
Kornibat, 132
Kovel, 242, 247
Krasnovodsk, 50, 117
Krasny (Red) Aksay, 44, 166
Krasny Kotelshchik, 4, 48, 49
Krein, Mark, 8, 241, 244
Kreisky, 179
Ksenofontov, 258
Kuban steppes, 48
Kuibyshev, 44
Kulak(s), 24, 29, 43
Kurasov, Gleb, 19, 22, 34, 97
Kursk, Kursk Battle, Kursk Salient, 74, 75

La Roche-Sur-Yon, 62
Ladispoli, 192
Laos, 115
Latvia(n), 39, 97, 109, 157, 169, 170, 174 -178, 180 - 183, 194, 201, 206, 257, 258, 291
Latvian Institute of Advanced Training of Engineers, 178
Lebedev-Kumach, 53
Lebensraum, 40
Lend-Lease Program, 59, 67, 105
Leningrad, 17, 30, 56, 63, 64, 108, 121, 128, 131, 132, 135 - 138, 140 - 142, 189, 195, 196
Lenin (Ulyanov), Vladimir, Vladimir Ilych, 118, 119, 129, 132, 253, 255, 259, 260
Lenin's mausoleum, 58
Lermontov, 243
Levitan, Yuri, 57
Library of Congress, 30
Libya, 73
Lithuania, 39
Lichtenstein, 144
Lock, John, 114
Loktionov, 28
London, 20, 62
Lubyanka, 27, 66, 130
Lubrizol, 67
Luftwaffe, 45, 57, 65, 105, 106:
Messershmidts, 45
Junkers, 45
Fokke-Vulfs, 45
Stuka diving bombers, 45
Lyapunov, 8
Lyuba Model, 201, 202, 212
Luxembourg, 144

Magaziner, Lelya, and her husband Dolya Yasski, 165
Magdalene, Mary, and Magdaliniada, 164
Maikop, 53, 69
Makedonsky, 111

Makhachkala, 48–50, 69, 117
Malayan campaign, 73
Malenkov, 283
Mamaev Kurgan, 66, 165
Manchuria(n), 7, 57, 94, 142
Mandelstam, Leonid, 8
Mandelstam, Osip, 29, 30
Mao-Tse Toung, 28
Marat, 137
Marquis' Who's Who, VII, 216
Marshak, Samuil, 84, 114, 263
Marshal Budenny prospect, 40
Martov, Julius, 253
Marx, Marxism, Marxist, 253-255
Mauldin, Bill, 30
May, Josef, 19, 38
Mayakovsky, 138, 256
McHugh, Jimmy, 110
Mechnikov, 7
Medical Institute, 18, 79, 88, 95, 101, 158
Mein Kampf, 254
Mekhlis, Lev, 64
Mekinulov, Rafael, 142, 143, 151, and his children Alik and Allochka, 154
Memorial Day, 60
Mendeleev, Dmitri, 8, 138
Mengrel, 27, 257
Menikov, 63, 97
Mensheviks, 253, 255
Menzhinsky, Vyacheslav, 257
Meschanin, 273
Michoels, 130
Middle East, 73, 129, 243
Midwest, 206
Mikhailov, Sasha, 154
Miller, Arthur, 260
Mindlin, Sofa, 33, 41
Mineral'nye Vody (Mineral Waters), 69
Minsk, 171
Mischling(e), 260
Mitrofan, 42
Moiseiwitsch, Benno, 7
Moldavia, 39
Moliere, 9
Molnar, Ted, 229
Molotov, 39, 46, 130
Molotov-Ribbentrop Non-aggression Pact, 39, 46
Monaco, 144
Monchegorsk, 141
Monroeville, 200–206, 209, 221, 233, 234
Montgomery, 73
Moroz, Fanya, 18, 33
Morozov, Pavlik, 43
Morozov, Savely, 255
Moscow, 5, 6, 25, 26, 28, 31, 42, 44,
51, 57–59, 63, 64, 75, 85, 121, 128, 130, 132, 134, 142, 144, 155, 164, 179, 180, 184 - 189, 190, 195, 200, 201, 212, 217, 218, 242, 246, 254, 259
Murmansk, 85, 103, 105 - 108, 120, 121, 123, 124, 132, 135, 140 - 145, 147, 152 - 154, 157, 169, 170, 178, 201, 202
Murom, 117

Naples, Napoli, 67, 68, 78
Narodnaya Volya (The People Will), 255
Nazi propaganda, 31, 260
Nazi(s) (National Socialist

Workers Party), 45 - 47, 53, 55, 57, 59, 60, 61, 64, 73, 76, 77, 129, 261
Nazism, VIII
Nedorosl (The Minor), 42
Neiding, 142, 143
Nemirov, 136
Netherland embassy, 184
Nevelshtein, Solomon and his wife Tatiana (*née* Feldman), 5, 6, 9, 281 and children of:
Isabella, (see Shmulian Isabella)
Grigori and Tamara Nevelshteins, 6, 17, 56, 137, 138, 281
Nevsky prospect, 137
New Jersey, 188, 193
New York, 7, 154, 158, 171, 193, 199, 228, 255
New York Times, 31
New Zealand, 193
New World, 181, 188, 194, 202
Nicholas II, 255
Nicolini, Giuseppe, 77
Nietzsche, 114
Nobel Prize, 8, 30
Normandy, 60 - 62
Northern Atlantic, 59, 122
Northern lights, 106, 121
Novocherkassk, 47
Novogrudok, 20
Novorossiysk University, 1, 2, 273, 275
Nyandoma, 10

Odessa, 1- 7, 9, 17, 42, 52, 109, 110, 113, 118, 119, 164, 165, 207, 243, 252, 254, 273, 275
Odessa Café "Fancony," 118
Odessa State University, 4, 243
Oistrakh(s), David and Igor, 7
Olympic Games, 165, 179
Operation:
Barbarossa, 40
Baytown, 76
Citadel, 74, 75
Oak, 77
Overlord (Second front), title page, 61
Typhoon, 57
Orsha, 174
Osherovsky, Abram, 20, 96; his wife Leya, 20, and children of:
Clara, 21, 96
Ida, 20, 21, 79, 96
Iosif, 21, 96, 97
Lyuba, Lyubov Abramovna, 20, 21, 22, 23, 36, 46, 47, 50 - 52, 56, 70, 71, 72, 82, 83, 95 - 97, 132, 145, 160, 162 - 164, 166, 172, 281
Oscar, 21, 22
Rose, 20,
Vera, 21, 47, 56
Osherovsky, Yuri, 96
Osherovsky, Boris, 103, 106, 107, 121
Ostia, 192
Ostrovsky, 114

Palamarchuck, Vladimir, 132
Palestinian, 260
Panzer Group, 54
Pas-De-Calais, 61
Passport, 45, 48, 183, 184, 271
Pasternak, Boris, 29, 30, 178
Pedagogical Institute, 17, 56,

126
Pekurovsky, 145
Peter the Great, 17, 259
Philippines, 73
Pyatigorsk, 18
Pilsudski, 258
Pirogov, 8
Pittsburgh Opera, 209
Pittsburgh Carnegie Hall, 209, 239
Pittsburgh Philharmonic Orchestra, 201, 205
Plekhanov, 255
Poland, Polish, Poles, 6, 23, 39, 40, 55, 66, 122, 136, 248, 249, 257, 258, 285
Red Cross, 249
Politburo, 58
Poltava, 20, 41
Pompey, 192
Popular Mechanics, 40
Popular Science, 40
Potemkin Stairs, 6
Portniagin, Vladimir, 127
POW, 64, 73, 74, 76, 77, 94
Pravda, 134
Propiska, 184
Proskurov, 28
Protestant, 254
Provisional Government, 256
Pulitzer Prize, 30
Pushkin, 7
Putevka (pass, permit), 21, 22

Radek, 24
Radishchev, 259
Refusnieks, 181
Reds; Whites, 256
Remarque, 160
Republica Sociale Italiana (RSI), 77, 78
Revolution:
Bolshevik, 2
October, 163, 254
Ribbentrop, 39, 46, 76
Richter, Sviatoslav, 7
Riga, 97, 157, 169, 170, 176, 185, 188, 193, 199, 206, 219,
257, 277, 291
Riga Locomotive Plant, 177
Riga Poytechnical Institute, 170, 174
RISHM (Rostov Institute of Agricultural Machinery), 18, 85, 159, 160, 165, 170
River:
Amu-Darya, 117
Don, 40, 45, 64, 66, 158, 165, 166
Irtysh, 50
Mius, 54
Volga, 44, 64 - 66, 158
Volkhov's, 63, 64
Rhône, 76
Robespierre, 259
Romanian(s), 6, 52, 65, 66, 73
Rome, 76, 77, 113, 189 - 192
Röntgen, 220, 223
Roosevelt, Eleanor, 9
Rossinante, 111
Rostov-on-Don (Rostov), 17-22, 40, 41, 44 - 48, 50, 51, 53–56, 64, 66, 72, 74, 79, 85, 95, 96, 98, 100 - 102, 128, 140, 141, 145, 157 - 162, 165 - 168, 202, 262
Rostov State University, Mechanics-Mathematics

Department, 98
Rudin, 127, 135, 154
Rudzutak, 24
Russia (n), Russians, VII, 1, 4 -10, 17, 19, 20, 23 - 26, 30, 39 - 43, 47, 48, 56, 58 - 60, 62 - 65, 67, 68 - 71, 75, 79, 84, 85, 94, 97, 105, 108, 109 -116, 119, 120, 122, 124, 125, 129, 130, 132, 134, 136, 138 - 141, 144, 145, 154, 158, 159, 163 - 165, 166, 170 - 172, 174, 182, 185, 186, 189, 193, 195, 196, 201, 202, 205 - 207, 209, 217, 228, 231, 253 - 259, 273
Rychagov, 28
Rykov, 24

Sakharov, 178
Salerno, 76
San-Marino, 144
Sharif, Omar, 5
Shaw, Bernard, 71, 160
Sardinia, 77
Schopenhauer, 114
Scorzeny, Otto, 77
Sea:
Azov, 4, 17, 32
Black, 17, 21, 22, 63, 139, 140, 144, 148
Caspian, 48 - 50, 53, 65, 69
White, 25, 105
Sechenov, 8
Semipalatinsk, 50, 51, 72, 73, 78, 79, 83, 84, 86, 88
Sevastopol, 64
Severyanin, Igor, 114
Shcherbakov, 131
Shestihin, 136
Shmulian (*née* Nevelstein), Isabella Solomonovna; Isabella, Bella, VII, 1- 6, 8 -10, 13, 15, 17, 19, 23, 42, 43, 47, 48, 50, 51, 56, 78 - 83, 96, 107, 109, 110 -121, 124, 128, 136 - 138, 140, 143, 144, 162, 164, 165, 170, 173, 200, 204, 252, 274, 275, 281
Shmulian, Lev, Leiba, L., Shmulians, 1 - 6, 8, 10, 13, 23, 42, 81, 272, 273, 281
Shmulian, Theodor, and his son George (Zhorzhick), 4, 15, 19, 42, 43, 47- 50, 56, 70, 117, 118, 260, 281
Shmulian, Witold, VII, 4, 5, 8, 10, 15, 42, 51, 52, 70, 81- 83, 117, 220, 241 - 252, 281
Shtern, Grigori, 28
Shulikov(s), 24, 202, 217
Shumsky, I. G., and his wife Lidia, 164
Siberia (n), 56, 57, 59, 79
Sicily, 60, 76
Simons, Barbara, 234
Singapore, 73, 110
Sinyavsky, 178
Skladovska, Marie, 223
Slovaks, 73
Smakula, 8
Smirnoff, 7
Smolensk Oblast, 40
SMERSH, 70
Smushkevich, 27, 28
Solovyov, 138
Sochi, 139, 148, 149, 150
SOHNUT, 179, 188 -191, 194
Solzhenitsyn, 26, 178, 258

Songs:
Chanson d'Automne (Song of Autumn), title page, 61
"Chilita," 109
Comin' in on a Wing and a Prayer, 110
Dark Night, 84
Gaudeamus Igitur, 110, 111
In a Forest Near the Front, 84
Scowls Full of Mallet ('Song of Odessa'), 109
Song of Kakhovka, 69
Song of Sormovo, 110
Tango Magnolia, 110
The Sacred War, 53
Sorbonne, 2
Sorge, Richard, 58, 283
Southern Ural, 49
Soviet:
Armed Forces, 75
elite, 21
era, 7, 20,
culture, 8, 10
government, 25, 40, 45 - 47, 62, 70, 119, 120, 131, 179
occupation zone, 122
press, 20, 170
propaganda, 40, 46, 47
republic(s), 25, 39, 120, 178, 194, 195, 207, 256
State, 21, 132
Union, 2, 6, 7, 19, 20, 27, 31, 40, 44, 53, 59, 60, 65, 76, 94, 105, 106, 114, 128, 130, 163, 173, 179, 184, 202, 210, 247, 285
Union North Sea Navy, 106
Sovinform Bureau (Soviet Information Agency), 57
Sovnarkom, 27
Spinoza, 113
Spy, 28:
German, 3, 62; Japanese, 3; Polish, 66; Soviet, 58
the armored SS Divisions Wiking and Leibstandarte SS Adolf Hitler, 48
SSSI (Supplemental Social Security Income), 201
St. Petersburg; Petersburg, 6, 7, 30, 135, 206, 256, 259
Stalin, Josef (J. Djugashvili; 'Koba'), VIII, 2, 3, 5, 10, 24 - 29, 31, 39, 40, 43, 44, 57- 60, 63 - 66, 70, 74, 94, 107, 108, 117, 120, 121, 123, 127, 129 - 133, 134, 187, 247, 255 - 257, 259, 260, 283, 285
Stalingrad, Stalingrad Battle, 19, 64–67, 69, 73, 74, 76, 83, 93, 99, 165, 284
"Stalingrad Battle," 99
Steklov Institute of Mathematics (Steklov, Steklov's, Steklov Mathematics…), 5, 42, 51, 242, 244, 246
Stolyarsky, 7
Strait of Dover, 61
Strauss, 83
Student, Kurt, 77
Sukhomlinov, 127
Suzette, 41
Sverdlov, 255
Svetlov, 67, 68, 69, 291
Šveik, 112

T-34 tanks, 58, 85
Taganrog, 4, 17, 18, 32, 42, 43, 47, 48, 56, 117, 118, 158

Tamm, 7
Taranto, 77
Tarasov, 242
Tasso, Olga Grigoryevna, 109
Thackeray, 208
Timashuk, 131, 132, 134
Tomsk, 79, 88 - 91
TORGSIN, 8
Toulouse, 20
Trans-Siberian Railway, 59
Triolet, 160
Trotsky, Trotskyism, Trotskyte, 2, 10, 24, 26, 254
Tsipelzon, Anatoly (Tolya), 19, 97, 162
Tsipelzon, Moisey (Mosya), 162
Tsusima, 112
Tukhachevsky, 24
Turgenev, 243
Turkmen, 117
Turks, 6
Tymyansky, 97

U-boats, 58, 105
Uborewitz, 24
Ukraine, 39
Ukraine Famine, 5, 29, 31
Ukrainian(s), 6, 10, 115, 116, 129, 136, 185
Ulyanuk(s) Vladimir and Valentina, 202
Umilyanovsky, 23, 202, 217, 218
Umov, 8
United States, 58, 59, 60, 76, 106, 129, 130, 180, 188, 192, 197; USA, 54, 59
Unshlicht, 258
Ural Mountains, 44
USSR, VII, 3, 5, 8, 9, 25, 27, 29, 39, 41, 44, 45, 49, 51, 57, 59, 61, 67, 73, 75, 84, 87, 92, 105, 106, 110, 117, 128, 129, 131, 137, 142, 155, 163, 164, 169, 171, 173, 175, 179, 181, 183 - 185, 187, 189, 194, 195, 201, 202, 206, 242, 244, 246, 248, 249, 253, 257, 266, 277, 283
Utyosov, 7, 110
VAK, 175, 177, 277
Vasilevsky, 75
Vatican, 144
Venetia, 192
Verlaine, Paul, title page, 61, 62
Vertinsky, 71, 110
Vichy France, 73, 76
Victor Emmanuel III, 76
Vienna, 83, 179, 180, 184, 189 - 191, 193, 195, 200
Vietcong, 173
Vietnam, 115, 173
Vinnitsa, 118, 136
VKP(b), 27
Vladivostok, 59
Vlasov, 64
Vodovoz, 7
Volkovoy, 258
Voronezh, 29
Voroshilov, 117
Vysotsky, 7

Waksman, 8
War:
Civil, 28, 49, 121, 172, 256, 259
Great Patriotic, 27, 105, 130, 228, 241, 242
Second World, 53, 69, 75; WWII, title page, VII, VIII, 7, 19,

25, 27, 39, 46, 57- 60, 75, 92, 93, 97, 106, 123, 129, 136, 205, 207, 226, 253, 258
Six-Days, 184, 257
Russo-Turkish, 6

Warsaw, VII, 6, 40, 51, 184, 242, 248, 249, 258
Wehrmacht, 48, 57, 59, 61, 66, 69, 74, 106, 261
White Guard, 254
Wilde, Oscar, 114

Yagoda, 25, 26, 28, 253, 256, 257, 259
Yakir, 24
Yakovlev, 134
Yevtushenko, 170
Yiddish, 9, 130
Yurmala, 170, 199
Yurovsky, 255

Zaltsman, Ted, 18, 19, 41, 97
Zhana-Semey, 51, 72
Zharov, 164
Zhdanov, 131
Zhemchuzhina, Polina, 130
Zhvanetsky, 7
Zinoviev, 24, 26, 254, 257
Zionism, Zionist, 7, 258
Zlatoust, 49
Zmievskaya Balka (Snake Gulch), 55, 56
Zweig, 160

26381661R00177

Made in the USA
Charleston, SC
01 February 2014